CAREER DYNAMICS: MATCHING INDIVIDUAL AND ORGANIZATIONAL NEEDS

EDGAR H. SCHEIN
Massachusetts Institute of Technology
Sloan School of Management

ADDISON-WESLEY PUBLISHING COMPANY
Reading, Massachusetts • Menlo Park, California
London • Amsterdam • Don Mills, Ontario • Sydney

To Louisa, Elizabeth, and Peter

This book is in the Addison-Wesley series:

ORGANIZATION DEVELOPMENT

Editors:
Edgar H. Schein
Richard Beckhard
Warren G. Bennis

ISBN 0-201-06834-6
CDEFGHIJKL-DO-89876543210

FOREWORD

It has been five years since the Addison-Wesley series on organization development published the books by Roeber, Galbraith, and Steele, and it is almost ten years since the series itself was launched in an effort to define the then-emerging field of organization development. Almost from its inception the series enjoyed a great success and helped to define what was then only a budding field of inquiry. Much has happened in the last ten years. There are now dozens of textbooks and readers on OD; research results are beginning to accumulate on what kinds of OD approaches have what effects; educational programs on planned change and OD are growing; and there are regional, national, and even international associations of practitioners of planned change and OD. All of these trends suggest that this area of practice has taken hold and found an important niche for itself in the applied social sciences and that its intellectual underpinnings are increasingly solidifying.

One of the most important trends we have observed in the last five years is the connecting of the field of planned change and OD to the mainstream of organization theory, organizational psychology, and organizational sociology. Although the field has its roots primarily in these underlying disciplines, it is only in recent years that basic textbooks in "organization behavior" have begun routinely referring to organization development as an applied area that students and managers alike must be aware of.

The editors of this series have attempted to keep an open mind on the question of when the series has fulfilled its function and should be allowed to die. The series should be kept alive only as long as new areas of knowledge and practice central to organization development are emerging. During the last year or so, several such areas have been defined, leading to the decision to continue the series.

On the applied side, it is clear that information is a basic nutrient for any kind of valid change process. Hence, a book on data gathering, surveys, and feedback methods is very timely. Nadler has done an especially important service in this area in focusing on the variety of methods which can be used in gathering information and feeding it back to clients. The book is eclectic in its approach, reflecting the fact that there are many ways to gather information, many kinds to be gathered, and many approaches to the feedback process to reflect the particular goals of the change program.

Team building and the appropriate use of groups continues to be a second key ingredient of most change programs. So far no single book in the field has dealt explicitly enough with this important process. Dyer's approach will help the manager to diagnose when to use and not use groups and, most important, how to carry out team building when that kind of intervention is appropriate.

One of the most important new developments in the area of planned change is the conceptualizing of how to work with large systems to initiate and sustain change over time. The key to this success is "transition management," a stage or process frequently referred to in change theories, but never explored systematically from both a theoretical and practical point of view. Beckhard and Harris present a model which will help the manager to think about this crucial area. In addition, they provide a set of diagnostic and action tools which will enable the change manager in large systems to get a concrete handle on transition management.

The area of organization design has grown in importance as organizations have become more complex. Davis and Lawrence provide a concise and definitive analysis of that particularly elusive organization design—the matrix organization—and elucidate clearly its forms, functions, and modes of operation.

Human resource planning and career development has become an increasingly important element in the total planning of organization improvement programs. Schein's book provides a broad overview of this field from the points of view of the individual and the total life cycle, the interaction between the career and other aspects of life such as the family, and the manager attempting to design a total human resource planning and development system.

Future volumes of the series will continue to explore the connections between OD and other areas of management and organization theory—OD in the multinational context, a diagnostic framework for managers to use in starting up change programs, the role of alternative work patterns in increasing "the quality of work life," and the theory and practice of job redesign as a strategy of organization change.

It is exciting to see our field develop, expand, strengthen its roots, and grow outward in many new directions. I believe that the core theory or the integrative framework is not yet at hand, but that the varied activities of the theoreticians, researchers, and practitioners of planned change and OD are increasingly relevant not only to the change manager, but also to line managers at all levels. As the recognition grows that part of *every* manager's job is to plan, initiate, and manage change, so will the relevance of concepts and methods in this area come to be seen as integral to the management process itself. It continues to be the goal of this series to provide such relevant concepts and methods to managers. I hope we have succeeded in some measure in this new series of books.

Cambridge, Massachusetts   Edgar H. Schein
March 1978

PREFACE

The evolution and writing of this book have represented for me the pulling together of strands of work which have been going on for the last 15 years. I began with an interest in how organizations bring in and train their new members. The original purpose of the panel study which supplied much of the data for this book was to determine how people's values would change as a result of their organizational experiences. As I learned more about the evolution of careers and the problems which organizations face in developing their human resources, I realized that the early-career and training perspective was too narrow. One could not really look at the total problem of adult value changes or human resource management solely from the individual career occupant's point of view.

A second strand which is therefore reflected in this book is an interest in better understanding the concept of a total career. I have always been interdisciplinary in my approach to organizational problems and have found that to understand careers, one had to be both psychologist and sociologist/anthropologist. We do not have as yet a good set of concepts or a theory of how careers develop, and this book is not intended to provide such a theory, because we do not yet know enough. But major portions of this book are intended to illuminate how complex career dynamics really are and to forewarn readers not to accept too glibly some of the simple formulations of how to have a successful career which are circulating around. Most of the attention in this book is devoted to organizational careers, especially technical, professional, and managerial ones. The concepts evolved for career analysis should have some applicability to a broad range of other occupations, however.

A third strand of interest is reflected in the strong argument which I make throughout the book that organizations must be concerned with the total problem of human resource development for the sake of not only humanistic values, but organizational survival as well. My experience as an organization development consultant has revealed over and over again an insufficient sensitivity on the part of senior managers to the relationship between effective management of human resources and organizational performance and survival. Such effective human resource management must begin to take into account the long-range human issues—how organizational careers develop and evolve over time and how the organization must plan *for its own sake* to deal with the shifting needs of its people and the shifting nature of its work for which people will be needed. The link between formal planning and planning for human resources is increasingly becoming a matter of necessity rather than of convenience.

The fourth and final strand which is reflected in this book derives from my own aging and the recognition on a very personal level of how one's total life must be viewed in an evolutionary and total ecological context. The interaction of family, work, and more personal developmental concerns is very visible to me in myself, in my wife and family, and in my colleagues and their families. These phenomena are not really new, but changing social values have legitimized a more open discussion of them, and certain social trends, such as the trend toward dual careers, has made the issues more salient. The body of research on adult development is growing rapidly so that conjecture can gradually be replaced by demonstrated fact. But more important, both individuals as career occupants and managers who must make career decisions for others in organizations are becoming highly aware of the importance of thinking about the total adult in a total life cycle.

Because of the multiple strands which are reflected in this book, I have also written for multiple audiences. Some of the findings from my research panel have most relevance to young people entering organizations and to those managers who manage the entry and early-career phases. The developmentally oriented chapters are for those readers who want more insight into themselves and how their career and family issues can be put into a better personal perspective. The more organizationally oriented chapters, toward the end of the book, are written for managers who have to worry about organizational planning, especially human resource planning. All of the book is relevant to managers who wish to gain more insight into how to improve their own careers and how to deal more effectively with their own subordinates.

The ideas of this book derive from many sources, and I must therefore acknowledge a variety of intellectual debts. My many years of collaborative work with Richard Beckhard have deeply influenced my thinking, and Dick's editing of an early draft of this book directly influenced its present shape. My original mentor, the late Douglas McGregor, taught me what mentoring was all about long before I knew the term or its theoretical significance in today's adult development writings. Warren Bennis, Dave Berlew, Chris Argyris, and Dave Kolb were valued colleagues and collaborators on some of the early research and idea formulation on how individuals and organizations interact.

My main thanks, however, must go to my present colleagues Lotte Bailyn and John Van Maanen, who have been engaged with me over the past several years in an intense intellectual debate about work, family, career, organizations, and society. It is out of this joint intellectual effort that I acquired a real understanding of how work and family interact, how needs change throughout the adult life cycle, and how individual-organizational interactions must be conceptualized. We have done some joint writing, and each of us has pursued special interests within this broader context, but without the many hours of discussion, debate, testing of ideas, and joint research effort I would not have been able to formulate many of the arguments of this book. The arguments are my own, but their influence on my thinking is clear and central.

I owe a special debt to the 44 Sloan School alumni who were willing to become a panel in 1961, 1962, and 1963 and who were willing to return to M.I.T. in 1973 to be interviewed and surveyed about their evolving careers and lives. I found that the personal clinical approach was necessary to achieving an understanding of what career dynamics were all about, and I wish to thank the panelists for their continued willingness to probe with me into their lives.

The panel research would not have been possible without the support of the Office of Naval Research (ONR) and the special support of Dr. Bert King, who made the follow-up study in 1973 possible. In today's climate of publicly challenging many forms of government support for research, I think it especially important to express my personal view that ONR has always been truly dedicated to basic research in the social sciences and has made a tremendous contribution to the field of social and organizational psychology through its willingness to support projects such as my panel study.

My other major intellectual debt is to my many clients over the past 20 years. The opportunity to work on management development, organization development projects, team building at top corporate levels, and counseling individuals and groups about a wide range of human resource issues has provided some of the perspective I have needed to launch into this book. They, like the members of my research panel, must remain anonymous, but I freely acknowledge my debt to them for the ideas and stimulation which made this book possible.

In the process of rewriting, editing, and sharpening the book several people were especially helpful, and I wish to thank them at this time. Warner Burke, Bob Lee of the Exxon Corporation, Gene Dalton, Dick Beckhard, Lotte Bailyn, and John Van Maanen each made useful specific comments on all parts of the manuscript. However, Kirby Warren of Columbia University taught me a lesson in what true colleagueship can really be by not only challenging and enhancing ideas throughout the manuscript, but also giving virtually page-by-page editorial comments which immensely improved the final written version. I am extremely grateful to him for what must have been a very time-consuming effort.

I also wish to thank Marc Gerstein, who has been a helpful critic and, more important, has developed and applied in his organization many of the ideas about human resource planning and career development set forth in this book.

Work on the manuscript was tirelessly done by Madeleine Keyes and Brenda Venuti, and I thank them for their many hours of effort.

I also wish to thank my wife, Mary, who shared with me the running of an adult development seminar for Sloan Fellows and discussed at length with me what working, parenting of teenage children, and adult development are really all about and thereby helped to clarify many of the ideas which ultimately found their way onto the following pages. We have continued this seminar, which is now in its third year, and have found it to be a useful crucible for continuing to explore what happens to people and their families as their careers and lives unfold.

Finally, I want to dedicate this book to my children—Louisa, Elizabeth, and Peter—who watched with interest its evolution, but who have their own confrontations with its subject matter still ahead of them.

Cambridge, Massachusetts   E. H. S.
March 1978

CONTENTS

1
THE CAREER DEVELOPMENT PERSPECTIVE

Organizations are dependent on the performance of their people, and people are dependent on organizations to provide jobs and career opportunities. It is the purpose of this book to explore how organizations and people can match their needs so that both benefit.

Throughout this book I will be referring to the needs of organizations to recruit, manage, and develop human resources in order to maintain their effectiveness, survive, and grow. At the same time, I will be referring to the needs of people to find work situations which provide security, challenge, and opportunities for self-development throughout their entire life cycles. The problem for society, for organizations, and for people is how to match their respective needs, not only at the point of entry into an organization, but also throughout the entire career or life history of the person or the organization.

The concept of "career" makes it possible to explore how this matching takes place over time. The concept has meaning to both the individual pursuing an occupation—the "internal career"—and the organization trying to set up a sensible developmental path for employees to follow throughout their working life in the organization—the "external career" (Van Maanen and Schein, 1977). I will therefore organize the argument of this book in terms of what might be called a "career development perspective," a framework which will remind the reader throughout that one cannot understand fully the complex interaction which occurs between people and their employing organizations without a perspective that ties them together conceptually from the outset.

In adopting a "career development perspective" toward the interaction of people and organizations, I am trying to illuminate several kinds of problems which are of particular significance today: (1) the problem of improving human resource planning and development activities in organizations; (2) the problem of improving individual career planning and helping people who are caught in difficult work situations to cope more effectively with those situations; (3) the problem of improving the matching processes at all stages of the career so that early-, mid-, and late-career crises can be dealt with more effectively by both the organization and the individuals caught in these crises; (4) the problem of obsolescence, demotivation, and leveling off which occurs in mid- and late-career; (5) the problem of balancing family and work concerns at different life stages; and (6) the problem of maintaining the productivity and motivation of all those employees who are individual contributors and/or who are not motivated toward climbing the organizational ladder.

THE COMPONENTS OF THE CAREER DEVELOPMENT PERSPECTIVE

The essence of the career development perspective is its focus on *the interaction of the individual and the organization over time*. In order to analyze this interaction over time, it is necessary to spell out first a *basic model* of the total process of human resources planning and development (Fig. 1.1) and then to put this model into a temporal framework (Fig. 1.2).

Figure 1.1 shows the various elements which must be considered in analyzing fully the interaction of individual and organization. First, both the individual and the organization exist within a society—a social structure, a culture, a value system which defines occupations, criteria for success, and the expected paths through life. It is important to recognize that the culture, through its value system, influences both the organization and the individual in terms of what is considered to be a good career, appropriate work, a good place to work, an appropriate level of ambition, what success is, etc. As we will see, one of the dilemmas that surfaces when we take a developmental perspective is that the values surrounding work and career are themselves changing, which means that in a given organization there may be simultaneously several sets of values represented in employees and managers of different ages.

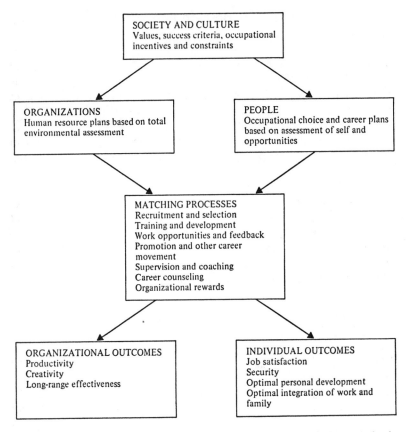

Fig. 1.1 Human Resource Planning and Development (HRPD): A basic model.

Society influences both organizations and people directly through government legislation, incentives, tax programs, the educational system, and other social institutions. These influences will not be a primary focus of this book, but they cannot be ignored. Both the organization and the individual have to cope within that total environment. For the organization this means attention to labor-market characteristics, economic conditions, laws governing equal employment opportunities, occupational safety and health, retirement policies and age discrimination, technological forces, and market characteristics which specify ultimately what kinds of skills will be needed in the employee pool and so on. For the individual this means attention to occupational and educational opportunities, and a balancing of career concerns

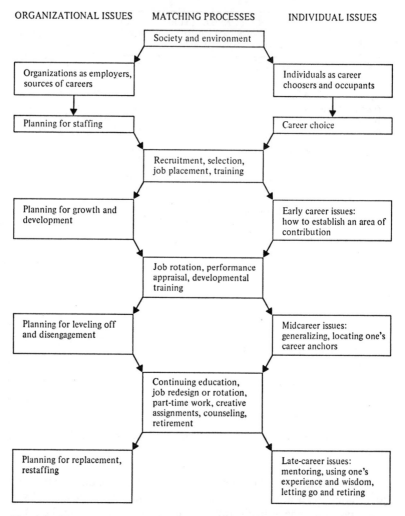

Fig. 1.2 Human Resource Planning and Development: A temporal development model.

with concerns for the family, self-development, and a life-style which has long-range viability. As more women enter the work force as full-time employees, both husbands and wives will have to give increasing attention to how to manage their "dual career" families (Bailyn, 1970; Rapoport and Rapoport, 1976).

In the center of Fig. 1.1 are depicted the "matching processes" which bring the individual and the organization together into, ideally, a mutually profitable relationship. Recruitment, selection, training, job assignment, performance appraisal, promotion, etc., are viewed here as matching processes, not processes which are solely the prerogative of the organization in fulfilling its own needs to get a job done. It is an essential argument throughout this book that how such human resource activities are managed will influence the long-range outcome for both the individual and the organization and that they are mutually dependent. For the long-range health of both their organizations and the individual employee, managers cannot ignore the consequences of how they manage people.

If the matching processes work optimally, both the organization and the individual will benefit—increased productivity levels, creativity and long-range effectiveness for the organization and job satisfaction, security, optimal personal development, and optimal integration of work and family for the individual. As we will see, the word "optimal" is important here because: (1) people vary in the degree to which they need to be career- or work-involved; (2) these needs change with stages of family and life development; and (3) these needs vary with the particular content of the work being pursued (Bailyn, 1977; Bailyn and Schein, 1972, 1976).

Figure 1.2 expands the concepts above into a temporal, developmental perspective. On the left-hand side of Fig. 1.2 we see the occupational/organizational processes; on the right-hand side, the individual processes; and in the middle, the matching processes. As I indicated above, society and the culture, through their laws, policies, social institutions, and programs, create the incentives and constraints which make up the occupational structure, or the labor market. Organizational recruitment and personnel development policies will ultimately reflect the environmental conditions which operate. These conditions identify as a major activity on the part of the organization its *planning* function in order to identify for both the short- and long-run what its needs for human resources will be. As Fig. 1.2 shows, these planning activities must take into account the career development cycle, focusing not only on initial recruitment, but also on the growth and development of human resources, leveling off and disengaging as people's needs change or as the nature of the work changes, and retirement and replacement. It is important to emphasize from the outset that such *organizational* planning must take place for the sake of *organizational* effectiveness, whether or not any individual career planning takes place. Too much career-planning focus has recently been given to helping individuals plan, and not enough attention has been given to human resource planning as a major and essential organizational activity.

Human resource planning as a key organizational activity becomes especially important as the rate of change in the world is itself increasing. Not only is it important to know what kinds of skills will be needed to fulfill particular organizational missions, but also the rapid change in key jobs such as those of functional and general managers requires more carefully thought-out training and development programs. Interdependence among various organizational specialities is also increasing, requiring a more careful assessment of how many of each kind of employee will be needed in order to maintain a reasonable balance. Finally, key specialities are coming to be more important to organizational performance, e.g., financial specialists, computer programmers, marketing experts, project managers, employees who can work at key organizational interfaces, and so on. Some of these specialists will be a scarce resource, requiring more careful planning in order to retain and challenge them.

The major stages of the internal career, which will be discussed in detail in subsequent chapters, are shown in the right-hand column of Fig. 1.2. By highlighting the dilemmas of different career stages, I am trying to indicate forcefully that needs change over time and that a good matching system must have the capacity to take those changing needs into account. Ultimately, the dilemma of an effective total human resource planning and development system is how to maintain a reasonable matching process when both individual and organizational needs change in response to changing environmental circumstances and to internal developmental processes.

In summary, a career development perspective as I am defining it here reminds us that both the individual and the organization exist in complex environments and that their interaction is partly determined by external forces. Furthermore, the interaction is dynamic and reflects changing needs on the part of both the individual and the organization. In the next section of this chapter, I will discuss some of the advantages of adopting such a perspective, in spite of its greater complexity.

WHY ADOPT A CAREER DEVELOPMENT PERSPECTIVE?

1. *Encourage Analysis of the Total Person*

The career development perspective encourages one to consider the *total person* who comes to work. In practice this point of view means that we must consider how activities related to self-development, career development, and family development interact throughout the entire life span of that person. Such a concern with the total person has become especially important in recent years because of societal value changes about the meaning and importance of work, how work and family concerns *should* interact, how one should measure one's success in life, the proper role of husbands and wives in dual careers, the importance of having children, how to care for them, and so on (Van Maanen, Schein, and Bailyn, 1977).

Much has been said in books on management about the need to manage the "whole" person, but not much help has been given to the manager to understand the whole person, to gain insight into how needs change throughout the course of life. One of the major goals of this book will be to provide some of this insight so that the manager can get a more realistic sense of what is involved in managing the whole person. At the same time, we will see that some of the changes which are occurring will necessitate that organizations begin to rethink and redesign some of their reward systems and personnel policies so as to remain more responsive to the needs which people are increasingly bringing into the work place.

2. Encourage Analysis of Different Careers and Occupations within Organizations and How They Interact

The career development perspective reminds us that individuals enter organizations through many kinds of occupations—engineering, sales, finance, accounting, production work, clerical and office work, and so on. Some of these occupations become more specialized and lead to staff or individual contributor careers in R&D, finance, or marketing; many of them level off into some skilled or craft level of work in manufacturing, service, maintenance, or sales; all of them constitute some kind of recruitment base for people to go into supervision, administration, and ultimately higher levels of functional or general management.

It is important to understand not only the paths and sequences within each of these occupations within the organization, but also their interaction, as the success of the organization becomes more dependent on such interaction. For most large organizations today, both the technology underlying what they produce and the marketplace within which they deliver or sell their product or service have become so complex that success is becoming increasingly dependent on effective interaction among technical, financial, and marketing people (Lawrence and Lorsch, 1969). Such interaction can best be understood from the career development perspective, which reminds us that each of these types of people will have developed a cognitive style, a set of values and attitudes, and a set of skills which reflects their particular occupation and career history. The manager who must integrate the contributions of such diverse and specialized resources must, first, understand that his or her people do differ because of their career history, and, second, learn how to take such differences into account. Individuals managing their own careers must be aware of the characteristics of their occupations and their unique career histories.

Furthermore, one cannot assess total organizational effectiveness over long periods of time without considering the interaction of different occupational groups over that period of time. For example, many companies' early growth and success stem from a technological edge based on the creativity of the entrepreneur and the skill of the engineering and production departments. Such companies become very sophisticated in managing the careers of technical people and manufacturing people. As such companies grow, acquire competitors, and sell in more varied markets, the relative importance of marketing, sales skills, and financial-control systems increases. For example, I am involved in several organization development projects in which the key issue is a power struggle among: (1) technical and manufacturing people who founded the company and believe that they really continue to understand the marketplace; (2) marketing people who came up through sales and are convinced that the marketplace has changed in ways that the first group cannot possibly understand; and (3) financial-control people who are trying to convince the other two groups that the declining availability of capital, strong competition from other companies, and insufficient attention to financial and other controls within the present system are the key issues to be managed. The power struggle works itself out in who is hired, what kind of person gets promoted, and whether or not talented people in the group that is losing power will continue to remain in the organization and make their contribution. Ultimately, the success of these organizations will depend on their ability to attract good people in all of these areas, create viable career paths for all of them, and manage them in a way that will integrate their efforts.

3. *Enlarge the Concept of Organization Development*

The career development perspective makes it possible to take a *more realistic view of how organization development and long-range organizational health can be related to each other.* Most writers on organization development emphasize the importance of creating "readiness for change," or the need for a "critical mass" before change will be sustained, or the need to "unfreeze" the system before a new innovation can be considered and implemented, but few of these writers (myself included) have given a clear picture of how such readiness can be achieved or how critical masses of committed employees or managers can be created or found (Beckhard, 1969; Bennis, 1969; Blake and Mouton, 1969; Schein, 1969, 1972).

Massive training interventions, e.g., putting everyone through a common training program, may be one method. A much preferable solution which I have observed in some companies is to expose a broad range of employees and young managers to relevant developmental experiences early in their careers, with the explicit expectation that such experiences may not pay off for five, ten, or fifteen years until those same people have reached senior positions. If they have been through the right kinds of developmental experiences early in their careers, they will be more ready to change the organization. And if *many* of them have had similar kinds of early experiences, they are more likely to support one another and to create that much-needed "critical mass." In other words, if an organization development program is to involve any real change in organizational culture, it probably must be combined with an explicit career development program which considers how such cultural change can be initiated and sustained over longer periods of time. Without such a career development emphasis, OD interventions run the risk of being just short-run fads or fail to get off the ground in the first place.

For example, both General Foods and Procter and Gamble started to send a wide variety of middle managers to sensitivity training programs in the 1950s as a kind of general investment in the development of these people. The debate about the utility of such training for the immediate improvement of management eventually led to a curtailing of such training, but not before a very large number of managers in both companies had been exposed to the values of increasing one's self-insight, learning how to observe and manage groups better, and improving their communication skills. In both companies, some specific payoffs came in later years, when programs of improving the productivity of plants were launched. Such programs were significantly aided by the presence of senior managers who, because of their own early developmental insights, had a feel for some of the more participative methods which were being attempted. In both companies I was later involved in projects which required a greater degree of teamwork because of the recognition of a growing interdependence among functions. The team-building efforts I helped to design worked much better with managers who had developed over ten years in a climate which put a positive value on such activities.

If one attempts to reconstruct how such a positive value climate arose in the first place, one would have to give credit to the early managers of management development who launched extensive career development programs which resulted in "seeding" new ideas in many parts of the organization. Because many managers were involved over many years, mutual support could develop for some of the new ideas of group dynamics, which in turn produced the critical masses needed to try specific new experiments such as those involving redesign of production work and new concepts of plant management.

To put it another way, the career development perspective forces one to look at organizational and individual effectiveness over longer periods of time—several decades—and to recognize that long-range changes must be embodied in the skills, values, and attitudes of the individual managers and employees who make up the key elements of the organization over that span of time. Too many organization development efforts are geared to fixing immediate problems with existing people; no provision is made for a change of people. For example, to redesign the work system of a factory without creating a career development system which will ensure that *future* plant managers will feel comfortable with the new work system is to invite failure in the long run. To restructure, through a team-building effort, how a top-management team works together, without worrying about management succession and the attitudes of future individuals who will manage or join the team is to do an incomplete job of organization development.

4. Facilitate the Analysis and Understanding of Organizational "Climate," or "Culture"

The career development perspective permits and encourages one to analyze that elusive phenomenon which we call organization "climate," "culture," or the "personality" of the organization. What we typically mean by such terms is that organizations differ, often dramatically, in their cultures—the kinds of goals they have, the kinds of styles they use, the values which underlie employee relations and manager/subordinate interactions, their stances toward the community, and so on (Schein, 1968; Schein and Lippitt, 1966; Schein and Ott, 1962; Allen and Silverweig, 1976). Visitors to organizations and new employees can feel such differences, which are often embodied in the architecture and physical layout of work (Steele, 1973), but it is often difficult to figure out how such differences arose in the first place.

The career development perspective leads us to two kinds of hypotheses about cultural differences among organizations. *First*, differences may be based on the *personality and career history of the founders and key members* of the organization (Gellerman, 1960). The values and attitudes of founders and early key members often become the source of later company policies, and one can understand those policies only by going back and analyzing the key people. In pursuing such an analysis of key people, it becomes important to consider not only their personalities, but also their occupational backgrounds and actual career development. For example, a company founded by an engineer (technical entrepreneur) will likely differ from a company founded by a venture capitalist whose entrepreneurial skills lie in finance and marketing rather than in engineering or manufacturing. A company founded by a person whose whole career history has been entrepreneurial will likely differ from a company founded by a person whose early history was in large organizations and whose entrepreneurial move resulted from disillusionment with such large organizations.

Second, differences may be based on the *cognitive, attitudinal, and value differences of the actual occupations which dominate that organization.* In other words, there is evidence that different kinds of occupations reflect differences in cognitive styles, values, and attitudes (Plovnick, 1976; Kolb and Fry, 1975; Lawrence and Lorsch, 1969; Schein, 1975; Keen, 1977). If two companies are built on two different technologies which reflect such occupational differences, one would expect that over a period of time the company "culture" would reflect the original differences in the technologies. For example, one of the differences between chemical engineering and electrical engineering is that the chemical engineer must live with higher degrees of uncertainty and longer feedback loops than the electrical engineer does; chemical processes change fundamentally as one goes from invention in the laboratory to pilot plant to final production plant scale, whereas a circuit design, once achieved, does not change fundamentally as one decides to produce more and more of them. In comparing process industries with electronics industries, one would therefore expect to find cultural differences which reflect this fundamental difference in cognitive orientation. To extend the hypothesis, one might expect to find characteristic differences among companies that are dominated by financial people, lawyers, engineers, salespeople, or other occupational groups. Such differences, if and when they are found, are usually the key to the managerial style and assumptions operating in the organization. If they are not understood, it is not possible to understand what kind of organization development program will work or what kind of person is more or less likely to succeed in the organization.

5. *Provide Perspective on Social Changes*

Finally, and implicit in much of what has been said above, the career development perspective focuses on some of the most important changes which are occurring in our society and in the world. Over the past several decades we have witnessed a number of changes which are tantamount to revolutions—major technological advances as exemplified in our ability to conquer space, harness nuclear energy, and conduct genetic experiments; major political and economic changes which have created more world markets and the opportunity for people to pursue careers on a broader, "global" basis; major social changes in our attitudes toward work, the rights of women and minorities to pursue careers on an equal basis with white males, the rights of workers to a safe and secure work environment, and the growing rights of workers to be legitimately involved in some of the decisions involving their own work and future careers; and major changes in social attitudes toward preserving the environment. All of these and other changes have occurred in a climate of economic growth and affluence which has created for many a much wider range of career options, including the option not to pursue a traditional career. Many young people today attach much less importance to a stable and secure career, have much less loyalty to their employing organizations, and have much less respect for the authority of position if that authority is not backed up by personal expertise.

As long as our society remains relatively "open," in the sense of continuing to provide many options, we will see a growing need for organizations to reassess their recruitment and management policies and their ways of rewarding people over the long haul. Alternatively, we may see much more acceptance of turnover, low motivation, second and third careers, part-time work, and other new work patterns. But career development issues are here to stay as social values place ever greater importance on the full development of human potential and as economic and technological conditions make it prudent for organizations to worry about such full development.

HOW THIS BOOK IS ORGANIZED

Part 1 of this book attempts to spell out the major dynamics of individual development as they apply to a full understanding of the career. This emphasis comes first because self-insight must precede insight into how to manage others. The manager concerned with HRPD must first understand himself or herself as a total human being before being able to think clearly about helping others to plan or manage their careers. Furthermore, the manager must understand the varieties of individual needs which operate throughout the life cycle in order to do a good job of organization planning.

Part 2 of the book deals with the dynamics of the career. Considerable attention will be given to the early career, where some of the most difficult and critical matching decisions occur. Each chapter in Part 2 attempts to elucidate career issues from both the individual and the organizational points of view, spell out possible negative consequences for the individual and the organization, and suggest some ways in which these negative consequences can be avoided.

Part 3 deals with the organization and the total process of human resource planning and development from the managerial point of view. A model of a total organizational HRPD system is presented and its various components discussed, with special emphasis on job/role planning and the linkage of various planning and development activities. This material is presented last because it presumes some insight into the complexity of the individual and the career, which is spelled out in Parts 1 and 2. However, the manager who feels that he or she already senses this complexity could jump directly to this portion of the book with profit.

The final chapter summarizes the individual, the career, and the organizational perspectives and indicates what employers, individuals in careers, and other institutions can do to improve the total HRPD process.

PART 1
THE INDIVIDUAL AND THE LIFE CYLE

In the next five chapters I will spell out the major life-cycle issues confronting a person. After a general discussion of cycles, stages, and life tasks, I will review the major tasks of the biosocial cycle, the career cycle, and the stages and states of the family, attempting to illustrate throughout the complex interactions of these various sets of life tasks. How the individual can better cope with life tasks is covered in the final chapter of Part 1.

2
INDIVIDUAL DEVELOPMENT

INTRODUCTION

Any human resource planning and development system must attempt to match the needs of the organization with those of the individual. If such a system is to work, much more effort must be devoted to fully understanding the needs and characteristics of the individual. Those needs derive not only from the individual's working life, but also from the *interaction* within the total "life space" of issues of work, family, and self-development. One of the weaknesses of traditional employee and management development systems has been the tendency to assume that employees can be conceived of as leaving family and self at home when they come to work and that therefore the organization need worry only about creating opportunities for *work*-oriented development activities. As the study of adult development progresses, it is becoming more and more clear that work, family, and self concerns interact strongly within people throughout their lives. This interaction simply cannot any longer be ignored. The organization, as Chester Barnard pointed out long ago, *pays* people only for certain of their *activities* (Barnard, 1938), but it is *whole persons* who come to work. How they perform those activities will depend on personal factors above and beyond the immediate work setting, organization policies, and how they are managed (Schein, 1970).

I can make this point in another way by relating what happened in a recent class session with a group of 27 high-level managers in the

MIT Sloan School ten-week Senior Executive Program. I presented the idea that it will become increasingly important for managers to know something of the details of their subordinates' family situations in order to know how best to manage those subordinates. Roughly one-third of the class objected violently to the very idea, asserting that this was not only unnecessary, but also an invasion of privacy and a violation of all kinds of traditional organizational values. While I was mentally preparing to deal with this set of counterarguments, several other members of the class jumped into the discussion with comments such as the following:

> "You may feel it's an invasion of privacy, Fred, but frankly I couldn't run my organization unless I know all about the family situation of each of my subordinates so that I can assess their mood and their readiness at any given time to tackle tough assignments. If they are having any problems at home, I want to know about it and help out so that my people don't have to pretend with me when they are preoccupied."

> "If I tried to give my subordinate an assignment which might involve a geographical transfer or even some small amount of travel without knowing how this would affect his immediate family situation, I would find myself having real trouble and, at worst, would create a situation where the person would do a lousy job because he resented being away from home."

I asked the total group how their companies were viewing these phenomena and learned that roughly one-third of them did have the traditional "hands-off" view, roughly one-third did not see the issues as very strong one way or the other, and roughly one-third had well-developed, explicit programs of considering family and self-development issues as part of any job assignment or development activity at work. Some companies, I was told, do not make geographical moves unless the manager's spouse has been consulted and has had a chance to visit the new location. This company has found that the spouse's adjustment makes a major difference to the job effectiveness of the manager. As often as not, when someone fails in an overseas assignment in a multinational corporation, it is because the *spouse* could not adjust to the new culture.

To further test the involvement of companies in family issues, we interviewed 20 senior executives representing different large corporations both in the United States and overseas to determine to what extent their personnel policies gave consideration to family issues in relation to moving. In 18 of 20 companies the executive reported some kind of family-oriented activity, including explicit discussions with the spouse, trial visits, time delays to permit children to complete school, etc. (Hopkins, 1976).

The examples given so far deal with career/*family* issues, but the career/*self* issues are just as important. It is important for the organization to know when employees are having personal problems or when they are entering a phase of adulthood in which certain emotional issues are likely to be very salient. If those kinds of issues are ignored or actually ruled out of order, the potential cost is high to both the organization and the individual, because effective work is not possible when the person is emotionally preoccupied with some other issue. To give a trivial example, we would hardly want a 55-year-old airlines pilot who is having personal trouble with his wife to attempt to prove his manhood by continuing to fly under potentially hazardous conditions. If he is having emotional concerns, it might be best for him *and the company* for his boss to deal with those concerns directly, encourage some counseling, talk out the problem, or encourage him to take a two-week holiday rather than to insist on continuing to perform a difficult task when under emotional stress.

Many managers will rebel at this point, rightly arguing that they are not trained to understand all of these emotional issues, much less to engage in counseling relationships with their subordinates. I am not arguing, however, that managers should become diagnosticians, amateur counselors, or amateur psychologists; what I am arguing is that managers should become *aware* that in themselves, their bosses, and their subordinates, issues emanating from family life and from more personal concerns *do* influence how they perform their daily work and their longer-range career decisions. This awareness does not necessarily lead to anything more than communicating to others that you are aware and that the door is open to a discussion of what may be going on *in relation to task performance.* In other words, bosses should learn to create a climate that would make it possible for subordinates to feel free to tell them on any given day that they are having a crisis at home and would appreciate the day off; subordinates should be encouraged to reveal such information rather than being told to "solve their personal problems on their own time." If managers can accept the reality of the interaction of work, family, and self issues, they can at least help to alleviate some of the immediate pressures by managing their people more flexibly and understandingly, thereby increasing the effectiveness of the total organization in the long run.

The skills involved here for the manager are basically the same ones that lead to effective supervision—the ability to create a communication climate in which subordinates feel free to tell the truth, even if the truth is painful. Many managers unwittingly send the message that they do not want to hear about problems; they only want to hear that the problems have been resolved. If the subordinates cannot solve the problem, they will often simply hide from their boss the information that a problem exists. In the work area most managers can accept that this situation is undesirable—it is better to know about problems than to create a climate in which task-related information is hidden. The same logic applies to personal and family issues. If subordinates feel free to reveal problems, managers still have the option of saying, "I can't help you and don't really want to get involved, but if it is preventing you from doing a good job, let's figure out what you do need to get you back on the track." The manager can then encourage exploration of options—taking time off, seeing a counselor, doing nothing, etc.—without in any way getting involved in the content of the problem itself.

I am not saying that such skills are easily learned or easy to apply; I am saying that such skills are becoming more important in the total management of human resources. Much of the manager's ability to handle these areas will depend on an intellectual understanding of how work, family, and emotional issues interact and change over time. The rest of this chapter and the following ones in Part 1 are designed to sketch out some of the highlights of this area.

THE CONCEPT OF CYCLES AND STAGES

Every person can be thought of as existing in a world in which there are always multiple issues and problems to be dealt with. For most of us in Western society these issues can be divided into three basic categories:

1. Issues and problems that derive from our *biological* and *social aging* processes. As we grow and develop, predictable changes occur in our bodies and in our body chemistry which produce stages such as puberty and menopause. We also develop a variety of chronic illnesses, such as arterial disease, which lead ultimately to death. Many of our emotions reflect these basic changes in body chemistry and therefore can be thought of as being biologically linked. At the same time, our society and culture has a complex system of "age grading"—a set of expectations of what the individual should be doing and how he or she should be behaving at different ages (Neugarten, 1968).*

---

*It should also be noted that many of these expectations are changing rapidly as social values shift. Throughout this chapter I will be referring to traditional middle-class "trends" or "patterns," fully recognizing that they do not apply to all groups and, especially, may differ for men and women.

Thus "children" are expected to be emotional, impulsive, and playful; "adolescents" are expected to be confused and impulsive but also striving to reach adulthood; "adults" are expected to be "responsible" with respect to both their work and family obligations; and the "elderly" are expected to slow down, concern themselves more with leisure-time activities, and be accepting of their reduced levels of responsibility. These biological forces and the accompanying age-related social or cultural expectations make up the biosocial cycle—that part of the life cycle dealing with a person's *self-development*.

2. Another set of issues and problems concerns the person's *family* relationships. At an early age one's family issues relate to one's own parents and the problems of achieving independence. Sometime in the twenties one is typically expected to get married and to have children, commencing a whole new cycle of family issues, responsibilities, and problems. One's family of origin does not disappear at this point, however. Indeed, many of the most difficult problems of midlife stem from the fact that the demands of one's immediate spouse and children may conflict with those of one's parents, who are now older and becoming more dependent. So we all live in a family cycle in which our family of origin and our immediate family put various demands and constraints on us as well as provide nurturance, pleasure, growth opportunities, and, through our own children, the possibility of leaving something of ourselves behind to posterity.

Obviously the issues that derive from our families interact with the biosocial issues. But it is useful to think of these two sets of issues as separate cycles in interaction rather than as a single life cycle, because our parents, spouses, and children make demands and create opportunities which go beyond our immediate selves. Many of the forces emanating from the family are not under our control, and many of our roles, such as being a son or daughter or parent, are not reversible. We cannot quit such roles as we can quit a job; instead, we have to find a way to perform those roles.

3. The third major set of issues for most people in our society has to do with *work and the building of a career*. These issues have in the past been more salient for men, but they are increasingly coming to be equally crucial issues for women. Paid employment is the basic means by which society provides for the survival of the individual and the family unit. It is therefore integral to all of life, but it is separable from the other two cycles, because many of the constraints and opportunities which create the work/career cycle are not under the control of the individual or the family. Instead, they emanate from societal definitions of needs, economic institutions, traditions and policies

built into the educational and the occupational structure, and ultimately the specific policies of employing organizations themselves. The work/career cycle thus involves early occupational images, periods of preparation for work through education and training, a working life with many substages, and ultimately retirement and/or new work or career issues. The forces that act on people in regard to their work/career interact with the biosocial issues and the family issues, but each group of issues has an independent set of origins, therefore justifying the identification of *three* different cycles.

MILESTONES, CHOICE POINTS, GOALS, AND END POINTS

Each cycle contains smooth, even stretches as well as bumpy, obstruction-filled stretches. Usually each cycle is marked by milestones indicating where the person is and what he or she has accomplished. Finally, there are choice points where the person must decide which way to head. But the movement of life is always forward, linked to the biological clock and cultural norms. One can drift, stall, or stagnate, but there is basically no stopping and no turning back.

Each of the cycles has an ultimate goal or state to be reached, which is defined partly by human biological nature and partly by cultural norms. Thus the biosocial cycle involves growth, the culmination of one's abilities, and finally moves toward the end stage of death. The family cycle involves procreation, the education and development of one's children, and moves toward the "goal" of sending them off into independent lives of their own, so that the society as a whole and its culture are preserved.* The work/career cycle involves one's learning, productive contribution to an occupation or organization, and eventually moves toward retirement. Progress toward the end point is rarely smooth, and each cycle involves a period of peaking prior to a period of decline toward the ultimate end state or goal. Only the biological cycle has a clear end *point* of death; the family continues after the children have gone off on their own; retirement does not necessarily mean the end of working or productive involvement. The biosocial cycle, the family cycle, and the work cycle provide many options and choices after their peaks have been reached, and it is the quality of those choices—how we handle the period after the peak contribution—that ultimately defines the quality of our total lives and prepares us to accept death.

---

*It should be noted that values in American society around "normal" family life are rapidly changing, and in many dual-career families it is *not* taken for granted that one has children (Bailyn, in press).

The patterns of our lives, the choice points, and the milestones are shaped largely by society and cultural norms. However, the culture reflects to some extent the biological realities of human nature. Thus the period of adolescence and preparation for adulthood, work, and family responsibilities corresponds roughly to the biological onset of puberty and the period of emotional turmoil which accompanies biochemical changes in the person. The time when a person is expected to build a family and make a maximum contribution to society through work has tended to correlate with periods of maximum sexual potency and physical or emotional strength. Old age and retirement have tended to correspond roughly to periods of physical decline and ill health. But as we will see when we examine these periods in more detail, these cultural norms also create problems and incongruities. The most dramatic example is the situation facing women, who until very recently were forced, in effect, to choose either family or career, because cultural norms demanded maximum involvement in either one roughly during the decade from age 25 to 35. Such a conflict has not existed for men, because they can work while the women produce and care for the children. But even if the man was willing to care for the children, the period of pregnancy is unavoidably the woman's, and many organizations have justified their failure to give women responsible, high-level jobs on the grounds that they would become pregnant and have to take leave at times crucial to their careers.*

THE CONCEPT OF LIFE TASKS AND COPING

The cycles overlap and interact, and this interaction may be beneficial or problematic for the individual. We can visualize the situation in terms of the diagram shown in Fig. 2.1, which shows the three cycles in terms of peaks and valleys. A valley is a smooth, routinely functioning section of the cycle; a peak signifies either an obstacle or a choice point and thus poses a task which the person must deal with. Each of the cycles has associated with it its own set of tasks and choices (see Chapters 3, 4, and 5). If the tasks require a great deal of coping and emotional energy, it may make a major difference to the individual whether or not they are spaced out or come simultaneously. For example, if the person marries and takes a first job at the same time, as many graduating seniors from college do, he or she is taking on two major life tasks—one in the work/career cycle and one in the family

---

*The irony of such norms and policies is that unlike heart attacks or other unpredictable health problems for which sick leave is granted without question, pregnancy can be planned.

EXTERNALLY DEFINED CYCLES IN A GIVEN SOCIETY

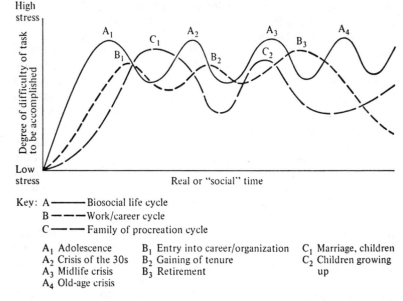

Key: A————Biosocial life cycle
     B— — —Work/career cycle
     C— — Family of procreation cycle

A_1 Adolescence	B_1 Entry into career/organization	C_1 Marriage, children
A_2 Crisis of the 30s	B_2 Gaining of tenure	C_2 Children growing
A_3 Midlife crisis	B_3 Retirement	up
A_4 Old-age crisis		

Fig. 2.1 A model of life/career/family cycle interaction. (Major hypothesis: Individual effectiveness is lowest when total difficulty of tasks is highest, but greater difficulty also produces greater opportunity for radical growth.)

cycle—both of which require investments of time and energy which may be beyond what the individual can muster. In this case the individual may cope by reducing involvement in one or the other cycle, creating a more stressful work or marriage situation, or may cope by finding a new and radically different resolution of the work-family conflict.

How the individual copes with the tasks posed by the various life cycles will be a function of his or her *biological makeup* (health, energy level, native intelligence, temperament, and other genetically linked factors); *early childhood experiences,* both physical and emotional (nutrition, childhood health problems, emotional strains in the parents, etc.); *socialization* (the values and attitudes learned in the family, in school, and in the peer group and which determine life goals, ambitions, and values about legitimate means by which to achieve those goals and ambitions); *the accumulated experience* up to the point where a new task has to be faced and dealt with; and *family relationships.*

Some personality theories, primarily those stemming from Freudian models, emphasize the *continuity* of how the person copes. Personality styles learned in childhood continue to operate throughout life, and each major set of transitions, e.g., adolescence, midlife, and old age, tends to rekindle old conflicts and reactivate old coping styles. There is some evidence from longitudinal studies (Maas and Kuypers, 1974) that people who have had difficulty in their youth with health and adjustment problems have a more difficult time adjusting to retirement and old age. Some of the same health problems which plagued these people as adolescents or young adults but remained dormant throughout the bulk of their adult lives recur in old age.

Other personality theories, primarily those stemming from Jungian models, emphasize the *discontinuities* in personal lives, the unused potentials, the opportunities for growth throughout life. Though personal styles are learned in childhood, those parts of the personality not engaged or used do not disappear. Rather, they may be dormant for long periods of time, only to emerge at midlife or even later. Life is seen as a continuously unfolding process in which each person has at least the opportunity to continue to develop unused potentials. For example, many people find in later stages of their lives that they have creative urges and talents they never exercised because of the necessity to be involved in practical, day-to-day work concerns. A research project at Boston University is studying the lives of 30 people who were successful first in a traditional career such as business or law and who switched after the age of 30 into the creative and performing arts as full-fledged second careers. To be included in the study each person had to be successful in both the first and second careers, which meant that a high degree of talent and motivation had to be displayed in a brand new area. The researcher had relatively little difficulty locating people who had made such a transition successfully (Osherson, personal communication, 1976).

The evidence is mixed on which model of human nature is more accurate, largely because not enough longitudinal research has been completed to test how stable or labile the human personality really is. Most likely we will find in every person areas of stability which reflect the core learning and socialization of early childhood, but we will also find that such core learning does not limit the person in other life areas (Schein, 1971). The opportunity to develop new areas of skill, new values, and new personality traits will probably be found to be an important part of each life, but how the person uses those opportunities will, in turn, reflect earlier experiences.

To help people in such coping will ultimately involve changes in cultural norms, early-childhood socialization, and increased opportunities for health, nutrition, and education. In addition, we must develop systems of education and training for adults which not only enable people to accurately diagnose their opportunities for growth, but also teach coping skills which make it possible for them to take advantage of those opportunities once they arise. Adult education, sensitivity training, and other recent experiments with "personal growth" in adulthood show that it is indeed possible for people to increase their capacity to grow and to take advantage of new opportunities throughout their lifetimes. The film *Harry and Tonto* makes a critically important point when it shows how Harry in his seventies turned the adversity of eviction and the loss of his best friend into an opportunity to develop some unused parts of himself and build a new life-style. As I will attempt to show later, such learning often involves critical yet *small* adjustments in one's manner of living, not always major revolutions such as changing jobs, divorce, or physical relocation.

Having identified the concept of stages and tasks and having pointed out the importance of their interaction, let us next look at each of the major cycles from the point of view of the major tasks they involve.

3
THE STAGES AND TASKS
OF THE BIOSOCIAL LIFE CYCLE

Over the past several years researchers have begun to identify the major developmental stages that all people go through in some form or another and have attempted to pinpoint specific transitions, often called "crises," which reflect particularly difficult life tasks (Erickson, 1959; Levinson *et al.*, 1974; Gould, 1972, 1975; Vaillant and MacArthur, 1972; Vaillant, 1977). Much of this research builds on earlier studies in developmental psychology (Baltes and Schaie, 1973; Datan and Ginsberg, 1975; Sze, 1975), but it is only recently that "adult" stages of development have been specifically pinpointed. Gail Sheehy's book *Passages* (1976) has brought popular attention to this field, and a number of textbooks have begun to summarize and delineate those stages (Troll, 1975; Kimmel, 1974; Kalish, 1975; Bischof, 1976). Since much of the research has been done on men, there is likely to be some male-oriented bias in the stages and crises that have been identified. It should also be noted that any attempt to derive general stages ignores the considerable differences which probably result from socioeconomic levels and other features of society which affect cultural norms. Finally, one cannot ignore the fact that these norms are themselves rapidly changing; thus what may be a "normal" stage today may be considered very unusual a decade from now.

Most of the researchers working in the area of adult development have found that the major tasks are roughly correlated with age, probably because of the two factors which were mentioned previously—age-related biological changes and the powerful cultural norms about what is expected of people at different ages (Neugarten, 1968). In our culture many of these norms revolve around the decades, and we tend to think of becoming 30, 40, 50, or 60 as major milestones in our lives. Some milestones derive from *laws*— becoming 18 or 21, when one is allowed to enter bars, obtain a driver's license, enlist, or be tried in adult rather than in juvenile court; others derive from *organizational* and *social* policies—the age of mandatory retirement, when one is eligible to collect social security benefits, and so on. It should be remembered, however, that though there are correlations with age, there is also a huge amount of *individual* variation in both the sequencing of events and the ages at which they occur.

There is no easy way to summarize the vast series of events which make up the total life cycle. I have attempted to organize these stages in terms of a rough chronology, shown in Table 3.1. Note that the first major stage—from roughly adolescence through the late twenties or early thirties—is a period of getting away from home and establishing oneself in the adult world. One is building both a career and a family, and though one tends to be very sure of oneself in those years, the commitments made are in fact somewhat provisional and will be reviewed by the person in the next two decades. There are many difficult tasks to be accomplished in this period, but it is also a period of high energy, enthusiasm, and idealism, which make it easier for the person to cope.

The transition into the thirties is the first major time of reappraisal for most people. Ideals are reexamined and reestablished, provisional commitments are tested, and the person enters a period of either stabilization or major redirection. The realities of the world of work, marriage, child rearing, and coping with financial and other responsibilities displace the ideals of the twenties, forcing a whole series of choices. As these choices are made, the person enters a period of more permanent lasting commitments, usually described as "settling down" or "putting down roots."

In their late thirties or early forties most people face some kind of "midlife" transition or "crisis." Permanent commitments have now been made, and their consequences have to be assessed against the dreams, hopes, and ambitions of earlier times. What forces this self-confrontation is the recognition at some level of awareness of one's own mortality, of the fact that one has already lived at least half of one's life (Jacques, 1965; Rogers, 1974). The person now must not only continue to make choices, but also learn to live with the consequences of the choices made previously. As one accepts more responsibility for one's own unique life, one again becomes more open to the outside world and to new inputs. People at this stage get to know their

Table 3.1
The Stages and Tasks of the (Male) Biosocial Cycle

Age Ranges	General Issues to be Confronted	Specific Tasks
Adolescence to early thirties	1. Getting into the adult world 2. Making *provisional* commitments to various adult roles 3. Developing one's sense of self, thereby achieving a capacity for intimacy with spouse and friends 4. Becoming more discriminating in one's relationships 5. Establishing one's own life structure and style	1. Pull up roots and leave one's family of origin (ages 18–24) 2. Use the peer group for support without being overwhelmed by it 3. Make valid educational and vocational choices 4. Learn to get along with one's spouse 5. Establish one's own home and family without parental support or one's original home base 6. Establish new personal and group memberships, and community commitments 7. Develop a vision of oneself in the future—one's "dreams" 8. Find mentors and assimilate from them what is to be learned 9. Overcome the feeling of omniscience and the conviction that one's early choices are irrevocable and the only valid ones
Late twenties to mid-thirties: Transition	1. Dealing with the age-30 transition, whatever its specific meaning to the individual	1. Review all of one's provisional commitments about vocation, marriage, children, and social involvements

Age Ranges	General Issues to be Confronted	Specific Tasks
	2. First major time of re-appraisal: facing the questions "Am I what I want to be?" and "What do I want out of life?"	2. Begin the process of making more final choices which will lead to long-range, perma-nent adult commitments
	3. First recognition of one's own mortality	3. Choose major changes in direction, if indicated
The thirties	1. "Becoming one's own man"—widening, deep-ening, and stabilizing one's commitments	1. Put down roots and settle into the adult world
	2. Coming to terms with the fact that time is limited and finite	2. Come to terms with one's occupation, career —to either work extra hard to "make it" or give up a portion of the dream and settle for security
	3. Growing out of one's illusions	
	4. Preparing mentally and emotionally for the forties	3. Come to terms with one's marriage, substitut-ing a realistic assessment for the ideal vision of the twenties
	5. First concern with gen-erativity vs. stagnation via concern with one's own children and the parental role	4. Manage the potential conflict between family and career demands
		5. Become accepted by one's spouse for what one really is
		6. Manage the potential conflict between total absorption in family and work and continued involvement with com-munity and friends
		7. Learn to accept one's children for what they really are
		8. Learn to accept one's parents for what they really are—begin to feel

Age Ranges	General Issues to be Confronted	Specific Tasks
		responsible for one's own fate, destiny, and personality
		9. Work through one's relationship with one's mentors—deal with the gradual disenchantment, terminate unrealistic relationships, substitute one's own values and begin preparing to be a mentor oneself
Late thirties to early forties: mid-life transition or crisis	1. Facing the disparity between one's dreams and what one has actually accomplished or become—reliving of adolescent conflicts 2. Coming to terms with "aging" by recognizing first signs of bodily decline; more vivid recognition of one's own mortality	1. Review and come to terms with the elements of one's dream, the actual realities, and the disparity between them—become more aware of self and others as a basis for better future choices 2. Make new choices—to either accept and seek new meaning in work, family, and self or head in new directions
The forties	1. A period of reassessment and potential trouble, but also one of finding happiness and inner calm if properly coped with 2. Locating one's own life goals and values, achieving a more stable integration and life structure independent of prior role models or conformity pressures 3. Reopening oneself to the world after a period of being closed	1. Gain sense of autonomy and voluntary commitment—a sense that one is making one's own choices 2. Cope with overt depression, accept depressive feelings as part of life— "the die is cast" 3. Accept the uniqueness of one's life 4. Make final decisions about career—continue to climb, level off, or seek new career options

Age Ranges	General Issues to be Confronted	Specific Tasks
	4. Getting to know one's children as adults and to accept them in this role	5. Become a mentor—locate people to sponsor, teach, and support
	5. Establishing patterns of intimacy with spouse after parent role is over or dissolving the family and launching new life patterns	6. Deal with the empty-nest syndrome—helping spouse to adjust to loss of parental role and transition to some other role
	6. Becoming generative with respect to subordinates and other adults	7. Cope with fears of loss of competence and competition from younger people "on the way up"
		8. Cope with old age, dependence, and death of one's own parents
		9. Develop concrete plans for one's own self-development and balance such development with career and family demands
The fifties to retirement	1. A period of relative stability, but fraught with concerns about "running out of time" and bodily deterioration	1. Ensure that one stays in contact with one's friends, because of loss of interest in making new contacts and friendships
	2. A period of mellowing, warming up, and valuing spouse, children, and friends	2. Adjust to a general decline in sociability and a drawing into oneself and well-established patterns
	3. Finally accepting oneself for what one is and ceasing to blame one's parents for one's problems	3. Make life easier and more comfortable—avoidance of emotionally laden topics and issues
	4. Reviewing one's life work and contribution to the world	4. Establish adult relationships with one's children, which involves mutual reciprocity
	5. Growing concern with broader issues of so-	5. Learn to be a grandparent

Age Ranges	*General Issues to be Confronted*	*Specific Tasks*
	ciety and community, loss of specialization and growth of wisdom	
The sixties to death	1. Coping with occupational retirement	1. Adjust to reduced status and work roles
	2. A period of transition and uncertainty because of changes in bodily and mental functions, as well as social roles	2. Accept the fact that retirement and reduced roles are ultimately a reflection of one's own reduced capacities and motives
	3. Coping with declining health and capacities and the inward preoccupation that produces	3. Learn to change one's life-style in terms of physical and health concerns
	4. Adjusting to death of spouse	4. Adjust to increasing introversion and reduced communications with the outside world
	5. Adjusting to dependency on others such as children, friends, or institutions	5. Adjust to a reduced standard of living and coping with new financial problems
	6. Preparing for one's own death	6. Learn to compensate for loss of speed and physical competence by increasing use of judgment, tact, and accumulated experience
		7. Make concrete preparations for death—writing or rechecking one's will, deciding on funeral arrangements, etc.
		8. Make peace with oneself and others—to achieve some sense of integrity and avoid despair
		9. Die gracefully and at peace with oneself

children as adolescents and adults, bringing first a revival of their own adolescent conflicts, but ultimately a newly worked-through balance based on more self-acceptance.

It is during the subsequent period, generally the forties and early fifties, that people have to cope with the consequences of the "empty nest"—the growth and departure of their own children, the change in role for the nonemployed mother to potentially idle adult, the need to establish new patterns of intimacy between husband and wife as they suddenly discover that each other is all they have now that the children are departed.

As these problems are worked through, as self-acceptance and contentment grow, as people learn that their lives are really their own responsibility, there ensues a period of relative stability and contentment, usually associated with the fifties. The person mellows, warms up, values his or her old associations more than ever, but at the same time grows more troubled with the recognition of declining abilities, the intrusion of health problems, competition from younger people, and other symptoms of "aging." There may come a feeling that time is running out and that whatever one is going to contribute must be contributed now. As the person levels off, he or she must also begin to prepare for retirement and the potential change in life-style that may result from changes in financial, social, or health status.

The period of the sixties until death involves some major transitions. The most obvious one is retirement and the changes that may bring. For those who are well-prepared financially, this transition appears to be manageable. It is more difficult for those whose declining competence forces them into retirement and/or those who must reduce their standard of living markedly during retirement. Health problems can become more acute, and the person is faced with the major traumas of the death of close friends or spouse. Whereas one has spent one's life becoming independent, one now suddenly faces the possibility of once again becoming dependent. Death becomes a reality, the daily routine of life revolves increasingly around managing one's physical health, and withdrawal into self-preoccupation becomes a major threat to the person because his or her needs for others may continue to be high.

If the person can work through the various tasks of old age, take stock of accomplishments, learn to value wisdom and experience more as actual skills and competences decline, he or she can prepare for death with a feeling of integration and contentment. But the implication is clear—there are tasks to be accomplished right to the moment of death. There is never a time in the adult life cycle when the person can simply stop and coast. Instead, persons must learn throughout life to assess the tasks facing them and to cope with those tasks.

SUMMARY

This chapter has given a general description of the major tasks of the biosocial life cycle and the developmental issues which generate those tasks. In the next two chapters I will elaborate on the more specific issues and tasks which derive from one's working life and from one's membership in a family unit. Obviously these tasks overlap and interact within a given person, as was previously pointed out. Nevertheless, it is useful to distinguish the three basic cycles because the developmental issues in each cycle ultimately derive from different sources.

I have said little in this chapter about coping or the conditions which lead to better or worse management of transitions. The purpose thus far has been to describe the tasks; the issue of how to cope will be treated in Chapter 6.

4
THE STAGES AND TASKS OF THE CAREER CYCLE

The stages and tasks of the career cycle are closely related to those of the biosocial life cycle, because both are linked to age and cultural norms. But there are some aspects of the development of the career that need to be distinguished in order to understand, in particular, the tasks confronting individuals who are engaged in a full-time occupation in order to make a living. The term "career" is not meant to be limited here to professions or to occupations that have clear upward progressions associated with them. It applies just as much to the less skilled and more "level" occupations, which also have definable stages, transitions, and tasks associated with them (Van Maanen and Schein, 1977). And we are here referring to the "internal career," the stages and tasks as seen and experienced by the person in the career.

In identifying stages and tasks, I am abstracting the common elements which career occupants experience in a whole variety of occupations. Obviously there will be variations by occupation and by individual, but the basic pattern is visible when one compares people of different ages and ranks in many different kinds of occupations.

One of the most important differences between the career cycle and the biosocial cycle is that everyone has a life, but not everyone has an occupational career. Furthermore, one generally has more influence over one's career, and the career is more subject to external influences. Occupational careers can be aborted, truncated, changed, leveled off, and in other ways manipulated by the *individual* within the career and by the occupation or organization which provides the incentives, settings, and opportunities for the performance of that individual's career. People can remain unemployed, change jobs, or level off in a fairly low-ranking position; or they may make midcareer shifts, abandoning one career at one stage in order to pick up another one at a much lower stage. Organizations can eliminate careers, as when technological changes make certain occupations obsolete or unnecessary; they can fail to promote someone, lay people off, or in other ways intervene unilaterally in the career of the employee. Thus in talking about a career cycle, I am specifying more of an "ideal state," or a model of what a career would look like if pursued fully and successfully. In reality many people feel that they have "ruined" their careers or have "failed" in various ways. Perhaps when such feelings and images are aroused, it is testimony to the fact that the person feels some failure in coping with some crucial transition or in the performance of some crucial task.

DIMENSIONS OF THE CAREER CYCLE

The actual stages, issues, and tasks of the career development cycle are a synthesis of a range of developmental theories.* It is somewhat difficult to locate the common elements in the stages because of the variation which occurs in occupations and because of the relative sparsity of longitudinal career research. However, some basic *dimensions* can be identified which describe *external* career movement (Schein, 1971) and provide some of the external reference points for how the *internal* career is experienced.

Most people who work in organizations move along a *hierarchical* dimension during the course of their careers. That is, they achieve a certain number of promotions and raises to reach a certain level within the occupation or organization to which they belong. But some people rise to a very high level of leadership, continuing to climb until almost retirement, whereas others level off fairly early in their careers. In some occupations or organizations there are many steps, whereas others are fairly flat.

At the same time, everyone moves along a *functional* or *technical* dimension which describes their area of special expertise or blend of talents and skills. Those people who enter a specialty early and remain in it all of their working lives have relatively little movement along this

---

*For example, see Miller and Form (1951), Ginzberg *et al.* (1951), Havighurst (1964), Rapoport (1970), Sofer (1970), Super and Bohn (1970), Schein (1971), Hall, (1968, 1976), and most recently Dalton, Thompson, and Price (1977).

dimension. Others, who switch areas frequently, such as the person in an organization who moves from engineering to manufacturing to sales to marketing and eventually to finance and general management, move a lot along this dimension. When we talk of "second careers," we often mean a change in type of work, which implies movement along the functional dimension. Whereas movement *up* the hierarchy can be thought of as "vertical" career growth, movement along the functional dimension is one kind of "horizontal," or lateral, career growth.

A third, more subtle dimension, involves *movement toward the inner circle* or the core of the occupation or organization. As the person learns more, comes to be trusted by older members of the occupation or organization, earns tenure, and acquires responsibility, he or she is, in effect, moving toward the core of the organization along an *inclusion,* or *membership,* dimension. Usually movement up the hierarchy and movement in toward the center are somewhat correlated, but it is quite possible for a person to remain at a given hierarchical level, yet become more central and included as he or she acquires experience and is trusted more. It is also possible to move up and still remain at the periphery, as is nicely captured by the phrase "being kicked upstairs."

Movement along this third dimension toward the inner circle or core is another kind of horizontal, or lateral, career growth. For many people who are dead-ended on the vertical dimension, such growth is still possible and potentially very meaningful. Movement toward the core of the organization is most clearly signaled by being given access to special privileges and special categories of information—the "secrets" of the organization. Such "secrets" may involve anything from being told about the organization's policies and plans to being told more about the politics of how things are really done, how the organization views certain people, and especially what the organization really thinks of the person and his or her future (see Chapter 9).

If we combine these three dimensions, we can depict the organization as a three-dimensional cone to reflect the number of levels along the vertical axis, types of departments or functional areas as the segments around the circumference of the cone, and movement from the outside surface toward the center of the cone as movement toward the inner core of the organization (see Fig. 4.1). Such a general model permits one to consider the different types of boundaries which exist along each dimension and the filtering properties of such boundaries (Schein, 1971). That is, the criteria that will determine passage through a vertical boundary (promotion) will typically be different from those of a horizontal functional boundary (rotation) and those of a horizontal inclusion boundary (being given permanent member-

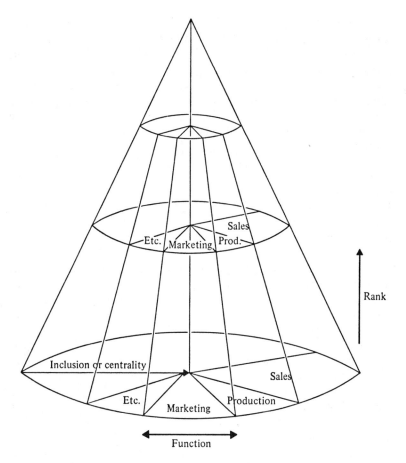

Fig. 4.1 A three-dimensional model of an organization. (E. H. Schein, "The Individual, the Organization, and the Career: A Conceptual Scheme," *Journal of Applied Behavioral Science* **7** (1971): 401–426.)

ship or access to special information). Critical career transitions can usually be associated with passage through one or more of these organizational boundaries.

Summary of the Career Cycle

The stages, issues, and tasks of the career cycle are shown in Table 4.1. The emphasis is on those stages and tasks which are particularly relevant to careers in organizations. People in professions or who are self-employed will have some similarities, but also some differences, in how the stages and tasks play themselves out.

Table 4.1
Stages and Tasks of the Career Cycle

Stages	General Issues to be Confronted	Specific Tasks
1. *Growth, fantasy, exploration* (age 0–21) (Roles: student, aspirant, applicant)	1. Developing a basis for making realistic vocational choices	1. Develop and discover one's own *needs* and *interests*
	2. Turning early occupational fantasies into workable realities	2. Develop and discover one's own *abilities* and *talents*
	3. Assessing the realistic constraints based on socioeconomic level and other family circumstances	3. Find realistic role models from which to learn about occupations
	4. Obtaining the appropriate education or training	4. Get maximum information from testing and counseling
	5. Developing the basic habits and skills needed in the world of work	5. Locate reliable sources of information about occupations and work roles
		6. Develop and discover one's own *values, motives,* and *ambitions*
		7. Make sound educational decisions
		8. Perform well enough in school to keep career options as wide open as possible
		9. Find opportunities for self-tests in sports, hobbies, and school activities in order to develop a realistic self-image
		10. Find trial and part-time work opportunities to test early vocational decisions

Stages	General Issues to be Confronted	Specific Tasks
	Passage into an Organization or Occupation	
2. *Entry into world of work* (age 16–25) (Roles: recruit, entrant)	1. Entering the labor market—getting a first job which can be the basis of a career 2. Negotiating a viable formal and psychological contract to ensure that own needs and those of employer will be met 3. Becoming a member of an organization or occupation—passage through first major inclusion boundary	1. Learn how to look for a job, how to apply, how to negotiate a job interview 2. Learn how to assess information about a job and an organization 3. Pass selection and screening tests 4. Make a realistic and valid first-job choice
3. *Basic training* (age 16–25) (Roles: trainee, novice)	1. Dealing with the reality shock of what work and membership are really like 2. Becoming an effective member as quickly as possible 3. Adjusting to the daily routines of work 4. Achieving acceptance as regular contributing member—passing the next inclusion boundary	1. Overcome the insecurity of inexperience and develop a sense of confidence 2. Decipher the culture, "learn the ropes" as quickly as possible 3. Learn to get along with the first boss or trainer 4. Learn to get along with other trainees 5. Accept and learn from the initiation rites and other rituals associated with being a novice (doing much of the dirty work, "mickey mouse" tasks, etc.) 6. Accept responsibly the official signs of entry and acceptance—uniforms, badges, identity cards, parking stickers, company manuals

Stages	General Issues to be Confronted	Specific Tasks
4. *Full membership in early career* (age 17–30) (Roles: new but full member)	1. Accepting the responsibility and successfully discharging the duties associated with first formal assignment 2. Developing and displaying special skills and expertise to lay the groundwork for promotion or lateral career growth into other areas 3. Balancing own needs for independence with organizational restrictions and requirements for a period of subordination and dependence 4. Deciding whether to remain in the organization or the occupation or to seek a better match between own needs and organizational constraints and opportunities	1. Perform effectively and learn how things are done, to improve 2. Accept partial responsibility 3. Accept subordinate status and learn how to get along with the boss and ones' peers 4. Develop initiative and realistic level of aggressiveness within the limits of the job, to show full commitment 5. Find a mentor, sponsor 6. Reassess original decision to pursue this type of work in terms of own talents and values and in terms of opportunities and constraints in the organization 7. Prepare for long-range commitments and a period of maximum contribution or for a move to a new job or organization 8. Deal with feeling of success or failure in the first job
5. *Full membership, midcareer* (age 25 +) (Roles: full member, tenured member, life member, supervisor, manager) (person may	1. Choosing a speciality and deciding how committed to become to it vs. moving toward being a generalist and/or toward management 2. Remaining technically competent and con-	1. Gain a measure of independence 2. Develop one's own standards of performance and confidence in one's own decisions 3. Carefully assess own motives, talents, and

Stages	General Issues to be Confronted	Specific Tasks
remain in this stage)	tinuing to learn in one's chosen area of specialization (or management) 3. Establishing a clear identity in the organization, becoming visible 4. Accepting higher levels of responsibility, including that for the work of others as well as one's own 5. Becoming a productive person in the occupation 6. Developing one's long-range career plan in terms of ambitions, type of progress sought, targets against which to measure progress, etc.	values as basis for decision of how specialized to become 4. Carefully assess organizational and occupational opportunities as basis for making valid decisions about next steps 5. Work through one's relationships with mentors and prepare to become a mentor to others 6. Achieve an appropriate accommodation among family, self, and work concerns 7. Deal with feelings of failure if performance is poor, tenure is denied, or challenge is lost
6. *Midcareer crisis* (age 35–45)	1. Major reassessment of one's progress relative to one's ambitions forcing decisions to level off, change careers, or forge ahead to new and higher challenges 2. Assessing one's career ambitions against more general aspects of midlife transition—one's dreams and hopes vs. realities 3. Deciding how important work and one's career are to be in one's total life	1. Become aware of one's *career anchor*—one's talents, motives, and values (see Chapter 10) 2. Assess realistically the implications for one's future of one's career anchor 3. Make specific choices about accepting the present or working for whatever future is visualized 4. Work out new accommodations with family around the specific choices made

Stages	General Issues to be Confronted	Specific Tasks
	4. Meeting one's own needs to become a mentor to others	5. Work out mentoring relationships with others
7.A. *Late career in nonleadership role (age 40 to retirement)* (Roles: key member, individual contributor or member of management, good contributor or deadwood (many people stay in this stage))	1. Becoming a mentor, learning to influence, guide, direct, and be responsible for others 2. Broadening of interests and skills based on experience 3. Deepening of skills if decision is to pursue a technical or functional career 4. Taking on more areas of responsibility if decision is to pursue general-management role 5. Accepting reduced influence and challenge if decision is to level off and seek growth outside of career or work	1. How to remain technically competent or how to learn to substitute wisdom based on experience for immediate technical skills 2. How to develop interpersonal and group skills if needed 3. How to develop supervisory and managerial skills if needed 4. How to learn to make effective decisions in a political environment 5. How to deal with the competitiveness and aggression of younger persons "on the way up" 6. How to deal with midlife crisis and the empty-nest problem at home 7. How to prepare for senior leadership roles

Passage through Inclusion and Hierarchical Boundary

| 7.B. *Late career in leadership role* (may be achieved at early age, but would still be | 1. Using one's skills and talents for the long-range welfare of the organization

2. Learning to integrate the efforts of others | 1. How to disengage from being primarily concerned with self to becoming more responsible for organizational welfare |

Age Ranges	General Issues to be Confronted	Specific Tasks
thought of as "late" in career) (Roles: general manager, officer, senior partner, internal entrepreneur, senior staff)	and to influence broadly rather than making day-to-day decisions or supervising closely 3. Selecting and developing key subordinates 4. Developing broad perspective, long-range time horizons, and realistic appraisal of the role of the organization in society 5. Learning how to sell ideas if in individual contributor or internal entrepreneur role	2. How to handle organizational secrets and resources responsibly 3. Learn to handle high-level political situations both inside and at the organization/ environment boundary 4. Learn how to balance continued high commitment to career with needs of family, especially spouse 5. Learn how to handle high levels of responsibility and power without becoming paralyzed or emotionally upset
8. *Decline and disengagement* (age 40 until retirement; different people start decline at different ages)	1. Learning to accept reduced levels of power, responsibility, and centrality 2. Learning to accept and develop new roles based on declining competence and motivation 3. Learning to manage a life that is less dominated by work	1. How to find new sources of satisfaction in hobbies, family, social and community activities, part-time work, etc. 2. Learn how to live more closely with spouse 3. Assess total career and prepare for retirement

Passage Out of the Organization or Occupation

9. *Retirement*	1. Adjusting to more drastic changes in lifestyle, role, standard of living 2. Using one's accumulated experience and wisdom on behalf of others in various senior roles	1. How to maintain a sense of identity and self-worth without a full-time job or organizational role 2. How to remain engaged up to one's level of energy and abilities in some kind of activity

Age Ranges	General Issues to be Confronted	Specific Tasks
		3. How to use one's wisdom and experience
		4. How to achieve a sense of fulfillment and satisfaction in one's past career

I can best summarize the career cycle by noting that there is a period of time prior to entry into a career during which the child or adolescent gains self-insight and learns about the occupational options available. The key process during the preentry period of growth and exploration is the obtaining of valid information about oneself and occupations and the making of valid choices which optimize one's chances of both using one's talents and achieving success and satisfaction.*

Entry into the occupation or organization is like growing up. On the one hand, the individual must be assertive, show initiative, and be willing to develop some area of skill which will make a contribution. On the other hand, the individual must learn how to be subordinate, learn the ropes, and be willing to be the "junior" member who often must do the dirty work of the organization. The ability to be both dependent and independent and to learn how to specialize in some area of contribution is the key to this early career stage.

As one obtains more permanent membership in the organization and leaves the learner role, one begins the long period of making one's contribution in some special area. The person must be prepared at this point in the career to become an expert in some area and to function effectively in that area without close supervision. Promotions and lateral moves across functional boundaries or parts of the organization may occur, but the major issue is some kind of ultimate testing between the individual and the organization of whether or not they can meet each other's needs in the long run. In this stage one must acquire self-confidence and the ability to judge one's own performance and act independently and reliably. If the area of work remains chal-

---

*There is a large amount of research available describing in greater detail the early process of choice (Zytowski, 1968; Super, 1957; Roe, 1956; Osipow, 1973; Pietrofesa and Splete, 1975). Much less is available on choices made in mid- and late career.

lenging, the person may well spend the rest of the career in that area in a craftsman, technical staff, or independent contributor role. This stage ends symbolically with the granting of permanent membership, the crossing of the organization's major inclusion boundary.

As one ages and/or gains experience, one moves into midcareer, which is characterized by two major new issues: (1) how to utilize one's experience and wisdom above and beyond one's technical, specialist skills (how to become effective at being a generalist); and (2) how to fulfill one's own growing need to be a mentor to others. Most people find that in the early career they have benefited in one way or another from the help, guidance, and support of more senior people in the organization or occupation. As they move into midcareer, they find not only that they have emotional needs to become helpful and nurturing to others, but also that their acquired experience and wisdom draw some attention from younger members. Becoming a mentor is, therefore, a very natural midcareer outcome. The form that mentoring will take may vary—becoming a teacher of more junior people, supervisory responsibilities, project leadership, taking on apprentices, etc.—but the interpersonal elements are the critical common feature (see Chapter 13).

For many people there is a period of crisis during which a major reassessment must be made of how one is doing relative to one's ambitions and how important work and/or career is going to be in one's total life space. As one recognizes where one's area of contribution is going to be (one's talents, needs, and values) and as one recognizes what one's likely future in the organization or occupation is likely to be, one has the basic information to rethink and reassess one's total work situation in relation to more personal and family needs and requirements. This can be a traumatic period if the needs of the family and those of the career conflict. Or, stress can result from the recognition that needs for money and security generated in the family can, in fact, not be met by the career, forcing the person to cut back in one area or the other or forcing all kinds of extra effort in the work area to meet family needs.

One other aspect of the midcareer crisis is the problem of how to remain up to date in one's area of specialty or even whether to attempt to remain up to date in the face of rapidly changing knowledge, competition from better-trained younger people, and declining energy levels in oneself. For those people who can make their experience and more generalized knowledge pay off or for those who move into administrative or managerial positions, this is less of a problem. It is most acute for those who wish to continue to make their major contribution in a specialty area (see Chapter 13 for a more detailed analysis).

The later stages of the career are harder to summarize because so much depends on the kind of career being pursued, the degree to which the person has moved toward managerial or leadership roles, the degree to which work involvement remains high, the degree to which the career is seen as successful, and the interaction of all of these factors with personal and family issues. Working out one's mentoring responsibilities and learning how to disengage when it is time to prepare for retirement are two common issues, however, which have to be confronted by everyone. How those issues are worked through will determine to a large extent the person's ultimate degree of satisfaction with the career.

As can be seen in Table 4.1, the age ranges for each stage are very broad, because people in different occupations move at different rates through the stages, and personal factors strongly influence the rate of movement as well. When and how people move through the various inclusion, hierarchical, and functional boundaries of an organization will depend on that organization's career development processes, the degree of talent and motivation of the individual, situational factors of who is needed where at what time, and other even less predictable circumstances. In analyzing career stages, therefore, it is better to view them as broad sets of common issues and tasks which everyone faces in some form or another rather than to attempt to link them systematically to particular ages or other life stages. It also follows from this that the actual interaction of career concerns with personal and family concerns is not easy to predict across a broad population. One will find patterns only within given occupations, socioeconomic levels, and organizational settings.

SUMMARY

In this chapter I have attempted to summarize and outline the major stages and issues of the career without going into detail on the actual dynamics by which some of these issues are worked out. In later chapters I will examine in greater detail the process of interaction between the organization and the individual, having laid out in Part 1 the more individualized perspective toward self and career.

5
THE STATES, STAGES, AND TASKS OF THE FAMILY

A developmental analysis of the family cycle is not as straightforward as the analysis of the biosocial or career cycles, because the family is a complex unit consisting of several individuals, each of whom exists in his or her own personal and career cycles. Families can have different structural configurations or states which are in part developmental, and for each state the developmental cycle may be different. For example, the states of being single, divorced, widowed, with or without children, with or without dependent parents all generate different issues and tasks. We can take the culturally expected "modal," or traditional, family pattern and analyze the cultural stereotype of how such a family develops, but clearly recognizing that for many this cycle and its tasks would be quite irrelevant. Also, since to review all of the vast literature on family development is well beyond the scope of this book, I will concentrate on some key issues which relate particularly to the career development perspective. I will begin with Table 5.1, which spells out the traditional pattern in our culture. Following this analysis, I will review some recent research which is particularly directed toward illuminating the complex interaction between work and family and will introduce some concepts which will be of increasing importance as organizations and individuals grapple with these issues.

Table 5.1
States, Stages, and Tasks of the Family Cycle

Stage or State	Issues to be Confronted	Specific Tasks
Dependent child	1. Learning to adapt to the environment created by one's own parents 2. Learning independence and mastery of the environment 3. Learning to get along with own parents while still dependent on them	1. How to decode the environment—parents' cues regarding what they want or don't want 2. How to get own needs met without creating too much trouble for parents; how to balance dependence and independence 3. How to learn from parents through imitation and identification
Transition to adulthood	1. Managing the delicate balance between total independence and partial independence to allow for some trial and error in an environment of safety and support	
Single adult	1. Managing relations with other sex 2. Deciding whether or not to get married 3. Finding a mate to marry or live with	
Married adult	1. Learning to live with a mate, accommodating to the needs of the spouse 2. Setting up own household 3. Deciding whether or not to have children 4. Making a long-range commitment to a certain family style and financial requirements	1. How to balance one's own needs and style with those of another person in an intimate relationship 2. How to manage finances, decisions about where and how to live, etc. 3. Assess own values around the meaning of children and own resources (financial and emotional) in regard to one's aspirations for them

Stage or State	Issues to be Confronted	Specific Tasks
Parent of young child	1. Adjusting to parenthood emotionally, especially the fact that one has taken on an irreversible legal, moral, and emotional obligation 2. Adjusting to the realities of child care 3. Dealing with the realities of multiple children 4. Reassessing own values and aspirations about children, especially their education, as a basis for further decisions on financial needs, life-style, etc.	1. How to set up a workable schedule of child care relative to work commitment and other activities 2. How to manage finances with additional cost of child 3. How to maintain intimate relationship with spouse 4. How to accommodate to the needs of the family as number of children makes childrearing task more demanding and complicated, especially in a period when career demands are also likely to be very heavy
Parent of adolescents	1. Dealing with the independence needs and rebellion of own children 2. Dealing with own feelings, which go back to own adolescence and are rekindled by children (one key aspect of midlife transition for adults) 3. Coming to terms with changing values as exemplified in the differences in life-style between oneself and one's children 4. Growing in one's own maturity from the experience of dealing with one's growing children	1. How to set reasonable standards and limits 2. How to enforce limits despite persistent tests of limits 3. How to cope with own feelings of frustration and anger if limits are deliberately ignored and violated 4. How to remain supportive and able to listen 5. How to develop empathy for the emotional struggles of adolescents 6. How to maintain intimate relationship with spouse under the potential strain of dealing with adolescents and the

Stage or State	Issues to be Confronted	Specific Tasks
	5. Preparing for the departure of children and the changes in role and style of life which may result	possibility of disagreeing on how to deal with them 7. Reassessing the work-family balance for both parents and deciding on new role as more free time becomes available
Parent of grown children	1. Adjusting to the departure of children—feelings of loss of parental role ("empty nest") and regaining of freedom ("finally free") 2. Building new relationship with spouse 3. Throughout the states above, balancing the needs of the family with needs for self-development and needs of career 4. Accepting responsibility for own parents, possibly financially or emotionally	1. How to fill in empty hours or emotional gaps with the physical departure of children 2. How to develop new work role, hobbies, or other activities which are *now* meaningful (one cannot automatically go back to what one did in the preparent stage) 3. How to assess and work on unfulfilled needs for self-development 4. How to make peace with own parents and provide them what they need in old age
Grandparent	1. Establishing a relationship with a small child 2. Dealing with own children in parent role, areas of congruence and conflict 3. Assessing own role as mentor and how to be most helpful to younger generations 4. Assessing the degree to which family roles can compensate for reduced work roles, building up the family roles	
Separated, divorced, or widowed	The specific issues and tasks here will be highly personal and dependent on specific circumstances surrounding the change of status and its meaning to the individual	

STATES, STAGES, AND TASKS
OF THE TRADITIONAL FAMILY

In our society there is an expected cycle of family life; most people are expected to leave their families of origin in late adolescence or early adulthood, get married and establish households, have children, educate them, take care of their own parents in old age, and be co-operative and supportive grandparents. At the same time, even a casual reading of the newspapers reveals how rapidly our values are changing in this area and how many new "life-styles" are evolving—couples living together without being married, explicit decisions not to have children, communal living in which early childrearing is done by people other than the parents, frequent divorce and remarriage, "marriage" between partners of the same sex, and so on. In spite of this variation, some common themes can be identified, and it is these themes which are highlighted in Table 5.1. The table presumes that everyone will form some kind of strong emotional attachment during the early adult years, will have some issues to work through with his or her family of origin, will have to face the issue of children in some form or another, and finally will have to face issues surrounding long-range commitments to another person and to one's own parents.

The most important point to be noted about the family cycle is that marriage and parenthood involve major commitments to other people and that these commitments impose constraints on the person far beyond those imposed by a job or career. These commitments are not only emotional and moral, but are also supported by the legal structure in terms of laws about divorce, desertion, or nonsupport of children. The potential conflicts between work and family are likely to be more severe than the conflict between work and self-development or self and family development, because work and family are likely to involve more extensive external commitments. To deal with those conflicts constructively requires more insight and adaptive capacity on the part of both the individual within the conflict situation (e.g., the parent who must decide whether to take an important business trip or stay home with a sick child) and the employing organizations (e.g., to become more aware of the emotional effects of asking people to arbitrarily separate all family issues from work issues). If either party to the situation fails to recognize and adapt to conflicts as they arise, both will ultimately pay a price in that the emotional strain on the employee will ultimately show up in reduced performance on the job and therefore reduced organizational effectiveness.

WORK-FAMILY-SELF INTERACTION

The analysis above of tasks introduces the major considerations involved in the development of the family, but does not illuminate sufficiently the potential problems which can arise for the person from various kinds of work-family-self interactions. We noted in Fig. 2.1 that this interaction is partly temporal—that various stresses occur in a cyclical manner and that it makes a large difference whether or not issues are coming up at the same time in several life areas. Another kind of interaction derives from more basic characteristics of the individual and the occupation or organization in which he or she is.

Figure 5.1 shows a basic model of the person in interaction with various external settings (Hall, 1971; Schein, 1971). For any given person there will be a degree of involvement with self-development (area A), reflecting activities such as hobbies, athletics, community activ-

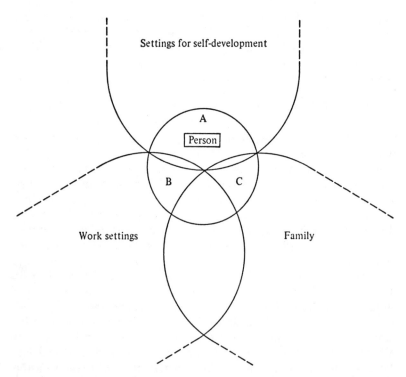

Fig. 5.1   A model for analyzing involvement in self, work, and family. (A = involvement in self-development; B = work involvement; C = family involvement.)

ities, friendships, etc. At the same time, and possibly overlapping, there will be an area of work/career involvement (area B), which will vary from person to person and also from one occupation to another. Finally, and again possibly overlapping either or both of the other areas, there will be the degree of involvement which the person has in the family (area C).

The areas within the person vary partly as a function of basic personality and early history and partly as a function of the degree to which the settings or activities "absorb" or involve the person (Kanter, 1977). For example, a person whose hobby is amateur theatricals may attend rehearsals seven nights a week and become totally absorbed in the activity to the point where neither family nor work captures much emotional attention. A large family may "demand" more involvement from the parent than a small family. And, as we will see, some occupations or organizations are more absorbing than others are.

The areas of involvement can overlap both inside and outside the person. Inside overlap occurs for people who perceive their work and family lives to be very closely related, e.g., they work only to "provide" for their families. An executive, e.g., a bank president, concerned about the company's image in the larger community may merge work and family to a great degree through the involvement of the family in business entertaining, volunteer work by the spouse, family appearances at public functions, and the like (Powers, 1977). On military bases or in company towns such a merging of the external settings is stimulated by the physical characteristics of those settings and the norms of the occupation. Sometimes a family merges the areas deliberately, as in "Mom and Pop" stores and husband-and-wife consulting teams. The merging of self-development with work is the goal of many people, but is difficult to achieve except in some occupations that afford wide opportunities for self-expression. How much family and self-development overlap similarly varies widely from person to person.

The degree to which settings absorb the person can be nicely illustrated in the occupational area by looking at a broad range of occupations and the demands they make on the family. As Table 5.2 shows, some occupations, such as farming or craft work, permit collaborative relationships between husband and wife, partly because the work and family settings are physically close to each other or actually overlapping. In contrast, in occupations such as engineering, management, clerical, and sales, there is no overlap between "office" and "home," there is less understanding on the part of the spouse of what the work setting involves or the demands it places on the employed

Table 5.2

Three Kinds of Relations between Work and Family,
Based on Degree of Occupational Absorptiveness of Husband's Work

Relationship between Arenas	Husband's Occupation	Occupational Characteristics	Husband's Family Role in Relation to Occupational Role	Wife's Role in Relation to Husband's Occupation
Work-home extension (positive relationship)	Farming, small shop or business, some professional or craft work	Home and work locales at least partly coextensive	Continuous with work	Collaborative
Minimal contact (neutral relationship)	Technical, routine, bureaucratic, clerical, low-/midlevel managerial	Low visibility of occupation to family	Alternative to work	Supportive
Work-home opposition and competition (negative relationship)	Mining, fishing, low-skill factory work	Psychologically or physically exhausting, damaging work	Recuperation from work	Peripheral

Adapted from Parker, 1967; quoted in Kanter, 1977.

person, yet the spouse is often required to play a supportive role. A third pattern derives from work settings physically removed from the home setting, requiring long periods of absence from the home and exhausting work, creating for the family the situation of providing a haven and a place for recuperation.

Beyond considering the external characteristics of the occupation in relation to the family, one can also assess the degree to which the nature of the work itself is emotionally or cognitively preoccupying or involving. For example, a survey of MIT alumni found that managers reported being highly involved in *both* work and family, whereas professors reported high work involvement but low family involvement. One possible explanation for this difference is that managerial work can more easily be left at the office (by delegating tasks, reaching decisions), whereas academic work (such as research or theory building) is intrinsically preoccupying, leading to low family involvement even when the person is physically at home with the family (Bailyn and Schein, 1976).

Above and beyond work involvement, other features of the work situation will have an impact on family life:

1. The *time* a job takes and how those hours are distributed will have an obvious effect on when husband and wife can be together, who will be involved in childrearing, and so on. A dramatic example can be seen in Spain and Mexico, where a work pattern from 9 to 2 and 5 to 8 makes it virtually impossible for fathers to see their little children except on weekends and on holidays.

The actual number of hours worked is probably closely related to the degree of work involvement, leading to concerns in some quarters about the deleterious effects of "workaholism." Some research studies suggest that lower-middle-class occupations involve the shortest actual working hours and exhibit the most "companionate" marriages involving much sharing of home chores. Professors, at the other extreme, have been found to work the longest hours, bring home the most work, be least likely to spend much time with their children, and be least likely to do household chores (Kanter, 1977, p. 32). Experiments with flexible working hours, sabbaticals, part-time work, and other time variations are obvious attempts by organizations to begin to deal with these particular work-family interactions.

2. The *geographical location* of the job and the *amount of travel* or *relocation* it requires is a second potential source of work-family strain. Though the research evidence is as yet sparse on the actual effects of travel and relocation on families, some consequences have been noted and must increasingly come to be considered seriously: "disconnected social relationships, especially for the men; increasing responsibility for the wives, since virtually no areas of family life could be assigned to the husbands who were away so frequently; guilt on the part of the husbands for deserting their families; fatigue stemming from the travel itself; wives' fears of being alone; and extra worry for one another while the spouses were apart" (Kanter, 1977 p. 36).

It has also been suggested that frequent relocation disrupts opportunities for the spouse to form any kind of permanent attachments, reduces opportunities to develop supportive friendships, and thus makes the spouse much more vulnerable to emotional upset (Seidenberg, 1973). On the other hand, it must be noted that many such mobile families find that they also improve in their ability to cope with varying realities of life and find it enriching to experience many different communities and settings. The effects on children are not clearly established, but there seem to be clear age-related issues, e.g., younger children are easier to move than teenagers. The mobility of a family unit thus may be primarily tied to the age of the children, the family being most mobile when the children are either very young or have reached college age and have left home.

3. The amount and type of *income* and *prestige* the career generates for its occupant obviously have a direct impact on the family. The family's daily life-style, the kind and quality of education available to the children, material possessions, travel, and leisure-time activities are all related directly to income and to organizational factors. Beyond the direct economic impact is the psychological impact of the job's providing prestige, self-esteem, and emotional well-being. Very exhausting or demeaning work may lead to tense family relationships. If the person is failing in some important way, the frustration and loss of self-esteem may directly affect how she or he handles family roles (e.g., the failing father who drives the children into certain occupations to make up for his own failure and begins to live vicariously through the successes of his children or the frustrated mother whose denial of her own frustration leads to distorted communication and tension in her home life).

4. The *type of work* itself and the *emotional climate surrounding the work* will have a direct impact on family life. For example, Kanter reports research that low job satisfaction is related to tension at home. People who work in low-autonomy situations or in jobs which "defeat" them may become more autocratic at home as a way of compensating for their defeat at work. People who work in intensive interpersonal encounters all day, such as personnel managers, may develop what she calls "interaction fatigue" and withdraw from contacts at home as though they had been "burned out" at the office (Kanter, 1977). As we saw in Table 5.2, different kinds of work will create potentially different roles for the family—as a haven and source of rest, as a unit that supports and enhances the work, as a source of emotional compensation for losses suffered in the work place, or simply as unrelated to the work.

ACCOMMODATION AND THE DUAL-CAREER FAMILY

It is likely that one of the major effects of women entering the labor force in greater numbers and at all levels in organizations will be an increase in "dual-career" families—those in which both husband and wife will be full-time paid employees pursuing a lifetime career. Bailyn (1978) has recently analyzed the possible patterns of accommodation which can arise in such dual-career families and has suggested some of the work/family strains which can arise.

The concept of accommodation refers to a person's conscious decision to subordinate work needs for the sake of the family. Thus a highly work-involved person who gives priority to work concerns would be low in accommodation; a person who gives priority to the family and reduces work involvement accordingly would be high in accommodation (Bailyn, 1977). In previous research Bailyn (1970) showed that self-reported marital happiness in dual-career families was primarily a function of the degree of accommodation of the husband. If he was nonaccommodative, it was difficult for the wife to fully pursue a career without causing strains in the marriage. However, if the husband was more family-oriented (high in accommodation), both partners could pursue careers and yet reported more happy marriages. In her more recent analysis Bailyn poses two further questions: (1) What kinds of options for distributing work and family tasks exist in dual-career families; and (2) How can strains in the dual-career family be reduced?

One basic option is for the couple to *differentiate* the degree of accommodation, to reach some consensus on which partner will be more work-involved and which one will be more family-involved. Such a decision can be permanent or can be renegotiated as needs change; e.g., the wife may be more accommodative during the child-rearing years, after which it becomes "her turn" to pursue her career more fully while the husband takes over more family responsibilities. The other major option is to equally *share responsibilities* and to maintain such sharing throughout the life cycle, a solution which obviously works best if both partners are at least to some degree accommodative. Figure 5.2 shows these patterns in terms of our basic work family diagram.

In the *differentiated* pattern the priorities are always clear as to who will manage family crises when they arise. This pattern is easier to manage, but involves potentially greater costs to the person who initially gives up some degree of involvement in either career or family. The *shared* pattern is harder to manage, but may be more rewarding in the long run. As Bailyn points out, there are various ways in which the dual-career family can reduce stress, particularly in the shared pattern:

1. *Limitation* of one area or the other—both partners can decide to be highly accommodative and to limit their career aspirations, or both partners can decide not to have children or to postpone the having of children until their careers have been well established (a solution which is made easier by the decision to adopt children at a later age, for example). Changes in the work setting, day-care centers, or alternative work patterns such as flexible hours, part-time work, or job sharing would make it easier for the couple to maintain both career and family involvement.

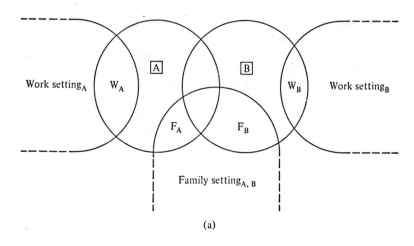

(a)

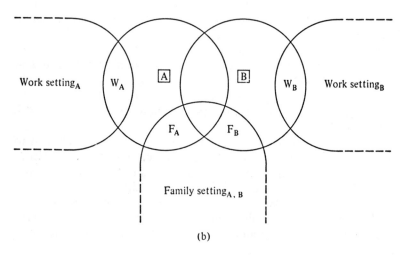

(b)

Fig. 5.2 Two basic dual-career patterns: (a) differentiated dual-career pattern, in which A is more work-involved ($W_A > W_B$) and B is more family-involved ($F_B > F_A$); (b) shared dual-career pattern, in which A and B are equally work-involved ($W_A = W_B$) and family-involved ($F_A = F_B$).

2. *Recycling*—both partners decide to emphasize the career (or family) at one stage of their life and the family (or career) at another stage of their life. The decision to postpone having children or the pursuit of "second" careers in midlife by either partner would be examples of this pattern.

3. *Segmentation*—both partners decide to clearly separate their work and family lives by keeping them physically and temporally apart so that each area can be given full attention when it is salient. The idea of "leaving one's work at the office" is the day-to-day expression of this strategy—the family takes absolute priority when the couple is at home. Long-distance commuting, for example, allows both partners to concentrate totally on the career when at work and totally on the family during the weekend. Such patterns would obviously be facilitated by organizational policies which permit more use of part-time work, sabbaticals, extended paternity leaves, and the like so that long periods of work involvement could be compensated for with longer periods of family involvement.

4. *Joint ventures*—both partners get involved in a career which permits more merging of the work settings and thus allows companionship and joint activities.

5. *Independent careers*—both partners decide to pursue their respective careers to the fullest and to cope with the consequences as they arise. This pattern implies a willingness to develop new life-styles such as long-distance commuting, periods of separation, full-time nannies, and other adaptations as needed.

As Bailyn's analysis shows, both organizations and individuals will have to adopt more flexible views toward career and family management if dual careers become more of a way of life. Personnel policies are today not well suited for the management of some of the patterns which have been identified. Similarly, the individual entering today's labor market may not have fully planned out the consequences of various kinds of career and family decisions. By remaining sensitive to the complex interactions which can arise between work and family, both individuals and organizations can protect themselves from initial decisions which may have irreversible and undesirable consequences.

SUMMARY

In this chapter we have reviewed the major states and stages of the family; have attempted to show how the issues of self-development, career development, and family development interact within the person; and have reviewed various kinds of interaction and dual-career families. This chapter and the two prior ones have sketched out the major developmental issues which persons face in the total life cycle. It remains in the last chapter of Part 1 to look at the process of coping by which an adult can identify and work on life tasks as they arise.

6
CONSTRUCTIVE COPING: WHAT THE
INDIVIDUAL CAN DO ABOUT LIFE TASKS

The previous three chapters outlined the major life tasks confronting the individual in the areas of biological and social growth, work and career development, and family life. For an ultimate understanding of these areas, one must have a better understanding of how they interact within the person, and one of the major tasks for future research will be a systematic exploration of such interactions. Here I will not speculate on the actual content of such interactions, since not enough is yet known about them, but will focus on the process of coping itself. In other words, whatever tasks face the individual and however those tasks interact, there is a process of coping which the individual must engage in to deal with them. Since the focus of Part 1 is the perspective of the individual, I want to define what the *individual* can do about any given situation.

This chapter will offer some observations and suggestions on how the *process* of coping can be made more constructive and effective. By "constructive coping" I mean the process of confronting tasks and developing responses which adequately deal with those tasks so that the individual grows and develops as a result of successive life experiences. It is a basic assumption of this whole approach to adult development that we do not cease to grow and develop when we are through adolescence. Instead, one can think of the entire period of adulthood right to the point of death as a continuing series of new developmental tasks which require constructive coping and which enhance the person's total repertory of responses.

The process of constructive coping will be conceived of as:

1. *Diagnosing what the problem is*—improving one's understanding of the situation which is causing stress;

2. *Diagnosing oneself*—improving one's understanding of one's resources, feelings, and needs in the situation;

3. *Selecting a coping response*—deciding how to deal with the stressful situation;

4. *Diagnosing the effects of the coping response*—evaluating whether it has achieved its purpose, whether the task has been faced and met, whether the problem has been solved.

It should be noted that this conception of the process of coping puts a heavy emphasis on *rational analysis* of the problem, oneself, and the environment. Though some of one's feelings and needs may have unconscious origins, it is important to recognize that *one can treat such feelings as facts to be rationally dealt with.* Even though we do not know the source of our anxiety in certain situations and may not be willing to invest in psychotherapy to find out what the source is, we have the rational choice of avoiding such situations if they make us too uncomfortable. In other words, whatever our personality, whatever our limitations, whatever the constraints which may be operating within the environment, and however high the stress level, *we always retain some choices.* The key to successful constructive coping is to diagnose our situation and ourselves sufficiently to identify what those choices are and to act as rationally as we can in exercising those choices.

DIAGNOSING THE PROBLEM

If we think back to the developmental cycles identified previously—the tasks which derive from self-development, career development, and family development issues—we can see that such tasks pose a variety of potential problems to the person. First we will categorize these problems into a logical framework, to facilitate a diagnosis of what sorts of coping responses may be needed. Three bases for categorization will be discussed: (1) the origin and possible interaction of tasks; (2) task difficulty; and (3) the source of the difficulty.

What Is the Origin of the Problem or Task?

When we confront a problem, it typically surfaces in the form of an unanticipated demand made on us or a response in others which is out of line with what we expected. One can think of these events as "lack of confirmation" or "disconfirmation" of our assumptions about the world and ourselves (Schein, 1973; Schein and Bennis, 1965). I may not have received a raise when I expected, or it may have been smaller than expected, or I discover an illness in myself or in a family member, or I find that I am not enjoying some activity in the way I used to, or I planned a move to get a better job and discovered that making new friends and settling in the new community is more difficult than expected, or my spouse announces a desire to return to school, which may require reorganizing the household routine, and so on. In other words, a problem or task surfaces when the smooth course of daily life is interrupted by something unanticipated—either an external event or some new feeling or response within us. Our first task, then, is to diagnose what is going on. Where is the problem coming from? What is the origin of the stress?

Because self, career, and family issues tend to interact in complex ways, it is not always obvious where stress is coming from. Is my disappointment about not getting a raise due to my feeling that my career may be stalled, or is it really a problem to me because the children are about to enter college and I need more money, or is it a problem because my self-image and pride are hurt? Until I have sorted out in which life area the event has its problematic impact, I cannot really begin a process of effective coping.* To give another example, if I discover at a certain point in life that I am feeling tired and depressed, is that feeling related to work issues, to my family situation, or to some internal emotional issue having to do primarily with me?

Even more important from a diagnostic point of view is the question of whether the source of the problem is in *one* of the areas or whether it is the result of some *interaction* among several such areas. My problem may be that not getting a raise came at the same time as the announcement of another child on the way. In this case the two tasks of regaining career momentum and building security for a larger family interact to create a potentially greater problem. I

---

*I am not implying that one can do this by oneself. Sometimes one needs the help of a counselor or friend to sort out the answers to these questions.

may not have the energy or the self-confidence to deal with both tasks simultaneously. I may not have the creativity or the information to invent new integrative solutions which might permit both the career and family problem to be dealt with by, for example, changing my job or changing my life-style.

One major hypothesis about coping is that it becomes more difficult if several life areas are involved. If I am simultaneously experiencing difficulties at work, with my family, and in my emotional life internally, I am more likely to become overloaded or conflicted to the point where any constructive coping may become impossible. Such situations also provide opportunities for major restructuring of one's life if one can take advantage of them, but such restructuring involves a higher order of coping which may be possible only if the person has both the internal resources and the help and support of the spouse. More will be said later about the role of others in aiding the coping process. For now the important point to underline is that a major diagnostic question is "which life area is the source of the problem and how are the life areas interacting in creating the problem?"

Diagnosing the source of the difficulty has a further aspect—identifying the *real* problem as distinct from surface symptoms or problems. When a disconfirming event occurs in a given life area, does that automatically mean that the problem lies in that life area? For example, assume that after several moves I have finally settled my family in a community and got my children in school, on the assumption that I will remain in that job for several years. Suddenly I am offered a promotion after nine months which involves another move. My first reaction may be to view this as a work/family conflict situation requiring some resolution of what I think are my career needs and my family's needs. That certainly seems to be the problem, but is it? How often in that situation is the *real* problem a conflict between self-development concerns and career concerns? I may be unsure about whether or not I want the promotion; I may not be confident that I can do the next job; I may feel that I have not had enough time on the present job to prove myself; though it is flattering to be promoted again, I may even feel some resentment at being uprooted so quickly from my present *job* situation (though I may initially experience it as a family uprooting). Or, perhaps such a move is an event I may actually have precipitated myself because I was not entirely comfortable in a settled situation. Though I may apologize to my family for uprooting them again, I may actually have set up the situation so that these events would come about, and my real problem is an internal conflict between my commitment to my career and my concern for my family.*

To illustrate the importance of accurate diagnosis, I want to cite a dramatic case of a highly successful manager of manufacturing in a very large corporation who suddenly resigned and launched a second career as a small entrepreneur in a small town in which he had long wanted to live. He was a high-potential manager who possibly could have become the president of his company. The key event in his decision to launch a new career was a diagnostic insight precipitated by his wife. He reports that he was having a series of family discussions about his future in the company when his wife asked him whether his ambitions and his hard work were connected to some *personal* goals, or to *family* goals of providing a level of income that would permit sending the children through school and living at an appropriate level in terms of their self-image. She further pointed out that the family situation had changed—the children were practically through school, the needs for money were rapidly diminishing, and they had achieved a life-style that was quite secure and satisfactory. In effect, the wife was saying: "If *you* really want this career advancement, I'll go along with the hard work and the life-style. But be sure *you* want it. If you are still doing it for *us,* we don't need it anymore. The kids are grown up, and our economic position is secure." The man reflected on these questions and decided that indeed he had got himself onto a treadmill which was originally motivated by personal and family needs. But his personal needs had changed substantially; he no longer wanted to climb the corporate ladder and was doing so only out of habit and the rationalization that he was doing it for his family. Once he recognized that his real problem was in assessing his *own* motivation, not the needs of his family, he realized that his *own* needs were not being met. It was then a fairly easy decision to re-think what he really wanted, i.e., to move out of the corporate job into an entrepreneurial one.

A key to identifying the real problem is to examine carefully one's internal reactions and feelings to the external events which are the precipitating factors. We are not really diagnosing the problem until we examine its impact on us, how we perceive it, how we react to it, what it implies for our self-image, what resources we will have

---

*It has been noted that some commuting couples who see each other only on weekends have adopted a life-style which may be the only one possible for them because of certain personality traits and relatively lower needs for family intimacy (Bailyn, 1978).

to bring to bear in coping with it—extra emotional energy, concentration, time, new skills, etc.

Once we have identified the real problem, we can assess whether the sources of difficulty lie in several life areas and whether the interaction among them is itself a problem. That is, the life tasks may be *independent* though acting at the same time (I may have a work problem of sorting out priorities among a number of work tasks and, at the same time but independently, may have to give some extra attention to a child with problems at school). Or the tasks may be *mutually reinforcing* (I may be getting feedback *both* at home and at work that I am not dealing effectively with some life area or some interpersonal issues). Or the tasks may be *conflicting* (I may be getting the message at work that in order to succeed, I have to work overtime and show more commitment and, at the same time, may be getting the message from my family that I am needed more at home. Or my own needs in the career area may be to seek a job which is more enjoyable and pays less at the same time that I am facing sending children to college and perceiving an increase in needs for money for the family). Having identified the sources of the problem, we can then turn to an assessment of its difficulty.

How Does One Measure the Difficulty of the Task?

Assessing the difficulty of a life task is itself difficult because it is hard to discriminate between some objective external criterion of difficulty (i.e., what most people facing a given task might find more or less difficult) and some internal subjective criterion of what is difficult in terms of a particular person's past history and personality. It is obvious that people's makeup differs in terms of how they will perceive any given task. Nevertheless, one can specify some general criteria for comparing tasks on degree of difficulty.

A *first* criterion would be *the degree to which the task requires the learning of new responses or skills.* The more the task requires coping patterns which are not in the person's repertory, the more difficult the task will be, simply because any new learning is always more difficult than an increase in effort around old responses. For example, adolescence is such a difficult period in the life cycle partly because the person must cope with brand new feelings related to sexual maturation. Similarly, the midlife crisis or old age is more difficult to the extent that each involves previously unexperienced events, such as unexplained depressions, loss of health and vigor, the loss of loved ones through death, having older people (such as one's parents) become dependent on one, and so on. In the career cycle the more difficult tasks by this criterion would be promotions or lateral moves into brand new areas of work, geographical moves into unfamiliar surroundings, changes in work group which require learning the new culture, a change in boss, a demotion, or other changes involving the need to learn new responses. In the family area leaving home, marriage, the advent of the first child, divorce, and the death of a spouse are some of the most difficult tasks, because we have no response set or coping patterns ready for such events. In other words, when in the face of a problem or tasks, we feel "I have never faced this situation before; I am not sure what to do," we are talking about intrinsically more difficult kinds of life situations.

A *second* criterion for difficulty is the degree to which *coping requires a large output of concentration and emotional energy.* Many life problems, particularly those involving *relationship* issues within the family or at work, are more difficult because they require a period of concentrated effort over time. If the problem is a neglected spouse or child, it may take weeks, months, or years of effort to rebuild a relationship; if the problem is a new and difficult boss or subordinate, it may take much effort and patience to build a relationship which will make effective cooperation possible. Whenever other people are involved, the coping process requires *mutual* learning, which is intrinsically more demanding of time and energy than if a person is simply dealing with some new element of his or her own internal environment.

A *third* criterion of difficulty is the degree to which *the problem results from a major disconfirmation of valued parts of the self or is a major disruption of emotional patterns from which the person obtains self-esteem and comfort.* For example, the loss of a loved one through death or geographical separation can be very "difficult" because of the degree to which the person depended on that other for confirmation, comfort, and support. Similarly, failure to get a promotion can be very traumatic because it may violate the person's entire self-image as a successful career occupant.

These kinds of problems can be doubly difficult because they may involve the other criteria as well; they may precipitate the person into a novel situation and may require new internal emotional learning, new interpersonal responses, and the building of new relationships.

A *fourth* and final criterion of difficulty is the degree to which *society or some valued reference group defines the task as a test to be passed to prove one's worth.* For example, getting into college can be a very traumatic, difficult task for a high school student not because it involves any of the first three criteria, but simply because parents, teachers, and the peer group use acceptance by a good college as a criterion of how good or worthwhile the student is. Such a process may not even be conscious, but may be very clear-cut in the degree to which positive statements attach to success and negative statements and expressions of disappointment accompany failure to get into good schools. In many such "test" situations, the outcome is genuinely unknown and the stakes are therefore very high. Failure can mean a clear message that the person had illusions which must now be given up, a costly and painful process of rebuilding the self-image on more "realistic" assumptions.

In summary, task difficulty can be defined by the degree to which it requires new responses, involves prolonged investment of concentration and energy, results from major disconfirmation of self-image or disruption of valued emotional patterns, and/or constitutes a major test of one's worth. Some of the most difficult life tasks involve all of the elements above, such as when one parent must, as a result of divorce or the death of a spouse, become breadwinner, father, and mother all at the same time.

Is the Task Difficult Because It Produces Ambiguity, Overload, or Conflict?

For any given life task one can identify several sources of difficulty which will help to identify how to go about coping, quite apart from the degree of task difficulty. These sources are the same as those identified by analysts of social and work *roles*. Thus the ability to perform effectively in a given role has been related to whether the person was suffering from "role ambiguity" (not knowing what was expected by others), "role overload" (knowing what was expected but being unable to fulfill all of the expectations), and "role conflict" (knowing what was expected but finding that different people expected contradictory things or that what was expected was incompatible with what the person wanted to do) (Katz, *et al.*, 1964).

Applying these ideas to constructive coping would imply that how the person copes will depend on whether the difficulty derives from not knowing what to do (ambiguity); from knowing what to do but having insufficient energy, time, or commitment to do it (overload); or from realizing that coping in one area conflicts with coping in another area or with one's own personal desires (conflict). If one is to arrive at a good diagnosis of the problem, it is obviously important to think out what difficulties are involved in planning to take some action in terms of criteria such as the ones stated. It makes a big difference whether I am feeling paralyzed in the face of the problem because I genuinely have no available response or because I am unwilling to do what needs to be done because of lack of energy or conflict. Often we do not know what the real problem is until we have identified within ourselves the options which may or may not be available for coping with it.

The sources of difficulty obviously interact with the degrees of difficulty outlined above. Tasks that involve previously unencountered situations are more likely to also involve response ambiguity. Until the ambiguity has been removed, the person will not know whether the things to be done will cause overload or conflict. Tasks that are difficult because of energy commitment almost by definition will cause feelings of overload and conflict, which must then be dealt with as part of the problem. In the case of tests of self, what is to be done is fairly clear, but the necessary responses to pass the tests may involve overload or conflict.

DIAGNOSING ONESELF

One cannot really fully diagnose a task or a problem without understanding clearly the impact of that task or problem on oneself—what feelings are triggered, needs aroused, resources or coping responses or energy levels are available within oneself to cope with the problem. Many people are very perceptive about the external sources of their stress, yet are quite unable to assess their own responses or what would be a realistic way for them to cope, given their makeup. For example, the failure to get a promotion may be accompanied by a clear message that one has failed a test and will not progress any further in a certain career direction. One may perceive that message quite clearly, but may then misperceive how much that is bothering one or may misestimate what kinds of alternative career options may work. It is essential for any constructive coping that the person have a maximum of self-insight and self-understanding, including insight into reactions to the problem situation and insight into the strengths and weaknesses (the resources) which can be used to cope with it.

Self-insight does not come automatically, just from having had a variety of life experiences. It is achieved through systematic self-study and effort to understand what is happening in oneself in a variety of situations. One of the most important results of focused training experiences, such as encounter groups, psychotherapy, transactional analysis, gestalt therapy, and the like, is that they interrupt the day-to-day life routines and provide a period of enforced self-study during which people can become more acquainted with themselves. For example, a common experience in such learning situations is that something frustrating happens, such as losing a game. By analyzing closely their reaction to such events, people become aware of some of their own defense mechanisms—the tendency to *deny* what happened ("I didn't really lose"); the tendency to *blame others* ("I lost because the judges didn't apply the rules fairly"; "John took advantage of me; he is just too aggressive"); the tendency to *project* one's problems onto others ("Look at what a bad loser Pete is, isn't that pathetic to take it so seriously"); the tendency to *blame oneself* and become a victim ("I always lose in games that require skill; I'm no good at those things"; "I blew it again and made John mad at me"; "I can't win"); and so on.

The crucial point is that each of the various ways of defending oneself are ways of avoiding the recognition of what the real problem is and what could be done about it. Until one becomes aware of one's own defensiveness and how it operates, one cannot realistically assess one's problem or what one's resources are to deal with it. And since each of us uses different defenses and uses them in different ways, it becomes crucial to learn about ourselves. We cannot really learn from the advice of others, whose pattern of defenses or coping may be quite different from our own. Only when we have self-insight can we listen to others and assess the value of what they have to offer to us in the way of guidance or advice. A good helper will therefore focus most of the effort on helping us to move toward self-insight as a step toward problem diagnosis and developing coping responses.

A practical guide to achieving some self-insight on your own is to take any given task or problem which may be confronting you and ask yourself the following questions:

1. What *feelings* is this task or problem arousing within me—anger, frustration, despair, relief, anxiety, or what?

2. Given my reactions and feelings, what is *really* the problem; what areas of *choice* do I have?

3. If my feelings are getting in the way of problem solving, do I have a choice about those feelings? Can I get past my anger, anxiety, etc., or can I get the feeling sufficiently under control to perceive and act on the problem? If not, the problem is *within me,* and what can I do about that?

4. What am I contributing to the problem by the way I am reacting to the external situation? Is there anything I can do about my reaction?

5. What are my options in terms of available coping responses which I know I have available within me? How will I feel about the use of these various options?

Note that the major emphasis in self-diagnosis is on the inner self. The hardest part of learning about yourself is to become aware of what you are feeling and to learn what triggers those feelings. Beyond that, it is important to learn whether your feelings are really based on subconscious forces and, therefore, relatively less under your control, or whether they are learned responses that can, in fact, be unlearned if you choose to do so and want to invest the energy.

One of the most powerful insights is to discover that we choose to feel in certain ways. When I am driving my car and someone cuts in front of me, I almost invariably become angry and competitive. It is hard to accept, but nevertheless true, that I am allowing myself those feelings because at some level I experience them in a positive way. In other words, I am choosing to feel angry and competitive. If I give in to the feelings and attempt to retaliate, I am *choosing* to put myself in a dangerous situation and would have only myself to blame if an accident resulted (as my wife has often pointed out to me in those situations). Similarly, if I am afraid to do something and therefore inhibit my action, I have to recognize the possibility that I am choosing to feel afraid and that I could have attempted to deal with the fear or to surmont it rather than giving in to it.

This section can be concluded with a few "tips" which may be helpful:

1. Try to be as *open* to your own feelings as possible; accept feelings as something to be owned and dealt with instead of being avoided or suppressed; recognize feelings as "normal" and not necessarily as bad or immutable.

2. Don't diagnose a task or problem situation without considering your *own reaction* to the situation; become as aware as possible of your feelings in reaction to whatever outside events are triggering the "problem."

3. Become acquainted with your *blind spots* and *defenses;* be suspicious of "denial," blaming others, yourself; recognize these as normal *initial* reactions to a problem, to be worked through until the real problem can be identified.

4. Examine carefully the *choices or options* available to you, including some choices about how you will feel in the new situation; become acquainted with your preferences or with options that make you too uncomfortable and choose with full awareness.

5. Take the *time* to reflect on and diagnose the situation and your own feelings about it; build in time for reflection and analysis and find ways of slowing things down enough to be able to reflect (you can't see down to the bottom of a muddy pool—let the water calm down enough to be able to see to the bottom).

SELECTING A COPING RESPONSE

A coping response is anything the person chooses to do in order to deal with the life task at hand. A response can be "doing nothing," letting the situation remain as is, or it can be an internal one, such as choosing not to be too upset about something or in some other way managing one's internal feelings about the situation. Deciding what to do will depend on the type of problem situation and its degree of difficulty. For example, problems that are new will require us first to decide whether responses used in other situations would fit the new one, or if not, how to develop a new response. During the mass layoffs of technical people in the early 1970s, for example, many engineers found themselves out of work, a situation completely new to them. Many of them chose to cope with traditional responses; they went to other companies in the hope of finding similar technical work, only to be frustrated repeatedly. With the aid of some government money and some innovative efforts from universities, some programs were developed which helped unemployed engineers to rethink their situation, redefine their self-image in broader terms than their specific area of technical expertise, rewrite their resumes to emphasize the broad, analytical skills they possessed, and reenter the labor market in new areas where such skills were needed more. This process could only work to the extent that the people involved could redefine for themselves their self-image and invent some new options and new coping responses.

Intimacy with Peers

The development of new coping responses usually requires some help from others. In the case of the engineers mentioned above, the help came from many outside sources. In the day-to-day coping with life tasks, we often do not need such a great amount of help, yet need some. The answer to many such problems is to open up communication channels with family members, friends, and peers in order to learn how they view problems and have coped with them.

In a seminar on adult development which I conducted with my wife for midlevel executives and their wives, a great deal of attention was given to the idea of "developing intimacy with peers." Everyone took it for granted that effective coping would be aided by more talking between husband and wife, but not everyone had considered the potential of community groups, church groups, social occasions, and other vehicles for individuals or couples to discuss problems they were facing and get ideas or perspectives from others who were facing similar problems.

Such sharing among peers without counselors or professional helpers would be the "blind leading the blind" and should therefore be viewed not as a source of *advice* for the person with a problem, but a source of perspective and ideas. From the managers and their spouses came many ideas which were a source of stimulation to others and which they could use in deciding for themselves how to cope better.

Serious Talk

Closely connected with the idea of "peer intimacy" is the idea of increasing opportunities for "serious talk." There was a great deal of consensus in the group that social patterns and occasions are often misused or underutilized by staying at a superficial "cocktail party" level of talk. Everyone in the seminar said that they went to such parties, enjoyed them, and gave them, but at the same time, everyone agreed that they were nonmeaningful and left one with an empty feeling. In contrast, the small dinner party or the church group get-together or retreat were often more meaningful, because people invested energy in serious talk. What was meant by "serious talk" was the sharing of life issues that were on people's minds and some discussion of different ways of coping with life tasks. The issues were not necessarily very deep or personal. No one was advocating some big "opening up" or "airing one's dirty linen." But there were many very important issues—e.g., how to help a 12-year-old child adjust to a new community, how to work out a better balance of time between work and family when the husband has to go off on frequent business trips, how to help a housewife become reinvolved in a career after the child-rearing years are over, how to deal with certain kinds of bosses, how to handle adolescent rebellion, and so on—which were meaningfully discussed from the multiple perspectives of the members of the group. They all agreed that they needed to find ways of setting up such groups in their own communities and to find ways of having more "serious talk."

Small Adjustments

Out of serious discussion came ideas for new ways of coping with problems—ways that either had not occurred to people or had not been seriously considered until they heard someone else talk about it. Many of these new ideas were not dramatic large changes, but rather "small adjustments" which had large psychological consequences. Some of the best examples occurred in the area of managing work-family conflicts.

A couple who found that they had too little time for serious talk with each other decided to get a dog and use the twice-a-day "walking the dog" period as built-in guaranteed private time.

A couple who felt that the husband's work and travel schedule dictated too much of their daily life agreed to a family vacation every year which would be scheduled, planned, and organized entirely by the wife. The husband reported that he was much more relaxed during the family vacation because he was not entirely responsible for planning and implementing it.

A couple adapted to the husband's traveling by having the wife meet the husband at a restaurant at the end of the trip. By meeting in town at a restaurant, the husband found it easier to decompress and reestablish contact with his wife in "neutral" territory. Going home first and greeting three little children, etc., was too overwhelming right after a trip. At the same time, it enabled the wife to get out of the house for a little while.

Several couples discovered the necessity to separate in their own minds the needs of the total family, including the children (e.g., taking total-family vacations), and the needs of the husband-wife pair (e.g., taking separate vacations away from the children, using money to hire more babysitting services, and in other ways protecting their own time).

These may seem like fairly trivial, nonoriginal ideas to anyone experienced with these matters, but the fact remains that many couples simply had not thought of any of these options or had not seriously considered them until they heard others talk about them. What the conversation sparked was a kind of creative coping, opening up options, letting their minds go to new ideas and new inventions for how to manage life tasks. Once this process was started, it was surprising how much innovative thinking came out of the group. People did not end up giving one another advice, but rather triggering one anothers' thinking, which then could become the basis for each person's or couple's developing some options. For many, a major conclusion was the necessity to build relationships with others which would permit serious talk so that one could at least find out what others were going through, how they were coping, and how they viewed life and its problems.

Supportive Relationships

Supportive relationships with other people not only aid in inventing new responses where that is needed, but also are necessary to sustain coping in situations which require a continuous output of energy over a long period of time or which involve severe threats to self-esteem. Coping with the loss of a job or the death of a loved one may be so devastating that the person needs to find some kind of supportive relationship as a first step in coping with the more general problem. In well-integrated communities such relationships are almost automatically provided through customs and rituals which surround traumatic events (wakes, funerals, etc.). For the more isolated nuclear family in a large city, life may be very impersonal and separate, therefore requiring more complex coping when traumatic events occur.

In summary, the essential aspects to selecting a coping response are self-insight and relationships with others which act as supports or sources of stimulation or perspective. Both are needed; neither by itself is enough. Therefore, the skills involved in developing self-insight and in developing relationships with others which permit support and serious talk become more general coping skills to be cultivated by every adult. Skills of listening, the ability to describe one's feelings to others, the ability to accept oneself and others as vulnerable, the skill of using time to reflect on things, the skill of gaining some control over one's own feelings—all are crucial to this enterprise of coping and living.

DIAGNOSING THE EFFECTS OF ONE'S COPING RESPONSE

Whatever we choose to do to cope with some life task or problem, we are not really solving the problem until we have checked out the effects of our actions. All too often we get caught in the trap of deciding to do something, doing it, and then relaxing, only to have the problem blow up in our face at some later time. Even worse, having decided to do something, we get overcommitted to that course of action and find it difficult to accept the possibility that the coping response we chose was incorrect and needs to be rethought. If we act and things don't work out, it is all too easy to blame others and the cruel world and to give up psychologically. It is at this moment that our need for self-insight is greatest. We must find a way to overcome our own distorted vision that makes us want to see success in our endeavors; we must find a way of overcoming the denial that if things aren't going right, we choose to ignore the data; we must find a way of surmounting the tendency to blame others for the failure of our own coping. All of these are difficult to do psychologically, yet all of them are part of what one might call growing up as an adult.

Coping can be thought of as a cyclical problem-solving process—it starts with problem identification and goes through to taking some action, but the results of the action merely cycle us back into another phase of problem identification. With each successive loop, I have learned something more about the nature of the problem and something more about myself. The trick is to allow this learning to take place.

SUMMARY

I have reviewed some of what I consider to be the key elements to effective, constructive coping—*diagnosing* the real problem, oneself, one's reactions to the problem, and one's feelings in the face of it; *selecting* an appropriate coping response; and *following through* by diagnosing and realistically assessing the consequences of one's coping efforts. There is no implication that these steps are easy. On the contrary, we can spend a lifetime attempting to achieve self-insight, gaining control over certain feelings, and solving certain chronic problems of living. But it seems increasingly clear as more becomes known about adult psychology that coping and living are largely one and the same thing. There will always be another task on the horizon, so *learning how to cope* is itself a major life task.

Relationships with other people—family members and friends —become especially relevant to effective coping, because we need ideas, perspective, and emotional support from others. Therefore, one of the most important skills to be developed in learning how to cope more effectively is how to establish more meaningful relationships with other people. This skill is of especial relevance within organizations, because it not only applies to increasing coping effectiveness generally, but also is a prime skill needed for people whose careers will be spent within organizational contexts. As will be seen in the remainder of this book, interpersonal competence is increasingly coming to be a critical skill not only for dealing with self and family development problems, but for career advancement as well.

PART 2
CAREER DYNAMICS: THE INDIVIDUAL-ORGANIZATION INTERACTION

In Part 1 I tried to spell out fairly clearly the issues confronting the individual throughout the life cycle. The person must find a way to balance and play out personal-developmental needs, needs to develop a viable career, and needs to develop a satisfactory family life. For most people in society a major portion of this "playing out" occurs in the context of building and maintaining a career, which brings the individual into direct interaction with "organizations." In the next several chapters I want to examine in greater detail this interaction and its consequences for both the individual and the organization.

An important outcome of the early career is a "career anchor," a self-concept that organizes and constrains career decisions. Data will be reported on the formation of such anchors based on a longitudinal study of MIT Sloan School alumni.

The final chapter in Part 2 will discuss midcareer problems and their underlying causes.

7
ENTRY INTO THE ORGANIZATIONAL CAREER

Every career transition can be viewed from two perspectives—the individual's and the organization's. As I have argued throughout this book, what makes "career" a complicated concept is that one can view it from the perspective of the *individual* developing his or her own life pattern of work or as an *occupation, profession,* or *organization* creating a "path" for people to follow. The same events will have a different meaning from the point of view of the manager in the organization who makes them happen (i.e., "putting someone through an initiation rite" or "teaching someone what the organization is ultimately all about") and from the point of view of the individual to whom they are happening (i.e., "getting a lot of mickey-mouse work which isn't contributing anything" or "doing the organization's dirty work because no one else is willing to do it").

Entry into the organization is, from the individual's point of view, a process of breaking in and joining up, of learning the ropes, of figuring out how to get along and how to make it (Van Maanen, 1975). The same process from the point of view of the organization is one of induction, basic training, and socialization of the individual to the major norms and values of the organization and of testing new employees to make it possible to place them correctly in a job and career path (Schein, 1968). The two processes can be seen as a kind of negotiation between the "recruits" and the organizational members with whom they deal, leading to a viable *psychological contract*—a matching of what the individual will give with what the organization expects to receive, and what the organization will give relative to what the individual expects to receive (Schein, 1970).

This transition can be more clearly understood by classifying it into three stages and analyzing each stage in greater detail. The *first* stage, *"entry,"* includes the period of preparation and training on the part of the individual, the recruitment and selection process which occurs prior to accepting a job, and the actual hiring decision and initial job placement. The *second* stage (discussed in Chapter 8) is *"socialization"* and includes all of the early process of "learning the ropes," how to make it in the organization, how to get along, how to work, and so on (Van Maanen and Schein, 1977; Van Maanen, 1975). This is a period of mutual testing by the individual and the organization; some of the details of the psychological contract are worked out, the individual builds a picture of the organization and his or her future in it, and the organization develops a picture of its new employee and his or her future.

The *third* and final stage (discussed in Chapter 9) can be called *"mutual acceptance"* and includes the various processes of formally and informally granting full membership to the new employee through initiation rites, the conferring of special status or privileges, more challenging and important job assignments, and the working out of a viable psychological contract. At the end of this period the new employee is a fully accepted member of the organization, but is still in the early stages of the career and has not yet achieved "tenure" or *permanent* membership. All that has been established is that there is enough of a match between what the individual needs and expects and what the organization needs and expects to continue the career in that organization. In fact, many midcareer problems stem from false hopes which are built up by both the organization and the individual in these early stages of the career.

These early career events can have one of two outcomes. The new employee either is successfully socialized into the organization or discovers that the degree of mismatch with the organization is so great that a job shift to another organization is necessary (initiated by either the employee or the employing organization). It is important to recognize that this transition involves a confrontation between two strong sets of forces: (1) the individual's talents, personality, prior attitudes, values, ambitions, and expectations formed by 20 or more years of childhood socialization and education; and (2) the organization's requirements and culture with its norms of what kind of work is valuable, how work should be done, what a good employee should be like, and so on.

In a period of economic affluence, in which job mobility is fairly easy, one might expect that neither the individual nor the organization will change its values where mismatches are discovered, thus leading inevitably to turnover. At the same time, it must be recognized that organizational culture is probably the more powerful force, which means that if persons for various reasons can *not* move to another organization, they will probably be subjected to strong pressures to conform to that culture and to change their own value system. The more they are constrained by various forces from leaving, the more likely it is that they will conform to the organizational culture and suppress their own creativity. As we look at the stages in greater detail, we must always bear in mind this inevitable confrontation between individual and organizational values and attempt to assess what kinds of resolution are optimal for both the individual and the employer.

TASKS OF THE ENTRY STAGE

The period of entry involves a number of developmental tasks for the individual.

Task 1: The first task is to make some kind of preliminary occupational choice, which will determine what kind of education and training to pursue.

Task 2: Next, one must develop a viable "dream"—an image of the occupation or organization which can serve as the outlet for one's talents, values, and ambitions. One must be able to develop a self-concept as a "manager," "financial analyst," or "entrepreneur," for example, which is reasonably consistent with what is known about both the world of work and oneself.

One of the major problems of this period is how to develop reality tests, i.e., how to determine whether one's view of the occupation or of oneself is realistic when both the individual and the potential employer tend to collude to hide reality, to avoid the person's getting turned off and going into another occupation altogether. Every occupation has its unpleasant realities and its dirty work, a fact carefully concealed from outsiders to maintain the idealistic myths which the members of the occupation build and foster (Hughes, 1958). The kinds of realities concealed about management have to do with how boring and difficult much of the work is, how much personal values might have to be compromised to get the work done, and how much politics and other nonrational elements determine outcomes (Dalton, 1959).

In discussing the problem of early career development, senior executives in management programs sometimes blame the university for failing to prepare students for the "realities" of life in organizations. They do not consider, however, that (1) those realities might turn too many high-talent students into cynics who might shift to other careers altogether, and/or (2) students wouldn't believe much of the information anyway, because they cannot afford to give up a dream before it has even begun to be actualized. We all need to idealize the occupations we enter, and we are therefore highly resistant to data that life in that occupation might be stultifying or even involve value compromises we might not be prepared to make.

Task 3: One must prepare oneself for the early career through "anticipatory socialization," in order to develop what one considers to be the attitudes and values necessary for succeeding in one's chosen occupation.   For a person entering business, such attitudes would include a commitment to the profit motive, a basic belief in the free-enterprise system and economic competition, possibly a belief in the particular products or services produced by the business or industry being entered, and so on. These beliefs may or may not be "realistic" in the sense of being a requirement for entry, but they are a necessary part of the preparation of the individual for any given career.

Task 4: As the period of education and training comes to a close, the individual is faced with "entry into the labor market," the realities of finding a first job.   Most schools support this process to some degree by making available the services of a placement office where recruiters from organizations and potential employees can come together or where information about jobs is available. There then ensues a complex interaction in which representatives of organizations and potential employees try to obtain valid information about each other. Through a few hours of mutual interviewing and possibly visiting the organization, the applicants are trying to determine whether to link an unknown number of years of their lives to a given employer and to assess whether their dreams and ambitions can be fulfilled there; the employer is trying to determine whether the candidate's talents, personality traits, attitudes, values, physical appearance, temperament, and energy level "fit" with the organization's needs. Mistakes can be costly on both sides, since each is investing time, energy, and money.

In a period of economic affluence, when plenty of jobs are available, individuals probably have less to lose if a mistake is made, since they will learn something valuable from their first year or so in *any* organization. For the organization, on the other hand, a recruiting/selection error is a no-return investment in human capital.

If jobs are scarce, however, individuals have more to lose from a bad choice, even though the pressures on them to take whatever is available are stronger. The danger in a tight labor market is that applicants will end up in an organization whose values are out of line with their own or whose opportunities are limited relative to their talents and that they will adapt to that organization by allowing themselves to be socialized to new values and by reducing their ambitions to the realities that are available. If that happens, both the individual and the organization are in a position of losing in the long run by under- or misutilizing the organization's most important resource—its human capital. Many midcareer problems can derive from an initial selection error combined with a failure on the part of the organization to manage such early mismatching. The employee overadapts, becomes complacent, and never achieves his or her full potential.

Problems in the Management of Entry Tasks

The recruitment/selection process creates several specific problems to which both the individual and the employing organization must be sensitive and with which they must cope.

1. The problem of obtaining accurate information in a climate of mutual selling.   Since the organization is trying to attract the best possible candidates and the candidates are trying to find the best possible jobs, there are strong incentives for both sides to distort reality by overemphasizing positive features and hiding or minimizing negative ones. But each party knows that the other is distorting and is therefore in a game of trying to outguess the other.

2. The problem of the organization and the individual unwittingly colluding in setting up unrealistic expectations about the early career.   Both are "future" oriented and are attempting to assess the *long-range* match between individual and organizational needs and resources, to the point where neither pays enough attention to the immediate *short-run events which will occur in the early part of the career.* This problem occurs especially with graduates of management schools, who are hired for their knowledge of and skill in *new* management technologies, e.g., the use of computers, mathematical techniques of analysis of financial and other problems, operations research, modeling, etc., but who are often brought into an organizational culture that will resist any of these techniques. Often the new recruit unwittingly becomes a change agent on behalf of one part of the organization that is trying to introduce new techniques into another, resisting part. For example, a graduate hired by a corporation specifically to introduce operations research techniques into a large plant was told within two weeks of arrival at his new assignment by the plant manager to "cool it." They were happy with how they were doing things, were hiding much of what they were doing from corporate headquarters, and were not about to let the new employee become either a spy or a boat rocker with his "fancy new techniques." He left the company roughly one year later, completely frustrated, and the plant continued to use its old methods of production.

3. *The recruitment process itself may build an incorrect image of the organization or socialize the individual to incorrect values.* For example, if the recruitment process creates a feeling in the recruits that they are a valuable resource being hired for their special talents, yet the first job turns out to be a period of indoctrination into company values, they may become very disillusioned about that company's commitment to using their talent. On the other hand, a tough period of recruitment and selection involving many tests can build a positive self-image and real commitment to the occupation in the recruit who passes the tough hurdles. As Van Maanen has shown in the recruitment of policemen, the very process of testing builds a commitment prior to selection. If recruits have invested heavily in getting into the organization, they will value their membership more (Van Maanen, 1973, 1974).

4. *The problems of deciding on a job without clear or reliable information about the future.* Assuming that one has a choice, one must make a decision which may commit one for an unknown length of time on the basis of very fragmentary and questionable information. Therefore, it is not surprising that there are nasty surprises ahead for both the individual and the organization. To minimize the negative consequences, it is important to provide many opportunities for mutual testing and validating in the early career. Ways must be found to make it possible for both the individual and the organization to communicate more fully and accurately their expectations, assumptions, and self-insights, even if some of this information is nonflattering. In the next section we will examine in some detail how this might be accomplished.

NEGATIVE OUTCOMES AND HOW TO AVOID THEM

In assessing outcomes, we must maintain three separate perspectives— that of the individual being recruited and attempting to launch his or her career, that of the organization trying to build up its human resources by hiring "good" people, and that of social institutions such as vocational or professional schools, counseling services, etc., whose function is to help society to maximize the utilization of its human resources by improving the process of matching individual talents with occupational and organizational needs for talent.

The Individual Perspective

From the point of view of the individual, the entry stage is a failure if it does not lead to a job in which there is the potential for talents to be utilized, needs to be met, and values to be actualized. Although individual talents, needs, and values vary, the goal of this stage must be for the individual to enter a work situation which is to some degree congruent with them. If the situation is either too challenging or too stultifying—lacking in opportunities for growth and development or demanding value compromises—one must either move to another organization or change some part of oneself. Adaptation is desirable only if one's self-image or needs were unrealistic; it is undesirable if one settles for less than one is capable of or compromises one's values and ambitions in the interest of the employing organization. Indeed, such compromise is undesirable in the long run for all parties concerned, since it represents wasted talent.

What can the *individual* do to prevent undesirable mismatching? *First,* it is obvious that as early as possible in their lives, people must develop a realistic appraisal of their talents, needs, and values and must attempt serious self-reappraisals at important times throughout their lives. Without *self-insight* there can be no realistic assessment of either occupational opportunities or illusions that must be abandoned. Programs of counseling starting in high school and continuing through college and graduate school should be utilized as much as possible by people before they enter the labor market. Self-exposure to varied experiences in extracurricular activities is probably a good source of self-insight if one makes a conscious effort to learn about oneself from each experience. One can use the growing number of self-diagnostic books available to obtain a picture of at least one's interests, needs, and values (see bibliography). For self-assessment of *talent*, it may be desirable for the individual to go to assessment centers or vocational counseling centers, which emphasize testing the person across a wide range of intellectual and other activities. But such activities will not provide a completely accurate basis for self-assessment of ability to perform in actual job situations. Part-time work, summer work, volunteer work, co-op work-study programs, and any other vehicle for getting into real work situations are highly desirable supplements to any testing or counseling.

In addition to exposing oneself to situations which provide potential feedback, one has to train oneself to *assess* such feedback information. No matter how sincere and dedicated the guidance counselor or vocational psychologist might be, his or her information cannot be taken at face value, because the predictive power of tests, interviews, and other diagnostics is depressingly low for complex occupations such as "management." People must learn how to interpret their own experience directly and to develop judgment criteria which tell them how they are doing. The earlier they learn to do this, the better, because feedback is always difficult to obtain, especially in organizational settings.

Second, people must learn how to *communicate* more accurately to others their own self-assessment of their talents, needs, and values. Self-insight is not enough; it must be accompanied by the ability to communicate one's insights to others so that the potential employer can assess more accurately the probability of a mismatch. Oral and written communication skills are critical for negotiating the interpersonal processes involved in any life transitions, whether they involve career, family, or self-development. Therefore, the earlier in life that people learn to communicate accurately about themselves, their feelings, and perceptions, the better off they will be in managing life tasks.

Communication skills of the kind I am referring to here apply to all kinds of personalities. I am *not* advocating that everyone learn to be more "open," because clearly individuals differ in ability to be open, and in many life situations openness is as much a handicap as an advantage. What I am advocating is that people develop ways of getting across to others their perceptions of themselves, particularly in transition situations such as those involving career choice. For example, a shy person is better off communicating this self-insight to a recruiter than ending up perpetually anxious or frustrated in a job situation which requires a high degree of extroversion. The more information the individual can get across to the recruiter, the better the match is likely to be, even if the recruiter is unable to reciprocate with good information about the organization. There is little to be gained in the long run by falsely selling oneself. The trick is to learn to be accurate—neither grandiose nor unnecessarily diffident or modest.

Third, people must learn to make *accurate diagnoses of potential job situations* from partial and often distorted information. In this area, especially, they can be helped by educational institutions' providing concepts and simulated experiences or cases to sharpen diagnostic skills. Whether or not the school provides such experiences, the individual must learn from interviews and visits how to assess an organization's culture in terms of both the short- and long-run job opportunities. The individual must also assess how realistic the recruiter is in assessing the individual's needs. Even though the job opportunity sounds glowing, is it safe to enter an organization without a clear feeling of being "understood" by that organization?

Student groups have been quite successful in improving their diagnostic skills by forming informal ad hoc seminars or discussion sessions during the job-search process. Such seminars can deal with the problem of how to draw inferences from the recruiters' behavior and what kinds of questions to ask which might reveal an aspect of the organization's culture. For example, one group developed the idea of asking recruiters about their own careers in some detail as a way of learning how the organization deals with people, but there is still much creativity needed in this area (Levinson, 1972).

To summarize, in order to avoid the negative outcomes of having to either move to a new job or change aspirations or values in an undesirable way, the individual must develop maximum self-insight, skills in communicating those insights accurately, and skills in diagnosing organizational settings from interview and observational data. Basically, one must develop one's own procedures for ensuring that each of these areas is optimally managed. An important by-product is that these skills are necessary for the management of any life situation and therefore represent an important area for people to invest in at all stages of their lives, not only during the early career.

The Organizational/Managerial Perspective

From the point of view of the organization, the preentry stage is a failure if any of the following occurs: (1) a high-potential recruit fails to accept a job offer; (2) a high-potential recruit joins the organization but soon leaves because of disappointment or disillusionment; (3) a high-potential recruit joins the organization but loses motivation and becomes a marginal performer; or (4) a seemingly high-potential recruit joins the organization but turns out to have low talent, low motivation, or values incompatible with those of the organization.

How can the organization manage the recruitment/selection process to avoid any of these negative outcomes? In a way, the solutions for the organization parallel those described above for the individual. *First,* the organization must have *self-insight;* i.e., those managers who initiate and manage the search for new employees must first have a very clear idea of what jobs need to be filled, what the characteristics of those jobs are both short- and long-run, how those jobs might change over time, and how someone who is successful in a job moves from that job to another part of the organization. In other words, the recruiting/selection system ought to be shaped in a manner consistent with how the parent organization works. If it is, then in screening interviews there is a greater possibility of accurately describing to recruits what they will be doing in both the short- and long run.

For such information to be available, the organization must do both *strategic and human resource planning*, even though that planning may not result in clear-cut forecasts. It is better to communicate to a recruit that the best planning efforts still leave his or her future career with the company "uncertain" than to (1) come across as not knowing what the future might bring because no one has thought about it or (2) reveal that the managers who have thought about it have failed to communicate with those who are doing the recruiting. And it is certainly not reassuring to a reasonably intelligent recruit to hear glowing tales of challenge and opportunity which are on the face of it nothing more than a sales pitch. Many recruiters do not know how their own organizations work in terms of typical career moves, average length of time of a job, possible and impossible rotational assignments, long-range possibilities for managerial or technical growth, etc. Instead, they operate by "motherhood" statements, e.g., "Everyone with potential who performs will get ahead," or use their own stereotypes of what *they* believe happens as a basis for what they assert. The danger is that the high-potential recruit will cross-check the information, will ask a friend who works for that company, and in other ways will gather data which, if they conflict with what the recruiter said, make it more probable that he or she will seek employment elsewhere.

In the long run, it is probably a better strategy to say, "I don't know how our promotional system works in finance, but I'll try to find out," than to make up something or give vague generalities. The ultimate example of this "truth in recruiting" philosophy is probably the West Coast company that ran a full-page ad in a trade journal; at the bottom of an otherwise blank page was the message, "We don't know what to say in this ad but are looking for good people," and then gave the company's name and address. The firm reported receiving as many or more applicants as when it ran more detailed ads and was told by many applicants that they appreciated the candor of the advertisement.

In summary, a good principle for recruiting might be, "Know as much as possible about the job, the organization, and the career paths within it, and then tell the truth as much as possible; admit uncertainty and gray areas if they exist; don't oversell, because a short-run success in getting bodies in the door does not solve the company's long-range human resource problems."

But what if the career development system of the organization is genuinely in flux and little accurate information can be provided to a recruit? I see nothing wrong with saying that point blank: "If you come to work for this company, we cannot guarantee what the situation will be like in one or two years or in which area of the company there will be opportunities for growth," if that is in fact the truth. It is indeed dangerous to set up false expectations by promising people promotions or new jobs on some kind of timetable, but there is nothing wrong with quoting historical facts that some people have moved up two levels in five years, others are still at the same level, and some have moved laterally. Whatever the facts are, they can be of value to the recruit without setting up false expectations, provided the recruiter quotes them simply as facts and not as part of a sales pitch.

Second, the recruitment/selection system must be able to *diagnose long-range growth potential in a person* as well as short-run performance potential. If the organization has done its homework and knows at some level what kind of people it needs for what kinds of work, it should then be possible to design interview, testing, and assessment procedures that are congruent with those requirements and with the organizational value system. I cannot in this book elaborate on the technology of diagnosing individual potential, which is a whole field in its own right (Schneider, 1976), but I do wish to make some comments about the necessity of making such assessment congruent with organizational values. Earlier in this chapter it was asserted that the recruitment/selection process is one of the primary bases on which potential new members form their image of their future employer. If the organization is seeking certain kinds of people, it must make sure that its own recruiting process does not turn those kinds of people off. For example, if a technical organization is seeking creative engineers, it might well be tempted to give psychological tests measuring creativity, but should resist the temptation until it has gathered data on what the impact would be on a potential creative recruit to be asked to take such a test. It might be that the *most* creative person would refuse to take the test or would refuse to work for an organization that would rely on such tests.

Finally, organizations must make more of an effort to *integrate the recruitment/selection activities with those of job placement and early supervision*, because lack of congruence at that interface runs the risk of producing early disillusionment and turnover (Schein, 1964). This integration can be accomplished in a variety of ways.

Probably the most common technique used by organizations is to actively involve in the recruiting process those line managers who will supervise the new employee. If line managers are the actual recruiters or parts of the recruiting team, they can deal more authoritatively with questions that candidates may have about the nature of the work they will be doing and provide examples through their own physical presence of what work in the organization would be like. On the other hand, the line manager is often untrained in interviewing and assessing the candidate based on the interview. Working as a team with a trained recruiter is one way of overcoming this potential weakness.

If the number of people to be hired is too great to involve line management in recruiting, the next best method of integration is to have frequent contact between the recruiters and the line managers who will become the supervisors of the new hires. This contact can be provided by planning meetings, reviews of candidates, feedback meetings on how past hires have worked out, etc. But *someone*, either in personnel or in the line function, must be accountable for bringing the two groups together on a regular basis.

Just integrating the recruiting and selection function is not sufficient. Planning must be integrated as well. As I have argued throughout, equal attention must be given to planning for human resources, analyzing systematically what the jobs are like for which one is recruiting, and estimating how those jobs will change in the future. Furthermore, as human resources become more specialized and expensive, plans must be made for the continued career growth of all new recruits. Even though no specific commitments can be made and even though no clear paths can be defined, it is nevertheless necessary to consider options and lay the groundwork for future career moves, whether those involve promotion or simply new lateral assignments. It is suicidal to attempt to stockpile high-potential people without considering specifically what they will be doing and how they will be managed five, ten, and twenty years down the road.

To summarize, for organizations to avoid the negative outcomes of inability to hire desirable candidates, losing good people soon after hiring them, demotivating and underutilizing high-potential people, or mistakenly hiring someone of low potential, it is first of all necessary for management to have maximum insight into the organization's needs and how its own career system works. It is also necessary for those involved in recruiting to be able to communicate clearly and accurately what the organizational situation is, and it is necessary for them to diagnose accurately the potential of a given recruit to meet the set of short- and long-run organizational needs identified. Finally, I have argued that it is necessary for recruitment, selection, and place-ment to be integrated as much as possible and have proposed several ways of achieving such integration.

The Institutional Perspective

The transition from school to work is sufficiently difficult that it must be supported by various social institutions and/or by special occupa-tions devoted to career transitions such as guidance counseling, voca-tional aptitude testing, etc. I will not review in detail all the things that such institutions or occupations can and should do, but can highlight one aspect. Because it is so difficult to anticipate what work will really be like and get accurate information during the recruiting process it-self, it would be highly desirable to improve the process of exposing students to real work situations before they have to make final com-mitments. Educational institutions can reinforce work/study pro-grams, work with employers to develop summer apprenticeships or internships, bring members of the occupation onto the campus or into the high school to talk about life in that occupation, arrange for stu-dents to visit local factories, and in various other ways ensure greater familiarity early.

SUMMARY

This chapter has reviewed the major tasks of the entry stage, the prob-lems likely to be encountered in the recruitment/selection process, the negative outcomes which may result from mismanagement of this pro-cess, and what the individual, the employer, and educational institu-tions can do to minimize those negative outcomes.

The entry stage ends with the decision to accept employment. Once the individual has made this decision and reports for work, he or she enters the next stage—"socialization."

8
SOCIALIZATION AND LEARNING TO WORK

The most salient feature of entry into one's first major job is what Hughes (1958) aptly called "reality shock." It occurs in different forms in most major occupations because no matter how carefully the work world has been explained in school and no matter how much part-time or apprenticeship work one has had, the reality of one's first full commitment is shocking because for the first time one confronts the gap between one's expectations and dreams on the one hand and what it is really like to work and be in an organization on the other hand.

The major developmental tasks of this period all derive from various aspects of the gap between expectations and realities and can be illustrated best by various comments of a panel of Sloan School alumni who graduated in 1961, 1962, and 1963 when they were reinterviewed after 9–12 months at work (Schein, 1964, 1968). The focus is on the tasks of a group entering business and industry.

TASKS OF THE SOCIALIZATION STAGE

Task 1: Accepting the Reality of the Human Organization

"All the problems I encounter boil down to communication and human relations. . . . " (consumer goods company)

"I thought I could sell people with logic and was amazed at the hidden agendas people have, irrational objections; really bright people will come up with stupid excuses . . . they have their own little empires to worry about." (aerospace company)

"The number of unproductive people there are in corporations is simply astounding." (chemical company)

"You don't have complete control over your own work; you have to work with other people." (manufacturing company)

"People are a nuisance. . . " (aluminum mining and manufacturing company)

"Having to check with everyone all the time." (chemical company)

"Working with people whom you can't control." (computer manufacturing company)

"Dependence on other people, which makes things move too slowly; someone is always changing what you write." (investment broker)

For many new employees, particularly those who entered in staff or managerial roles (as opposed to hourly work), reality shock consisted of the discovery, among other things, that other people in the organization were a roadblock to what they wanted to get done. Others in the organization did not seem as smart as they should be, seemed illogical or irrational, or seemed lazy, unproductive, or unmotivated.

As I listened to the group members discuss their first year at work, I had the feeling that at an emotional level many of them did not want to have to learn to deal with other people; they simply wanted them to go away. I got the impression that those few graduates who accepted the human organization, with all its foibles, as a reality soon learned to apply their analytical abilities and high intelligence to getting their jobs done within it, but that those who resisted this reality at an emotional level used up their energy in denial and complaint rather than in problem solving. The "selling," and "compromising," and "politicking" necessary to get their ideas accepted were seen as "selling out" to some lower value system. The same person who would view a complex technical problem as a great challenge found the human problem illegitimate and unworthy of his efforts. The unlearning of this attitude may be one of the key processes in becoming an effective supervisor and manager. At the time I interviewed the alumni, most of them were still in a state of shock and had not begun to reexamine or unlearn this attitude, however.

Task 2:   Dealing with Resistance to Change

> "You can't get agreement on a diagnosis, and then you get resistance to change . . . you are told 'stick around for 30 years and if it is still a problem, we'll look into it.' " (public utility)

> "I have to become a true consultant, because it is so easy to get a project blocked subtly. . . " (manufacturing company)

> "The works manager called me in and gave me a Dutch Uncle talk on the limits of my contributions; they don't really want the New York office to know how bad they are in some areas." (manufacturing company)

> "The company has a program of planned frustration, keeping you one step behind all the time; as soon as you master one thing, you discover several other barriers. You don't know how high the mountain is, but you do know that you are nowhere near the top." (consumer goods company)

> "I ran into conflict with procedures . . . the informal methods of handling things, shaped by people far higher up . . . you can't buck that." (consumer goods company)

Closely related to the first area is the shock of discovering that good solutions to problems are not automatically accepted. Recalcitrant and illogical people, formal and informal procedures, organizational politics, and plain disorganization all conspire to keep the new employee from implementing his or her prepared solution to things. Almost every alumnus interviewed in the study in one way or another stated that he was shocked by the degree to which his "good ideas" were undermined, sidetracked, sabotaged, or just plain ignored.

A typical first job was an assignment to look into some procedure being used by the organization, analyze it, and make recommendations for improvement. The new hire would do the analysis, find some flaws based on his education and newly acquired skills, recommend changes, and then discover that his recommendations were not implemented for one reason or another. Most of the alumni felt well-prepared technically to analyze problems, but completely unprepared to deal with resistance to change or the necessity to "sell" ideas and solutions (Avery, 1960). The degree to which people learn how to cope with resistance to change may well determine their future career path —whether they end up in more technical staff work, managerial work, or out of the organization altogether.

Task 3: Learning How to Work: Coping with too Much or too Little Organization and too Much or too Little Job Definition.

"Things are much more disorganized at _____ than I expected." (consumer goods company)

"Things move more quickly than I expected; they don't lie still." (manufacturing company)

"Your job is what you make of it." (oil company)

"The projects are not integrated; hence I have little control over the people from whom I have to get work out. Hence I have to become political to get my work done." (civilian consultant to military group)

"They let me go, and I'm going, but I don't know where." (aerospace company)

"I got no guidance from my own boss; had to define my own job." (computer manufacturing company)

"I did a lot of sitting around without a specific assignment, essentially training myself." (aerospace company)

"The company is extremely capricious in its style of decision making. You go for months with no decision, then a sudden stream of unexplained decisions." (manufacturing company)

"What do you do if the job assigned to you is nonsense; how do you influence upward?" (consulting firm)

"I had the problem of never having a problem which was clearly definable, hence had a hard time getting feedback, hence needed some direction on which problems are useful, which ones can be helpful to the company." (public utility)

"Not knowing whom to ask or what to ask; not knowing what the ball park is . . . the problem of not knowing what it is you need to know." (consumer goods company)

"It's hard to get a fix on what you are doing from a long-range point of view." (chemical company)

"Shallow-type boss whom you could not respect." (electronics company)

"Adjusting to routine, keeping time, filling out forms." (chemical company)

The quotes above highlight the frustration of not knowing what to do and how to contribute. Many of the graduates recognized that learning to live with ambiguity was something important which they would need in their future assignments, but that made it no less shocking or frustrating to encounter initially. Similarly, many were happy to have as much freedom to define their own work as they were given, yet were shocked at the degree to which the organization seemed to be abdicating its responsibilities of defining the job.

This area is especially shocking to the new employee, because in school things are typically well organized, highly structured, and rational. Problems are clearly defined and either have a solution, or, in case discussions, everyone at least knows that there is no solution. The failure to be guided in the first job was often seen by the alumni as incompetence on the part of the boss or as evidence of disorganization and inefficiency, leading to disillusionment with the organization in general. In school the students had learned that organizations should be efficient and effective in the pursuit of profit. Once in an organization, however, the new hires learned that things moved more slowly and much less efficiently than they had imagined and not always in ways that were profit-oriented.

Some of the graduates found themselves having to not only define their own jobs, but also help their bosses define theirs; others felt such a tight rein on them that they did not feel free to make any mistakes. In either case, the new hires felt prevented from learning anything about their own capacities; in the former case they usually got no feedback, and in the latter case they got so much guidance that they were hardly acting on their own at all.

A number of graduates were satisfied with the amount of autonomy they enjoyed, but still had problems obtaining adequate feedback on their own performance. What fed the dissatisfaction in all these cases, of course, was the underlying expectation that they *should* learn something on their first jobs and that their supervisors *should* feel responsible for teaching them. It is not surprising that this expectation would be held by a group so recently out of school. The important ultimate learning for them may be how to obtain valid feedback in a situation in which it is not automatically forthcoming from others—i.e., *how to become a good judge of one's own performance*. In this sense all of the alumni expressed a degree of dependency on the organization which might be unrealistic; by ignoring this need in new employees, on the other hand, the organization may be missing an important opportunity to train them.

In summary, carving out one's own job is an essential aspect of the more general task of learning *how* to work—how to define problems, look for relevant information, overcome resistance to change, and be able to judge one's own performance validly.

Task 4: Dealing with the Boss and Deciphering the Reward System—Learning How to Get Ahead

"The thing that surprised me was the tight rein that was kept on you; you were not really allowed to make a mistake." (consumer goods company)

"You are evaluated silently without being given any feedback for the first six months, then suddenly terminated if you are unacceptable." (manufacturing company)

"Technical people around here are first-class citizens, and staff people like me are second-class citizens." (R&D lab)

"I was told you have to learn to behave yourself. 'If you don't think this is right, there is the open door.' " (manufacturing company)

"You get ahead by having the ability and working hard." (engineering company)

"Make your boss look good, sell as hard as possible, use any available levers, and be an effective communicator." (chemical company)

"It's whom you know that counts." (aerospace company)

"What's important is 'who knows you,' you have to have high visibility, get along well, be important to the boss, make yourself more attractive through performance." (R&D lab)

"It's whom the boss knows that matters." (aerospace company)

"It's a dilemma, should you make the boss look good and go up the ladder with him or work on your own visibility?" (oil company)

"Do a good job, impress people, and be there a long time." (consumer goods company)

"Fellows who get ahead are those who have a quality of critical thinking beyond hard work." (furniture manufacturing company)

"Nice appearance, glib tongue, outgoing personality. The general level of incompetence in the whole industry makes competence less relevant." (advertising agency)

As the comments above indicate, one of the major problems of this stage is deciphering the boss and the reward system. There is first the immediate problem of how to get along with the boss—he or she may be overcontrolling or undercontrolling, too absent or too present, too incompetent or too competent. No one in the first job was entirely satisfied with the boss, because the very fact of having a boss was inherently uncomfortable after the autonomy of student life. The new employee was likely to experience a conflict between needs for dependence and needs for independence. In the early part of the career new employees are still learners; hence a certain amount of dependence is desirable and appropriate. On the other hand, in order to succeed, new employees must display an ability to function on their own, to take initiative, to define problems accurately by themselves, and even to evaluate their own performance to some degree. So the ability to handle the conflict between dependence and independence is one of the major accomplishments of the early career.

Beyond learning how to relate to the boss is the problem of how to decipher the reward system—what is really expected of one, what is really rewarded, how much one can trust the official formal statements. As the quotes above indicate, different graduates saw very different kinds of things as important to getting ahead, covering almost the entire spectrum of possible alternatives from pure ability and performance to pure politics and "image control." One reason for the ambiguity is that managerial careers are themselves highly variable, and it is possible to succeed in organizations in different ways. Another reason is that new employees must evaluate the accuracy and relevance of much of the information offered by older employees or supervisors, because the situation may have changed.

The early part of the career is a kind of mutual testing and exploration period; it is not clear at this point what mix of talent, personality, motivation, and values will lead to high long-range performance. It is as if the organization is saying, "Let's take in some high-talent people and watch them for a while before we attempt to match up specific people with specific career paths." At the same time, the individual is facing from his or her perspective a similar question: "Let's see what this organization has to offer me in the way of options and types of work, before I decide where to put my commitment."

Given this mutual-exploration process, it is not surprising that criteria for advancement are very ambiguous at this early stage. Indeed, from the point of view of the organization, either too much or too little concern with how to get ahead could be viewed as inappropriate at this stage; the new employee should be learning how to perform well in the new culture, not be overconcerned about "promotion." On the other hand, complacency also raises concern because it might reflect lack of long-run motivation. As we will see later, the learning of complacency is one of the dangerous negative outcomes of this period.

Task 5: *Locating One's Place in the Organization and Developing an Identity*

"What is your appropriate reference group? To whom do you owe allegiance or loyalty? What is the relevant domain or empire?" (manufacturing company)

"I had a real problem of status, with reference to which group around here do I judge myself?" (public utility)

"I'm the man without a home, changing departments every three months because of this training program; first I identified with the trainee group, then had split loyalties between them and departments." (consumer goods company)

"When you are a consultant (he is an *internal* consultant), where does your identity lie? People in the research department don't understand, the boss often doesn't understand, you have to stand outside and look at the company as a whole, identify with operations research as such." (manufacturing company)

"I wasn't committed to the data-processing department when I started working there, but was reminded by my boss that I should be; now I feel more committed to it." (manufacturing company)

"I work in an economic-analysis group. We find ourselves trying to sell the total company perspective to various groups. My total company identification is carrying over into my social life as well." (oil company)

"There is no question of my identity or loyalty what with owning a chunk of the company." (This man entered the family business.)

"I have become a cynic. Every man is a liar and a fraud among businessmen in my industry; they either don't know what they are doing or are cheaters." (furniture manufacturing company)

Entering a new organization involves a process of gaining acceptance from both the hierarchy (the boss) and the peer group. For those new employees who have a clear assignment in a well-defined group, the only problem is how to match their own needs and talents with the requirements of the group. However, for many new employees there is a prior problem—locating an appropriate peer group and deciding with which of several groups to align oneself. This problem arises because of the common practice of bringing management trainees into the organization through rotational types of training programs or in vaguely defined administrative, staff, or consultant roles which permit them to roam freely in the organization and to define their own jobs to a considerable degree. They may be given the task of examining procedures in a given department and then selecting on their own some area where they see a problem. Or they may be hired into a staff group that does analytical studies for various line groups, confronting the new members with the potential conflict of loyalty to either the staff department or the line group for which the project is being done. Some of the graduates went into administrative groups in R&D organizations and found themselves in conflict between helping the technical person get his or her job done even if administrative procedures had to be subverted, or, conversely, upholding the administrative procedures even if that meant slowing down technical progress on a project. If a new employee was identified as on a "fast track," he or she had the dilemma of whether or not to identify with the department in which the current rotational assignment was located. Some alumni expressed this as a problem of status—placing themselves in the pecking order could not be done without deciding which reference group to use, partly because it was not clear which group had how much status. An important part of the learning process during this stage, then, is to decipher the status system and to build one's own membership and sense of identity accordingly.

Summary

The various tasks described above interrelate and can be seen as an effort on the part of the new member to form what has been called by sociologists of work "a perspective" toward the organization and one's role in it. The major problem in developing this perspective, as Van Maanen (1975) has pointed out, is to locate oneself in time and space—to get a sense of one's own progress, likely future, and relationship to the hierarchy and to the peer group. The perspective one forms is what gives meaning to one's work and one's career; it is the subjective inner learning which accompanies one's external work life and which influences one's future behavior in the organization. For this reason, the particular perspective one learns during the socialization stage has important consequences for the future career.

PROBLEMS IN THE SOCIALIZATION STAGE

Just as there are problems in the recruitment/selection process, there are similar kinds of problems in the early induction and socialization process, and these problems need to be identified and assessed so that the perspective arising from this process optimally meets individual and organization needs.

There is likely to be a mismatching or mutual misperception of the needs of the new employee and the needs of the organization (Schein, 1964). The recruitment/selection process, as I indicated, encourages each side to *sell* itself. In that process the new employee is likely to emphasize traditional job values, such as "a challenging job," "opportunities for advancement," "money," "opportunities to use special aptitudes and skills acquired during the educational process," "responsibility—a job in which one's contribution makes a difference," and "opportunities to be creative and original." All of these are valid job values, in the long run. But they gloss over some important immediate needs that the new employee has and which are more difficult to admit to oneself and to others. The deeper-level need of the new employee is to obtain answers to the following set of questions which may or may not be conscious, but which need to be answered in the early stages of the career.

Underlying Questions for the Individual

1. Will the job give me an opportunity to *test myself*? Can I really do the job? Can I stand the pressure of working on real things which matter? How will I deal with my own anxieties and tensions generated by the job? Will I be any good at it? Will I like it?

2. *Will I be considered worthwhile*? Will I be given an opportunity to show what I can do? Will I be able to make a contribution? Will I be liked? Will my contribution be appreciated?

3. Will I be able to *maintain my individuality and integrity*? Will I have to compromise any of my values or ethical standards? Will I have to conform to undesirable organizational norms?

4. Will I be able to lead a *balanced life*? Will I have time for family and personal interests? Will my career make demands on me beyond my ability to meet them?

5. Will I *learn and grow*?

6. Will my membership in this organization meet my own ideals and *enhance my image of myself*? Will I be proud to be associated with this occupation and/or organization?

For its part, the organization also has a set of deeper questions which must be answered in the early stages of the career before a final investment is made in the new employee or "tenure" granted.

Underlying Questions for the Organization

1. Will the new person *fit into our organization*? Will the person's style of working, attitudes, values, and personality mesh with our culture? Is he or she "our type" of person? Will the person be able to conform to the pivotal organizational values without overconforming and becoming complacent?

2. Will the new person be able to learn the ropes and *make a contribution*? Will the new person be able to innovate to improve our organization?

3. Will the new person *learn and grow*? Will the new person become a leader, an independent contributor, able to take on high levels of responsibility?

Resolution of Socialization Problems

Both sets of needs are legitimate, but the actual process of entering an organization, being given a first job assignment, and going to work for a given boss rarely creates a setting within which either set of needs can be openly addressed. There is a danger that neither set of needs is perceived by the main actors—the new employee, the boss, and the immediate peer group. New employees may not even recognize that they have such needs for self-testing and self-evaluation, and the organization may be too busy socializing and "initiating" the new member to pay much attention to these deeper needs.

There is also growing evidence from studies of the early career that the first boss is critical to how this period is negotiated. This person can unwittingly make it very difficult for the new employee to have an adequate self-test, by assigning work that is either too difficult—leading to premature failure—or too easy and meaningless—leading to discouragement and boredom (Schein, 1964; Berlew and Hall, 1966; Bray *et al.*, 1974). This phenomenon occurs most often because the boss feels threatened by the new employee, who often comes in with a better education or a better starting salary than the boss, leading the boss, sometimes unconsciously, to attempt to prove that the employee is not so great. Giving too difficult a task quickly proves the new employee's incompetence; giving too easy a job or meaningless work is typically rationalized as necessary because the new employee could not be trusted with important work until he or she has learned how the company "really" operates. This assumption may be valid initially, but a great trap is the concomitant false assumption that such learning will take many months or years, when in fact it might only take a period of weeks.

The organization often stereotypes the new employee as over-ambitious, unrealistic regarding advancement, too theoretical, idealistic, naive, immature, inexperienced, and unwilling to learn how to sell ideas and work within the human organization. Much of this stereotype is built up in the recruiting interviews, where mutual selling dominates, and much of it may in fact be correct, but it masks the other important needs which the new employee has and which were mentioned above. The danger in the early socialization process is that the first boss and others with whom the new employee comes into contact will feel the need to "straighten him or her out," "show him or her what life is really like," "put him or her through an initiation rite," etc., which often comes across to the new employee as a way of being put down.

Many of the Sloan School graduates interviewed commented on what it felt like to be a new employee:

"You have to remain quiet, have to listen, don't make comments." (manufacturing company)

"You feel held down, can't make the changes you want to make." (government agency)

"Certain bosses, because of their personality, don't respect youth." (manufacturing company)

"They accept us but give us only lip service." (aerospace company)

"I'm seen as an outsider, an academic, the golden gifted boy." (manufacturing company)

"You are seen as academic, idealistic, not practical or experienced." (computer manufacturing company)

"The new man is seen as a dreamer who doesn't know the realities." (electronics company)

"Quantification and an analytical approach is threatening to the senior man because it displaces his sense of experience." (manufacturing company)

"You must be ready to take on whatever comes, yet you're supposed to be a self-starter." (manufacturing company)

"I blew my stack once when an older man started on the 'smart young kid' stuff; I came back with "stubborn old man.' " (public utility)

One of the commonest techniques used by bosses to "initiate" the new employee was what was labeled by the new employee an "upending experience." Though some upending experiences were accidental, in many instances they were a conscious strategy on the part of the boss. The essence of this strategy is to involve the new employee in a task which drastically violates his or her expectations about self or the organization in order to teach certain "realities" quickly and dramatically. The best example came from an engineering manager who gave every new college graduate who entered his group the task of analyzing a special circuit which violated some textbook assumptions and therefore looked as though it could not work, yet which had been sold for years. When the new employee would announce that the circuit could not work, he was told that it did and was asked to figure out why. He typically could not explain it, which left him thoroughly depressed and chastened about the value of his college education. The manager felt that only at this point was the new employee "ready" to learn something and to tackle some of the "real" problems on which the company was working. If the new employee's self-esteem can survive upending experiences, it is probably an effective way of introducing him or her quickly into the organization, but for many it could lead to discouragement and demotivation or so much disillusionment that they would seek a job elsewhere.

NEGATIVE OUTCOMES AND WHAT TO DO ABOUT THEM

In assessing negative outcomes we must again distinguish between outcomes for the individual and outcomes for the organization and, by implication, for the society as a whole.

The Organizational Perspective

In the discussion of the recruitment/selection process, I emphasized the individual perspective first because it is the individual who has the initiative in choosing a job. However, once the person has decided on a job and reports for work, the initiative shifts to the organization and the boss. The organization has now made an investment to be protected and developed. The major negative outcomes for the organization, then, are that the person: (1) quits before he or she has made a contribution (given the organization a return on its investment);

(2) becomes complacent and demotivated so that the organization never obtains a contribution in line with the person's potential; and/or (3) does not quit when he or she should and becomes "dead wood" at an early age. Turnover is a relatively visible cost, easy to measure. The learning of complacency and failing to quit are potentially more dangerous because they may be invisible, and their true consequences may not surface until the employee is well embeddded in the organization. Some examples from the panel study highlight how complacency can creep in even during the first year:

> "I can't convince them when I think I am right, and I don't know how people will react if I am wrong, because I get no feedback, so I am easing off. I have learned not to try so hard." (manufacturing company)

> "I have learned to adopt a mild-mannered approach to change, because I might be wrong. I don't really have any evidence that I'll get punished; I'm just playing it safe." (public utility)

> "Hedging is cultivated in this company, and people try to do it with style." (R&D company)

> "I don't know how much frustration is supposed to be normal around here; how do you decide when it has reached a point where you should either give up or make a move?" (automotive manufacturing company)

> "My real frustration is that the outcome is the same; anticompany behavior gets just as far as procompany behavior." (advertising agency)

> "They are crazy over flip-charts here; they had to be done just so, dry run five times. Thinking gets to be so unrefined with all the focus on the presentation." (automotive manufacturing company)

> "It takes two years to find out where the back door is in a company. Personally, I'm giving myself another year. . . . I see my frustrations as challenges right now." (manufacturing company)

The solution to this set of potential problems is to: (1) *give the new hire some challenging work as soon as possible,* and (2) *ensure that the new employee gets feedback on whatever he or she does.* This strategy does not necessarily mean full-time, high-challenge, high-risk work. But some *mix* of training and "real" working seems essential, and valid feedback is crucial if the new employee is to learn anything.

The organization must discover lack of competence, if it exists, *early* in the career. One of the real dangers of periods of prolonged training and "safe" assignments is that the organization never tests the new employee, so that neither the employee nor the organization obtains accurate information on the person's capabilities. In other words, it is in the best interests of *both* the organization and the new employee to become involved in some amount of challenging real work as soon as possible, so that if a real mismatch exists between what the organization needs and what the individual can provide in the way of talent, it can be identified early enough before either has invested too much in the mismatched relationship. An early termination is, in the long run, less expensive than "dead wood" from the point of view of the organization. Similarly, from the point of view of the individual's self-esteem, the pain of going through several jobs early in the career is less than that of either remaining in an organization in which one is not valued and to which one cannot make a contribution or being laid off in mid- or late career.

Another possible negative outcome for the organization is that the new employee learns norms and values which are out of line with those that will be needed later in the career. It is not uncommon for organizations to have different values at different hierarchical levels. For example, top management may value creativity and initiative in higher levels of the organization, but its own managerial practices may have created a climate for middle management and below which teaches conformity and complacency. The employee's first supervisor and first peer group are the representatives of the organizational culture and will shape the employee's view of the total organization and how to get along within it. In order to avoid the possibility that the wrong things will be learned, it is essential that higher levels of management diagnose and assess the culture which is operating at the bottom of the organization and explicitly monitor the early induction and socialization process. For example, in one company that relies heavily on engineering there has been a conscious tradition to have every design engineer follow his or her project through into production and the marketplace. As the company has grown and as the products have become more complex and dependent on many engineering groups, the engineer has had to become more of a specialist, working on similar aspects of many different products. But a new engineer coming into the organization might be socialized very differently, depending on whether he or she was assigned to a project run by (1) an "old-line" engineer who still believes in seeing each product through to the marketplace and who encouraged the new engineer to become broad in outlook, or (2) a "new" supervisor who believes that the way to succeed in engineering is to become highly competent as a specialist in some specific aspect of product design. Both kinds of socialization are simultaneously going on in this company, probably without higher management's clear awareness that this is happening.

The implication is that the first supervisors of new employees must be chosen carefully in terms of several criteria. (1) Will they feel secure enough so that the destructive behavior of giving too hard or too easy work is minimized; i.e., can they deal realistically with the new employee without their own feelings and needs distorting the relationship? (2) Will they be innovative enough to find the right mix of learning tasks and meaningful, challenging tasks to permit the new employee to experience realistic self-tests? (3) Will they be able to make a valid assessment of how the new employee is doing and give valid feedback on performance? (4) Will they transmit the right kinds of values and norms to the new employees in terms of the long-run contribution that is expected of them?

Many organizations are recognizing that supervisors of new employees have a very special and important role to fulfill in inducting and socializing the new employee and therefore should be trained for their jobs. Seminars involving group discussion among supervisors, workshops involving opening up communications between new employees and their bosses, lectures on the problems of being a new employee or the boss of a new employee—all have been utilized in the effort to minimize the negative consequences in this crucial encounter stage (Schein, 1964; Kotter, 1972, 1973).

The Individual Perspective

The worst outcome from the point of view of the individual is that the needs for a self-test are still not met after some period of time in a job. Work that is too difficult or too easy, meaningless, or purely "practice" or exercise (what trainees call "mickey-mouse") leads to this negative outcome. One reason why many companies have abandoned lengthy, full-time training programs in favor of early assignments to challenging jobs is that so many high-potential employees were demotivated and quit if they were kept for too long in a training program. If the company does not have the insight to deal with this problem, what can the individual do to help himself or herself?

Probably the most important thing one can do is to learn that one must be *both* dependent and independent, *both* a learner and a self-starter. The early part of the career revolves around the *balance* between: (1) learning and responding to the demands of others, and (2) identifying and acting on opportunities to take the initiative and develop challenging activities of one's own (Dalton, Thompson, and Price, 1977). One must avoid the trap of trying to get along at either extreme—waiting for things to be done for one or trying to do every-thing for oneself. The key is to find the right balance and to pace one-self optimally to overcome feelings of being dependent, to achieve the feeling of being relatively more independent.

The more insight one has into the dynamics of entering a new organization, the less likely one is to become a victim of some of the traps outlined above. New employees should talk to one another, their bosses, and others in the organization to get perspective on what is happening to them, not simply draw their own conclusions silently. If they do not check out what they are perceiving and learning, they can-not correct for biases which may emanate from a particular boss or a particular group or may result from fortuitous events. As one insight-ful panelist put it, "I am pretty frustrated right now, but am not sure that my experience up to now is representative. I figure I'll give it one more year before drawing final conclusions about this company and deciding whether to move or not."

The Institutional Perspective

The process of socialization and learning to work occurs pretty much within the boundaries of an organization or occupation and is rela-tively little influenced by outside forces. However, from the point of view of society and its educational system, it is highly desirable that human resources be used optimally. The more that educational and re-search institutions can study the process of organizational socializa-tion and the more they can educate both new employees and those already in positions of power to understand the dynamics of the early career, the better the chances of reducing costly mismatches. The prime effort probably must come from the educational institutions to teach their graduates how to manage the early part of the career by recognizing clearly what their own needs are and how best to protect themselves from socializing experiences which may be destructive. One example of efforts in this direction is the growing number of courses in business schools directed toward career counseling, orga-nizational diagnosis, self-analysis of career aspirations, etc. If new hires have a clear insight into the process of socialization, they will be in a better position to negotiate realistically with their employing orga-nizations as the career unfolds.

SUMMARY

This chapter has reviewed in some detail what events transpire in the socialization stage and has attempted to illustrate with quotes and examples some of the problems and negative outcomes which can occur in this stage. From the organization's point of view, it is important to avoid the negative outcomes of: (1) turnover of high-potential new hires; (2) demotivation and the learning of complacency; (3) failure to discover incompetence early in the career; and (4) the learning of values and attitudes which are out of line with what will be needed later in the career. The best remedy is to carefully select and train first bosses to provide optimal learning experiences, challenging work, and good feedback. For the individual the major negative outcome is not to have a chance to test oneself and determine what one can do. One must seek out opportunities for self-tests if they are not provided by the organization.

If the new employee weathers the reality shock and begins to learn how to work, deal with people, manage resistance to change, deal with the boss and the peer group, and get a sense of identity in the organization, he or she is becoming a full-fledged member. As the organization learns more about the employee and sees whether, where, and how she or he can contribute, it gradually grants full membership. Though the process is psychologically gradual, this mutual acceptance is organizationally symbolized by specific events, such as a promotion, raise, new assignment, or formal performance appraisal. These events signify that a psychological contract has been negotiated. The next chapter looks at this process in greater detail.

9
MUTUAL ACCEPTANCE: DEFINING THE PSYCHOLOGICAL CONTRACT

Mutual acceptance is a major transition during which the relationship between the new employee and the employing organization becomes more clearly defined. Through various kinds of symbolic and actual events, a "psychological contract" is formed which defines what the employee will give in the way of effort and contribution in exchange for challenging or rewarding work, acceptable working conditions, organizational rewards in the form of pay and benefits, and an organizational future in the form of a promise of promotion or other forms of career advancement. This contract is "psychological" in that the actual terms remain implicit; they are not written down anywhere. But the mutual expectations formed between the employee and the employer function like a contract in that if either party fails to meet the expectations, serious consequences will follow—demotivation, turnover, lack of advancement, or termination (Schein, 1970).

In terms of the organizational model presented in Chapter 4, this transition is the crossing of a major "inclusion" boundary, a movement toward the inner core of the organization and symbolizing a higher degree of acceptance of the employee by the organization. It is important to distinguish this transition from the career movement embodied in promotion, which indicates the crossing of a hierarchical boundary, or a functional (rotational) move, which indicates the crossing of a functional boundary, though such moves can occur simultaneously. But one can, as we will see when we look at how this transition is symbolized, move toward the core of the organization without being promoted or making a lateral move. At the same time, the employee must "accept" the organization by accepting the higher degree of responsibility or trust conferred on him or her in this transition process.

How soon this transition occurs varies by type of job, the new employee's performance, and a host of fortuitous circumstances, but it typically occurs during the first few years of employment. It is preceded by a period in which both the individual and the organization have had a chance to test each other, to find out whether there is enough of a match to warrant a continuation of the relationship. The new employee decides that she or he can perform, that the work is challenging and satisfying enough, and that the culture is compatible enough with his or her own personality and value system to continue to invest in the organization; the organization decides that the new employee has enough talent to make a contribution and the right kind of personality and values to fit in. The process of mutual acceptance, then, communicates and ratifies these two sets of perceptions and feelings.

EVENTS SYMBOLIZING ORGANIZATIONAL ACCEPTANCE

The process of mutual acceptance is highly variable, depending on the nature of the work, the kind of department, the style of the boss, and the culture of the company. To understand it one must look at a variety of examples which illustrate how different new employees experience the transition and what kinds of events symbolize the organization's acceptance of the person.

Most of the initiative for mutual acceptance lies with the organization. The new employee may feel good about his or her new job and *hope* that it continues, but does not have the license or power to "accept himself or herself into the organization." Instead, one must wait for some evidence that one's own feelings about oneself are shared by the boss or others in the organization. This period of waiting can be quite painful because one may not be able to relax until one has been reassured that one is acceptable, and such reassurances are often followed by more severe "tests." As we have seen above, getting feedback in an ongoing situation is difficult. So even if one feels one is doing a good job, one knows that in someone else's eyes one may be "messing up." How, then, does one learn that one has been accepted?

Positive Performance Appraisal

One of the commonest events indicating organizational acceptance is positive feedback in the first formal or informal performance appraisal. At this time the boss has an opportunity to communicate how the new employee has performed so far and what he or she can look forward to. However, the process is by no means automatic, because many performance appraisals are perfunctory and leave the new employee as confused as ever about his or her status. The boss may say, "You're coming along fine," in a tone of voice which makes it very clear that the employee is still very much on trial. One of the most important areas of training for supervisors of new employees is how to use the performance-appraisal situation constructively to give valid information. This involves learning how to share feelings of uncertainty if they are there, how to give *accurate* feedback whatever it may be.

One of the commonest traps in this process is the assumption that the boss must come out with black-and-white statements about performance. Instead, bosses might well train themselves to say that they are "not sure," that in one area of work the employee is doing a good job but that in another area improvements are needed or not enough evidence is available. Performance-appraisal forms can be designed to facilitate more accurate communication by asking the boss to list critical incidents or to think of actual behavior on the part of the subordinate which formed the basis of the judgment.

Supervisors of new employees often do not realize how critical these first performance appraisals are in shaping the attitudes of the new employee and, therefore, how important it is to be accurate in one's observations and feedback. The new employee will be looking for signs of acceptance or rejection. The boss must therefore be careful to communicate accurately what his or her feelings actually are in this regard.

Salary Increase

Another symbolic event which can signify acceptance by the organization is a nonperfunctory raise. I say "nonperfunctory" because new employees know very well that the information of how they are doing is carried more by the *size* of the increase than by its presence or absence. Once they get a raise, they have to decipher its meaning— whether it is routine and therefore means only that they have put in their time, or whether it is enough higher than routine to indicate that the organization has accepted them and is looking forward to a future relationship. Often the deciphering is aided by the fact that the communication of the raise is combined with performance appraisal or at least a brief conversation with the boss in which the reasons for the size of the raise are discussed. But unless the boss is motivated and able to give accurate information during this encounter, it does not necessarily illuminate matters for the new employee. Here again some training of supervisors on how to give feedback with raises would be very beneficial. The most damaging feedback is the vague hedging which gives no information or permits the receiver to read in wrong information.

New Job Assignment

In many work situations the most important event symbolizing acceptance into the organization is to be shifted from one's initial assignment (which is often defined as "provisional" or "training") to a second assignment which is more permanent and/or more challenging and/or more obviously important to the total performance of the organization (i.e., one which carries more "responsibility"). As a recent analysis of the "socialization of engineers" has shown (Jacobson, 1977), even if the first assignment is challenging and involves responsible work, the new engineer still feels on trial and does not really feel like a member of the organization until he or she has been given a *second* assignment, one that is more responsible than the first. The *change* in status is the important message, not the absolute status level of the first or second job. The new employee knows that the first assignment is given on limited information based on interviews and past record. The second assignment, however, is based on *observed* performance and therefore is a measure of how the person has actually been doing.

It should also be noted that the work the person is given is a more reliable measure of his or her worth than judgments delivered in performance-appraisal situations, because the new employee correctly assumes that the organization will not assign work which is important unless it perceives the employee as capable of doing it. In this connection, a dilemma can arise if the organization evaluates a new employee as being very capable and as having high potential, but there simply is not enough challenging, important work to do. Such a situation has often arisen during periods of rapid economic or technological change when, for example, a company hires good engineers for future growth in spite of having no immediate work for them. In that situation the performance-appraisal process bears a special burden. The high-potential person must be convinced of his or her worth even though no challenging, important work is forthcoming.

Many of the alumni in my panel study talked about the pros and cons of rotational training programs in relation to the issue of feeling accepted. In many such programs, the new trainee is rotated through several departments for a period of six to twelve months, whereupon a more permanent job assignment is made to one of those departments based on both the preference of the person and the opinions of the department supervisors. These first regular assignments did *not,* however, function as symbolic acceptance events, because the alumnus knew that he had not yet been really tested; the training situations were too often "make work" or "watching others work." Though the training was seen as useful, it still left the new employee after six to twelve months with a feeling of being untested and untried, which for many was extremely frustrating. It was only after additional months in a department doing "meaningful" work that they began to get data about their own abilities and acceptability.

If an organization wants to speed up the process of integrating its new employees, it must find ways of giving them responsible, meaningful work as soon as possible, maybe even at the same time as they are undergoing a training program, so that the intrinsic feedback which comes from actual performance and the granting of new assignments can provide the message of acceptance on the part of the employer.

Sharing of Organizational "Secrets"

One of the commonest and most meaningful ways of accepting a new employee is to give him or her privileged information which is obviously shared only with someone who can be trusted not to take advantage of it. As new employees prove their ability to perform and their acceptance of pivotal organizational values, it is likely that their bosses and peers will begin to share with them some of the more invisible and private aspects of what goes on in the organization. The employee will then be allowed to look "backstage" and to learn some of the "realities"—what "really" goes on and how people in the organization "really" perceive and feel about things.

Organizational secrets fall into several categories. One has to do with specific *work-related information*, such as specific technologies, marketing techniques, or production methods, which must not be revealed to competitors. When they first enter the organization, employees are often asked to sign agreements not to reveal such information, but they do not learn anything which would in fact be damaging until they have worked for some time and have earned the right to work on sensitive projects which may involve "secret" methods. In this area there are, of course, layers of secrets, and some categories of information, such as secret ingredients of a specific product, may be shared only with a very small inner circle of people who have been in the organization for a long time.

A second category of "secrets" is a more frank discussion of *what others really think of the new employee*, how he or she compares to others, and what the future prospects really are. Information may be communicated about specific timetables when promotions or further moves may be expected, the fact that "others are watching his or her progress and have various kinds of expectations about career development and future areas of contribution."

A third category of "secrets" concerns *"how things really work"* and *"how one really gets things done."* The new employee is told about political situations, informal procedures which have to be followed to get work done, key people to "watch out for" or "to get on the good side of," and how to deal with the boss or other power figures. This information is different from "learning the ropes" in that it involves appraisals of the working situation which may be uncomplimentary or embarrassing to the organization or may reveal information which could give a competitor organization an advantage if revealed. How things *really* work, therefore, is information reserved for those who have proved themselves worthy of being entrusted with potentially sensitive information, and it is precisely the knowledge on the part of the new employee that he or she is being given such "secrets" that indicates acceptance into the organization.

A fourth and perhaps most significant category of "secrets" is a more frank accounting of *"what really happened" around key historical events* that the employee may have been aware of but may never have fully understood. Why a certain product or program was "really" discontinued, what "really" happened to the person who retired unexpectedly, why someone did or did not get an expected promotion, why certain decisions were made in the way they were made, and so on, are "secrets" of this type. In discovering these histories the new employee may also learn a great deal about the more personal aspects of key people in the organization, their strengths and weaknesses, personal troubles, what kinds of help or support they need, and so on.

This category of information "rationalizes" the organization once again for the employee. I pointed out in Chapter 8 that one of the most difficult aspects of socialization is the acceptance of the fact that decisions are not made "rationally" in terms of the principles found in textbooks or organization theories. One of the reasons this process is frustrating is that the "real" reasons, which have to do with the more personal aspects of how the organization actually functions, *cannot be revealed to the new employee because he or she cannot be trusted with the information.* Paradoxically, the new employee must prove his or her trustworthiness in part by *taking it on faith* that there are in fact good reasons why things are done the way they are, even though they may seem irrational at first. Only later will those actual reasons be revealed. This process of having to take things on faith until one has passed further inclusion boundaries continues on up and into the organization in that there are always other layers of "secrets" which have to do with how things work as one moves higher up and more toward the core of the organization.

The sharing of secrets has an especially powerful effect in symbolizing acceptance, because it is something which once granted cannot be taken away. The organization is making itself genuinely vulnerable and is, through this process, emotionally involving or coopting the employee in an irreversible way in that the employee knows that he or she is now in a position of being able to hurt the organization by revealing those secrets.

Initiation Rites

In many organizations the acceptance of the new employee as a full-fledged member is symbolized by a ritual event—a party, hazing, or granting of some special privilege or symbol, e.g., uniform, club membership, credit card, or private office. Such events usually accompany performance appraisal, a new assignment, or a raise, but they also serve to cement the relationship among the new employee, the boss, and the peer group through some emotionally involving event or the giving of some scarce resource associated with membership —secrets, stock options, etc.

Initiation rites are very important and meaningful precisely because they involve some overt investment on the part of the organization and change the emotional relationship between the new employee and the other members of the organization. The new employee now knows that he or she has crossed an important organizational boundary, has moved "into" the organization to some degree even though his or her work, salary, or formal status may remain the same.

Promotion

Being promoted is the most obvious, tangible reward the new employee can obtain as proof of his or her acceptability. Unfortunately, too many employers as well as employees assume that promotion is the *only* tangible sign of acceptance. If the employer puts too much emphasis on promotion, the new employee may stay in limbo for much longer than is necessary. Performance appraisal, salary increases, new assignments, sharing of secrets, and initiation rites can all function to effectively integrate the new employee. Indeed, it is a dysfunctional aspect of many organizational norms to conceive of "career growth" or "progress" or "success" *only* in hierarchical terms. In fact, it is possible for people to grow and make progress *laterally* across different functions through progressively more challenging work assignments in different areas without change in rank; it is also possible for people to grow and make progress by becoming more effective within a given job, and it is possible for people to grow and make progress by becoming more "central" in the organization even though their formal job titles or job descriptions do not change.

HOW THE EMPLOYEE ACCEPTS THE ORGANIZATION

The employee's acceptance of the organization is more invisible but no less important than the organization's acceptance of the employee if a viable, long-range psychological contract is to result. Employee acceptance is manifested in a variety of ways.

1. *The decision to remain* in the organization is, though often implicit, a signal that the employee accepts the organization and its employment terms. Especially in a fairly open labor market and in a society increasingly approving of a whole variety of life-styles, including not working at all, organizations must recognize that if they are able to retain good people, such retention may imply real acceptance on the part of the employee of the work situation. Unfortunately, this decision is often not discussed, and the employee who decides to leave finds it necessary to be fairly secretive about it until it is too late to renegotiate the psychological contract. It might be prudent for both the employee and the organization to discuss more explicitly, as part of the performance-appraisal discussion, how the employee is feeling about remaining in the organization.

2. *A high level of motivation and commitment,* as displayed by high energy, long working hours, willingness to do extras, and overt enthusiasm for the work, is a second and more visible sign that the employee has accepted the work situation and the organization. However, organizations often err in viewing this kind of visible commitment as the *only* measure of employee acceptance, failing to pay attention to other signs of acceptance. As was indicated in previous chapters, people differ greatly in the degree to which they are "work-involved," and it is possible for someone with low work involvement to be doing good work and to accept his or her work situation. It is a mistake for organizations to use the highly work-involved individual as the standard

against which to judge everyone else and to assume that someone who displays less commitment is therefore *un*motivated or unaccepting of the organization.

3. *Willingness to accept various kinds of constraints, delays, or undesirable work* as a "temporary" condition is a third type of signal of employee acceptance. For example, the organization may promise challenging work, salary increases, or promotions at some time in the future, but ask the employee to accept the duller work, lower pay, or lower rank for the present. An employee who feels accepted and accepts the organization may be willing to put up with these constraints and delays for a period of time. However, the boss must be very aware that such acceptance may be provisional and that if the promised rewards are not forthcoming, the psychological contract has been violated and may lead to the employee's loss of commitment, anger, and possible decision to leave.

It is in this area that there is a danger for both the individual and the organization to be tempted to "play games" by miscommunicating, making false promises, or attempting to substitute psychic rewards for economic ones. The organization, for its part, may in effect say to the employee, "We know that we are asking you to do a boring or meaningless job for low pay, but we will let you know what is really going on and share some secrets as compensation." If the employee remains under these conditions, the illusion may exist that the psychic reward of being given secrets is adequate compensation. What is often going on in reality is that the employee is feeling increasingly angry, but at the same time is for various reasons trapped in the situation. It is under these conditions—a psychological contract which the employee regards as basically unfair—that the seeds for unionization, sabotage, absenteeism, and other undesirable consequences are sown. In other words, just the willingness to accept constraints or delays does not automatically signal acceptance on the part of the employee, though under some conditions they are regarded as fair.

THE PSYCHOLOGICAL CONTRACT

The working out of the psychological contract is an ongoing process of negotiation and renegotiation between the employee and the employer, but much of the process remains implicit and rests on assumptions about the future, the degree of credibility of what is overtly said, and the actual events which transpire as the career unfolds. The process of mutual acceptance is one important milestone in the unfolding career. It is a time when the psychological contract is first ratified. But the dynamics of this process are such that neither the employee nor the employer can trust entirely the information which is exchanged, thus leaving the situation psychologically ambiguous. For example, even though the employee is allowed to share organizational secrets or is given an important and challenging assignment, she or he may still have doubts about the organization's acceptance and whether the organization's definition of the work can be trusted or is instead an attempt to sell itself to elicit higher levels of motivation. On the other side, highly valued employees can assure their employers that they are committed, yet be plotting to get a better job elsewhere at the same time. Many of the alumni in the panel study indicated that they had decided to leave an organization long before they felt free to tell anyone about it in the organization. They felt strong disappointment that they were not getting what they expected in terms of work or rewards, yet felt that they could not "level" with their boss in the process of negotiating what they would have regarded as a fairer psychological contract. Unfortunately, in many of the cases which led to turnover, both the organization and the employee ended up the loser.

Though it is implicit, the psychological contract is real in the sense that both the employee and boss (and work group) have strong expectations of each other after some period of "learning" or "socialization" has passed. Both parties are therefore vulnerable to disconfirmation and disappointment—"things didn't work out the way we expected." Such disappointment and its later consequences can be ameliorated somewhat by various efforts to make explicit as much of the psychological contract as possible. For example, as part of a performance-appraisal discussion the employee and the boss could attempt to state explicitly what their assumptions and expectations are about each other over the next six to twelve months. The philosophy of Management By Objectives as applied to performance appraisal asks boss and subordinate to set joint targets, which often encourages the surfacing of implicit assumptions and expectations.

Some organizations are using focused workshops to help groups of subordinates in a department to discuss and share their expectations of what they expect to give to the organization and what they expect to get in return; supervisors go through the same exercise in the workshop, identifying what they expect to give and to receive. The lists are then shared, and a joint effort is made to identify areas where there are mismatches. These areas are then discussed in an attempt to locate a resolution in the form of adjusting expectations or behavior or both. Though most of the efforts in this direction have been focused on the initial socialization period (Kotter, 1972, 1973), there is no reason why one could not have such facilitative workshops with people three to five years into their careers or even later. The point is to locate a vehicle to open up the discussion between the employee and the employer so as to explore the psychological contract more openly and thereby to reduce the chances for mismatches and disappointment.

The psychological contract changes in important ways as the person goes through a career and life cycle, because his or her needs change in important ways. Similarly, what the organization expects of the individual changes with changes in job or role. Thus one might expect that in the mid- and later career there is a growing likelihood that new disappointments will arise because the individual's effort and the organization's rewards may be based on assumptions which were more appropriate to an earlier career or life stage. For example, organizations commonly assume that if a person has high work involvement at an early stage of the career, such work involvement should remain high. The demotivated or plateaued individual is seen as a "problem" rather than as a possibly normal mid- to late-career phenomenon. Many managers talk about remotivating people, even though they acknowledge when pressed that the present level of motivation is "adequate" and the work quality "sufficient to make a contribution." Rather than remotivating the person, a better solution might be to renegotiate the psychological contract and to adjust expectations on both sides to new realities (Bailyn, 1977). To take another example, people's willingness to be relocated changes with their family circumstances and their personal life-styles. Rather than assuming that a position which was true at one career stage will remain stable, ways should be found to reassess every few years what needs and expectations both the employee and the employer have of each other and to determine how best to meet both sets of needs.

SUMMARY AND CONCLUSIONS

The major potential hazard of the period of mutual acceptance is that insufficient information is generated for either the organization or the individual to determine whether to accept the other. The early career must generate sufficient opportunities for testing of the new employee to permit everyone to learn whether a potential match of individual and organizational needs exists. Second, the process of negotiation or dialogue must facilitate the exchange of accurate information. Many alumni complained bitterly that after several months they still did not know where they stood, though interviews with their bosses had revealed that they were doing very well or very poorly. On the other hand, bosses complained that they did not know how the new employees felt about the organization and their jobs, even though interviews with those same new employees revealed that they had clear and definite feelings. In many cases the new employee makes a mental decision to leave the organization, but feels no obligation to communicate this decision to the boss. Similarly, bosses mentally write off new employees as having no long-range potential, yet feel no obligation to get this message across. Each party may find itself second-guessing the other, and nasty surprises result in the form of sudden resignations or terminations.

Even more costly, because neither the individual nor the organization is willing to confront a situation of mutual dissatisfaction, the employee is carried along with the vague hope that he or she will improve while the employee clings to the job with the vague hope that it will become more interesting and challenging sometime in the future. It is such mutual avoidance that creates "dead wood" in organizations.

If human resource planning and development is to become effective, it must address the problems of the early career as outlined in Chapters 7–9. Managers at all levels must become aware of the pitfalls and dilemmas and must: (1) educate themselves as individual performers to do a better job of bringing new people on board; and (2) work with others in the organization to create better systems and procedures for integrating new employees. These problems involve line managers intimately and therefore cannot be completely delegated to such staff departments as personnel, training, and recruiting. The beneficiaries as well as potential victims of mismanagement of this stage are the line managers themselves, and therefore they must become involved in the early stages of planning for effective recruitment, selection, job assignment, socialization, performance appraisal, and further integration of new employees through the negotiation of a viable psychological contract.

10
THE DEVELOPMENT OF CAREER
ANCHORS: TECHNICAL AND MANAGERIAL

Consider the following dialogue:

> Interviewer: Are you still at the Acme Company?
>
> Respondent: No. We had this program of Management By Objectives at Acme, and I realized that I wasn't meeting my *own* objectives. So I started to care less about *Acme's* objectives and left.

INTRODUCTION AND DEFINITION

In the previous chapters our focus was on entering the organization and achieving a viable psychological contract. This process involves deciphering the norms of the organization, learning to get along with peers and authority figures, and most important, learning how to work. The subsequent early career can be viewed as a time when the career occupant undergoes a whole series of learning experiences which gradually define for the new employee and for the employing organization the employee's areas of talent and long-range contribution.

New employees typically come into the organization with some specialty based on their school work or on training obtained as part of their induction into the organization. But until they are actually working, neither they nor the organization can really know whether or not their abilities will be commensurate with the present and future requirements of their jobs and potential careers. Furthermore, new employees do not know how they will like the work or how their values will fit with those of the organization within which the work is performed.

The early career can therefore be viewed as a time of *mutual discovery* between the new employee and the employing organization. Through successive trials and new job challenges, each learns more about the other. Even more significantly, however, the new employee gradually gains *self-knowledge* and develops a clearer *occupational self-concept*. This self-concept has three components, which together make up what I will call the person's *"career anchor"*:

1. Self-perceived *talents and abilities* (based on actual successes in a variety of work settings);

2. Self-perceived *motives and needs* (based on opportunities for self-tests and self-diagnosis in real situations and on feedback from others);

3. Self-perceived *attitudes and values* (based on actual encounters between self and the norms and values of the employing organization and work setting).

Several things should be noted about this concept of career anchor. *First*, it is *broader in its definition* than the typical concept of job value or motivation to work. Many analyses of occupational choice place exclusive emphasis on motives and values, failing to take into account the critical role of self-perceived talents and abilities based on actual work experience.

Second, because of the emphasis on actual work experience, it is *not possible* to predict career anchors from tests. The concept emphasizes evolution, development, and *discovery* through actual experience. Though the person may have all kinds of latent talents and abilities based on school performance, they do not become an active part of the self-concept until tested in real situations in which the outcomes matter. In many cases the person does not know what his or her talents really are until they are tested in real-life situations. Career anchors, then, are clearly the *result* of the early interaction between the individual and the work environment. They are "inside" the person, functioning as a set of driving and constraining forces on career decisions and choices. If one moves into a setting in which one is likely to fail or which fails to meet one's needs or which compromises one's values, one will be "pulled back" into something more congruent —hence the metaphor of "anchor."

Third, the concept emphasizes the *interaction among abilities, motives, and values in the total self-concept*. They are mutually interactive in that we come to want and value that which we are good at, and we improve our abilities in those things that we want or value. In trying to understand a career, it makes little sense to try to reduce everything to just one concept such as motives, values, or abilities. The purpose of the career-anchor concept is to highlight the gradual integration of motives, values, and abilities in the person's total self-concept.

Fourth, career anchors can only be discovered over a number of years during the early career, because one cannot know until one encounters a variety of real-life situations how one's abilities, motives, and values will in fact interact and *will fit the career options available.* For example, one may believe oneself to be talented and motivated toward a consulting career and have some evidence that one would like it, only to discover that one's needs to stabilize one's life are in complete conflict with the life of travel characteristic of a consultant. Or one may enter a certain kind of company in a job for which one is well suited only to discover a real incompatibility between one's own values and those of the employer.

Finally, the concept is intended to identify a *growing area of stability within the person* without, however, implying that the person ceases to change or grow. It may well be that career anchors are the source of stability that permits growth and change in other areas. It is also possible that anchors themselves change. But it should be recognized that the concept is designed to explain that part of our lives which grows more stable as we develop more self-insight based on more life-experience.

ORIGIN OF THE CONCEPT

The concept of career anchor evolved out of the longitudinal study of Sloan School alumni previously referred to (Schein, 1968, 1975). The 44 male panelists in the study were reinterviewed by me in 1973, approximately 10 to 12 years after their graduation. These interviews focused on the actual detailed job history of each person and the reasons for the choices or decisions which he made—decisions such as whether to leave an organization, seek additional education, and so on. When I examined the *reasons* for the actual decisions, there emerged in almost all cases a clear *pattern* of responses. One might see little consistency in the actual job histories, but there was a great deal of consistency in the reasons given for decisions. Furthermore, the reasons became more clear-cut, articulate, and consistent with accumulated job experience. During the first year or so, the person might be seeking broad concepts like "challenge," "more earnings," or "more responsibility." After a few years of experience, he would refer to specific kinds of work or responsibility or job settings which attracted him.

The concept of career anchor emerged as a way of explaining the patterns of reasons given by the 44 panelists. The person being interviewed usually did not see the pattern spontaneously, but would readily see it once it was pointed out. The alumni usually attributed their lack of self-insight to lack of opportunity to sit down and analyze their own careers systematically. They felt as though they were making arbitrary, short-run kinds of adjustments and could not see the consistency in those adjustments which gave a pattern to their behavior, though they became more and more clear as to what they wanted out of their careers. The labels eventually chosen for the career anchors reflect those needs or wants.

Once the concept had been developed in the panel study, it was "tested" in a variety of other settings. First, I attempted to predict the pattern of attitude and value *changes* in the panelists over the 10–12-year-period of the study. These changes made sense only if the group was divided by the different career anchors. As I will show in Chapter 12, the direction of change of attitudes reflected the kind of socialization which one would expect to accompany different kinds of careers. Second, I developed a biographical form (see Appendix 1) to enable a person to analyze his own career and found that a group of 50 middle managers could use it to develop a fairly clear picture of their own career anchors. These self-ratings were not validated by interviews, but did indicate that people could discover patterns in their own careers. Third, an interview study of 20 senior executives (Hopkins, 1976) revealed that it was possible to sort them unambiguously into anchor groups based on a half-hour interview on career history and future career aspirations.

In summary, the *career anchor*—the pattern of self-perceived talents, motives, and values—serves to guide, constrain, stabilize, and integrate the person's career. Based on the research conducted thus far, I would hypothesize that career anchors will remain stable throughout the person's career, though this hypothesis has not as yet been tested.

The career anchor functions in the person's work life as a way of organizing experience, identifying one's area of contribution in the long run, generating criteria for kinds of work settings in which one wants to function, and identifying patterns of ambition and criteria for success by which one will measure oneself. As we will see, people really differ in how they view their careers, even from a fairly homogeneous background such as a graduate management school. It becomes crucial for managers as well as career occupants to come to recognize these differences so that psychological contracts can be developed which accurately reflect the needs and expectations of the person in the career.

TYPES OF CAREER ANCHORS

The panelists' patterns of responses could be sorted into five basic categories. Some alumni found themselves increasingly unable to work in large organizations and ended up in essentially "autonomous" careers. Others organized all of their career decisions around the need to create something—a product, a company, or a service—of their own. These entrepreneurs were anchored in "creativity." Both of these groups operated outside of large, traditional organizations as their careers unfolded.

Alumni in a third group organized their careers around their specific areas of technical or functional competence and made job moves essentially by the criterion of maximizing their opportunity to remain challenged in their specific content area. A fourth group was preoccupied primarily with career stability and became more oriented toward the extrinsic issues of security and stability. Finally, alumni in a fifth group were concerned with climbing the corporate ladder to positions of general management, where they could exercise large amounts of responsibility and link organizational achievement to their own efforts.

The numbers in these groups are not as important as the types, because the numbers probably reflect the sampling bias of Sloan School graduate students. The five types, however, can probably be found in all occupations and must be clearly understood because, as we will see, they want quite different things out of their careers, measure themselves quite differently, and therefore have to be managed quite differently. It is also important to note that these are self-image patterns, not externally defined. Therefore, it is not valid to judge the relative success of the people in the different groups unless one imposes external criteria. In doing so one may miss the more significant fact that some of the alumni specifically rejected some of the external success criteria and attempted to develop more meaningful inner standards of how they would regard their career success.

The career anchor can be viewed as that concern or value which the person will not give up, if a choice has to be made. In many careers it is possible to meet a variety of needs and to express a variety of talents. One's anchor may not then be highly visible until one faces choices. If such choices have not had to be made early in the career, the person may go through a considerable portion of life without clear awareness of what his or her anchor really is. Yet it is increasingly important for people to gain self-awareness in this area so that they can make more informed choices at critical decision points in their lives. By the same token, it is important for managers to become more aware of the career anchors of their subordinates so that rational career moves are made by the organization.

Let us now examine the five anchors in greater detail, looking at technical functional competence and managerial competence in this chapter and at security, autonomy, and creativity in Chapter 11.

Technical/Functional Competence as a Career Anchor

Nineteen of the 44 alumni in the panel study made it very clear throughout the interview that their primary concern in making career choices and decisions was the actual technical or functional *content* of the work they were doing—whether that work was engineering, financial analysis, marketing, systems analysis, corporate planning, or some other area related to business or management. The self-image of people in this group is tied up with their feeling of competence in the particular area they are in, and consequently they are not interested in management per se, though they will accept management responsibility within their technical or functional area of competence. But they make it very clear that it is the area of work which "turns them on" and indicate that career growth for them means continued advancement within that area only. For example, a young financial analyst anchored in that area aspired to be treasurer or controller of his company. When I asked him what he wanted in the way of a position beyond that, he said that he would want to become the treasurer or financial vice-president of a larger company. This person imagined the pinnacle to be financial vice-president of General Motors, but he could not imagine himself in any other functional area, and he resisted strongly the idea of going into *general* management.

Not only are the roots of these people in the actual analytical work they are doing, but they also actively disdain and fear *general* management, viewing it as a "jungle," a "political arena," and a type of work that does not permit the exercise of what they consider to be their skills. They view functional management as necessary to the performance of their skill and as a way to advance, but they are not attracted to management per se. People anchored in their technical or functional area of competence tend to leave companies rather than be promoted out of their area, but they experience considerable conflict because they know that the traditional career path in American organizations is to move from functional to general management. Many of them said in the interview that they did not feel free to reveal to their bosses their strong desire to remain in their technical or functional area, because they would be viewed as lacking in ambition, which might hurt their career in general. Some of them feared that they would not have the courage to turn down a general management job if it was offered, even though they felt sure they would fail in it because of their dislike of what those jobs entailed as they saw them. This group is perhaps the spawning ground of future victims of the Peter Principle.

Alumni in this group covered a wide spectrum of types of work in organizations. Their titles are given below to illustrate the fact that such titles alone do not tell us about their career anchor. Only by talking to the individuals was it possible to discern the pattern described in this section and to differentiate it from the other career anchor patterns:

1. Project manager and part founder of a large consulting firm;

2. Research associate to the vice-president for academic affairs of a medium-size university;

3. Director of required-earnings studies in a large national utility;

4. Manager of engineering in a large product line of a medium-size manufacturing company;

5. Member of the technical staff of the R&D division of a large, national utility;

6. Principal programmer in a technical unit of a large systems design and manufacturing company;

7. Market development engineer in a new-venture group of a chemical corporation;

8. Project manager of an aerospace division of a large electronics corporation;

9. Treasurer of a small growth company;

10. Commerce officer in a large department of the Canadian government;

11. Assistant professor of operations research in the management department of a military academy;

12. Senior consultant in a small management consulting firm;

13. Assistant director of a government office of telecommunications;

14. Plant manufacturing engineer of a large consumer products division of a large corporation;

15. Manager of market support systems for Europe in the information services division of a large corporation;

16. Teacher and department head in a regional rural high school;

17. Project supervisor in a technical division of a large chemical company;

18. Director of the cost analysis group of a large technical systems consulting firm;

19. Principal in a large management consulting firm.

Case Illustration: Terry Furniss   When I first met Terry as a second-year graduate student in 1961, he struck me as a handsome, articulate, somewhat diffident but confident young man. Large and imposing in manner and bearing, he spoke in a relaxed and comfortable manner during the interview, communicating maturity and integrity in the extreme.

Terry is the oldest son in an Irish immigrant family that settled in the Boston area in the 1920s. His father worked in a variety of semi-skilled jobs, and his mother was a domestic in the home of a department store president. He has three sisters and two brothers. After attending public elementary school, Terry went to Junior Seminary in a nearby city, thinking that he would like to be a priest.

During his high school years this aspiration waned, because he realized that he was just not cut out for the life of routine and strict discipline the priesthood would entail. He transferred to Boston College High School with the help of a friend and began to do excellent academic work in physics and the classics because of some tough, challenging teachers. His good senior year earned him a scholarship to Boston College, where he majored in physics. After two years there he realized that he wanted to get into a managerial position sometime and that this would require some graduate work—either a Ph.D. or graduate management school. Terry applied for and won a General Electric summer scholarship at Rensselaer Polytechnic Institute following his junior year at college. During this summer he spent a substantial amount of time at the G.E. laboratories, which gave him an insight into how companies work and reinforced his desire for a graduate management degree.

Terry applied to several schools and was admitted to MIT's Sloan School in 1956. After one term he received an offer from a local R&D company to work as a field engineer. He accepted the offer because the draft was hot on his heels, and the job carried a draft deferment with it. He worked in this organization for three years and then returned to graduate school.

Based on the 1961 interview (during Terry's last semester at MIT), we drew several conclusions about his values and aspirations. He put a very high value on *task accomplishment, getting a job done, and doing it right.* Beyond that central value he wanted some challenge and adventure in his life, expressed particularly in terms of some ideas of starting up a business venture in Ireland, but he also put a great deal of emphasis on having a career which would not be so demanding that it would interfere with family life. He did not, for example, envision himself in a large corporation and being moved every few years, because this would be bad for his children (he expressed these views at a time when he was still single). Terry also put emphasis on being fair and honest in one's dealing with people.

In talking of his career in 1961, Terry was almost apologetic about his inability to be specific about his goals. He interviewed over 20 companies—some in relation to an overseas job, some in relation to data processing, which he had become interested in after his summer work for G.E., and some in relation to the plan to go to Ireland. In the end he settled for the R&D company that had employed him prior to graduate school and worked in R&D administration. The job ended up being a kind of "odds and ends" situation involving the writing of technical proposals, setting up management systems for various R&D projects, and contributing to contract sales efforts.

Terry stayed with this company for two and half years, first in administration, which he found "too vague," and eventually in marketing, which he "grew to dislike very much."

> It involved finding money for people to conduct research, and I knew that I was never good enough to do the research for which I was out ringing the doorbells [various government agencies]. . . . I was never good enough to do the research myself, yet I was always forced to go out and dig up the money for somebody else to conduct the research. . . .
>
> I grew to dislike it very much, and I thought for six to eight months before I finally decided what I wanted to do, so I wrote 20 letters blind to 20 different companies, and Acme Electronics was one of the few that I got any response from at all. [Acme is a very large electronics firm doing consumer and government contract work.]

The work in Acme was as a "simulation analyst" in a small staff group which was developing some new concepts about how to use computer simulations. Terry knew that this was a risky area and that if the work ran out, he would be the first to be laid off. One day about two years later, the leader of the group told Terry that he was thinking of starting a new consulting company and invited Terry and another member of the same work group to go into it with him. The group leader, John, asked Terry if he would be able to invest some money in the new concern and offered Terry a position on the board if he could raise more than $5000. Terry convinced several of his friends to invest in the new venture and put up some of his own money to help launch it. John and the other man started the company while Terry continued at Acme for another six months, finishing off projects. He worked in the new company some nights and weekends, writing proposals, debugging programs, and otherwise helping in any way he could.

The new company became successful quickly through its contract research for government agencies. Terry joined with the title of Senior Analyst and put his main energies into helping the data-processing effort, using computer applications. In a questionnaire sent out some years after he joined the consulting company, he said:

> I have gradually reached the point where I can clearly define what I need in a job to make it interesting and challenging to me. In the years ahead these needs may vary slightly, but I am zeroing in on them. Briefly, what I need in a job is a specific goal, e.g., a computer system or program to solve some problem, or a production schedule to be met which involves producing a concrete product, within fixed dollars and time limits—using people and machines in an efficient fashion.
>
> Right now I enjoy projects involving substantial intellectual challenge (e.g., systems analysis/programming), but I may eventually prefer production-oriented work where the major challenge is not intellectual. In any case, I am convinced that I would never enjoy a position in sales—regardless of product or level in the organization. I much prefer to do the job—design the system, produce the car, etc.—than to sell it.

What is striking about this statement is not only the rejection of sales, but also the absence of any reference to management per se. In the new consulting firm, though he is a part owner and on the board by virtue of his investment in the company, he has continued in a technical function, writing proposals and directing projects concerned with technical assistance, conducting research and evaluation on social science areas ranging from manpower and health to housing and criminal justice. Almost all of these projects are federally funded, with contracts awarded on the basis of competitive procurements. The projects extend from six months to several years, with budgets ranging from $100,000 to over a million dollars, and employ two to ten staff members. Terry's specialty, as he sees it, is "project management."

Terry was married in 1968, now has three children, and is very family-oriented. He lives on a large lot in a rural area, where he spends a lot of time with his children and on gardening. He is an adventurous person, as his original intentions to go to Ireland had indicated, and engages in sports such as canoeing, mountain climbing, and tennis, though he admits that in recent years he has had less time for these things because of the demands of his family.

To summarize his career situation, a major theme throughout his interviews is that he likes the technical work he is doing and sees himself as continuing to do such work. He described the changes in himself over the 12 years of the study as primarily getting more awareness of and insight into the fact that he needs to do technical, production-oriented work with clear boundaries and deadlines associated with it. He is definitely unwilling to sacrifice closeness to technical work in order to climb the promotional ladder. He turns down jobs which might involve long hours of work or traveling, and hence promotion, in order to preserve the well-balanced situation he has achieved.

Summary.   To recap, the alumni anchored in technical/functional competence have oriented their careers around their areas of competence and have explicitly avoided situations which would remove them from those areas or push them into general management. They have entered what Driver (in press) calls "steady state" careers where the major growth, as in craft work, is increasing skill in the area of competence but not much hierarchical rise. Success for people in this group is determined more by feedback that they are expert in their areas and by increasingly challenging work in those areas rather than promotion or monetary rewards per se, though these are obviously important as well.

Managerial Competence as a Career Anchor

Eight of the 44 alumni had in common a strong motivation to rise to positions of managerial responsibility, and their career experiences enabled them to believe that they had the skills and values necessary to rise to such general-manager positions. Unlike members of the previous group, people in this second group have as their ultimate goal management per se. Specific technical or functional jobs are seen only as necessary interim stages on the way to the higher, general-management levels. They see the necessity of becoming competent in one or more functional areas, but no one area captures their commitment. Instead, they perceive their competence to lie in the *combination* of three more general areas which they referred to and which I labeled as follows:

1. *Analytical competence: the ability to identify, analyze, and solve problems under conditions of incomplete information and uncertainty.* In talking about their past and future careers, these graduates referred frequently to their ability to take a mass of information of varying quality, recognize the relevant and valid portions, come quickly to the heart of the problem, state it in a way that it can be worked on, and then facilitate the analysis and solution of the problem. This ability requires sensitivity to the environment, the ability to assess the validity of information, conceptual tools to analyze the information and put it into useful frameworks, and problem-solving skills.* The same analytical skills were referred to whether the person was working in finance, marketing, information and control, engineering, or whatever. It is in this skill area that formal education seemed to make a contribution in that the conceptual models and skills in analysis were typically perceived to have been learned in school.

2. *Interpersonal competence: the ability to influence, supervise, lead, manipulate, and control people at all levels of the organization toward the more effective achievement of organizational goals.* The analytical skills referred to above do not by themselves produce an effective manager, as the panelists saw it. Rather, analytical skills must be combined with interpersonal skills, since most of the work of the manager, especially at higher levels, is carried out through other people. The manager must not only analyze problems, but also be able to communicate that analysis to others, elicit motivation to work on the problems, and monitor progress toward problem solution. The skills of working with other people include not only supervision, but also running meetings, dealing with interpersonal or intergroup conflict, influencing peers over whom the manager has no direct authority, influencing the boss and others higher in the hierarchy, and managing interpersonal relationships with people outside the organization. These skills appear to be becoming more important as the complexity of organizations increases. Consequently, the learning of interper-

---

*Dill *et al.* (1962) put special emphasis on this skill in their longitudinal study of young managers.

sonal competence, or the discovery that one has it, becomes a crucial event in the development of a manager.

3. *Emotional competence: the capacity to be stimulated by emotional and interpersonal crises rather than exhausted or debilitated by them, the capacity to bear high levels of responsibility without becoming paralyzed, and the ability to exercise power without guilt or shame.* This third component of managerial competence is the most elusive, yet possibly the most important in identifying the kind of person who will succeed in *high*-level managerial roles. The emotional component was discussed by these alumni most often in the context of crises which they had faced and weathered. People reported that they were "surprised" that they could take on a difficult interpersonal situation, such as firing someone or supervising someone much older than they, and not only handle it effectively but also "feel good" about the manner in which they handled it. The very things which the alumni anchored in technical/functional competence feared or deplored as "politics in the executive suite" or the "jungle" were seen by the managerially anchored panelists as "stimulating" and the place "where the action is." Politics, in-fighting, wheeling and dealing, making things happen, having the ultimate responsibility was seen by them as the very thing they wanted and would be stimulated by.

From my observer perspective listening to the panelists, it is, of course, obvious that different occupational roles require *different kinds* of analytical, interpersonal, and emotional competences. The systems analyst facing an intractable intellectual problem and sustaining a high level of intellectual energy for 48 hours until the problem is solved is showing a kind of emotional competence; the doctor making life-or-death decisions about a patient is displaying another kind of emotional competence.

What appears to distinguish those in the managerially oriented group is the fact that *they explicitly drew attention to the emotional aspects of their job* and saw as part of their own development the evolution of the insight that they could deal with emotionally tough situations. The emotional-competence component—being able to make decisions under conditions of risk and uncertainty, being responsible for acting on whatever crises arise, being liable for the consequences of one's own decisions and those of subordinates—was much more visible to these alumni and therefore something they felt they needed if they were to succeed.

I did not investigate the lives of these people from a clinical point of view and therefore cannot judge how they actually handled their feelings, what kinds of defenses or coping mechanisms they used, how they dealt with their tensions, and when or how their ability to handle particular emotional problems was learned. It was clear, however, that they were not feelingless people with "icewater in their veins" or "machinelike" in their dealings with people. This group of alumni was as or more emotional than any other group, but its members did not feel crippled or bothered by certain of their emotions; rather, there seemed to be an ability to express these emotions and discharge tensions so that they would not simmer under the surface. For example, a person who had the difficult job of firing someone would recognize the difficulty, face up to it, do it as humanely and sensibly as possible, feel badly about it, talk it out with a friend or spouse, and then feel some relief at having done the job. People in this group did not avoid the situation or procrastinate to avoid the discomfort, nor did they feel great anxiety or guilt afterwards. They accepted the fact that their decision might influence the welfare of many people or involve the risk of losing many dollars, but they would make the best decision possible and then watch the outcome with *appropriate* tension.

The emotionally competent manager would be less likely to develop psychosomatic or other symptoms of health and emotional problems. The emotionally less competent manager might look calm on the surface, but might well be developing ulcers or hypertension, which would ultimately interfere with work performance. In listening to these managerially anchored panelists, I got the impression that the ones who came across as emotionally competent were more "realistic" about life and more willing to confront whatever was happening, including their own tensions. For example, several of the successful managers reported that they had at one or another time faced personal and family crises, had gone to psychiatrists, and had worked out their problems. What distinguished them was not the absence of such crises, but rather their willingness to face them and do something about them.

An aspect of what I am calling emotional competence in managerial roles which did not come out in the interviews but which one sees in looking at the biographies of great leaders is the ability to make tough decisions where no integrative solution is possible, where one has to take the lesser of two evils or sacrifice something in the short run for some greater good or longer-run gain. Perhaps the best examples occur in the realm of politics. In World War II, for example, there is evidence that Winston Churchill knew, because of the breaking of the German codes, that Conventry was to be bombed. However, if he protected Conventry, he would be revealing that the codes had been broken. In order to protect the secret, he had to decide to let

Conventry be bombed and to live with that decision (Winterbotham, 1974).*

To summarize, as the alumni saw it, the person who wants to rise to higher levels of management and be given higher levels of responsibility must be *simultaneously* good at analyzing problems, handling people, and handling his or her own emotions in order to withstand the pressures and tensions of the "executive suite." This kind of person "needs" to be in an organization and to rise to a level within that organization where these various competencies can be exercised. He or she will seek opportunities to express the combination of analytical, interpersonal, and emotional competencies.

The notion of a *combination* of abilities, skills, or competencies is critical to a true understanding of the managerial role and the determinants of success in the role. People with strong analytical competencies could do very well in various kinds of staff roles within organizations. If they *combine those analytical competencies* with some interpersonal skills and if they like to work with people, they could rise to fairly senior functional-management roles. Someone with *primarily* interpersonal skills and relatively low analytical competence would probably be more successful in lower-level line jobs, such as first- or second-level supervisor in a "people-intensive" kind of work such as "shift foreman." Without the emotional competence to make tough decisions and the self-confidence that arises from the recognition of one's own emotional competence, it is difficult to conceive of a person's either aspiring to or being successful at higher levels of general management. At the same time, it is clear that such emotional competence is not enough. To be successful in those higher-level jobs also requires the analytical and interpersonal skills and the self-confidence that arises from the recognition that one has those skills. It is the need for this *combination* which makes it so difficult to locate and "develop" general managers, because it is not even clear when and how the kinds of competencies which have been described develop in a person's life.

Once one has a clear recognition of one's own managerial competence anchor, one still faces some difficult choices, especially in mid- to late career. I did not observe these dilemmas within the panel group directly, because the panelists are still too young, but they clearly exist in organizations. For example, as one rises into general-management

---

*It has been asserted that managers must be able to take risks. In these terms what that means is the ability not only to make a risky decision, but also to follow it through emotionally.

jobs, such as "product-line manager," "division general manager," "president of a subsidiary," and so on, one increasingly finds oneself in positions where one does indeed have the high levels of responsibility and authority which one is seeking. In a large complex organization the next level *up* for this kind of a person can pose a serious dilemma, because that next level may involve a *reduction* in direct authority or influence even though it is at a "higher" level of responsibility within the corporate structure. Specifically, managers face this dilemma when they have to decide whether or not to remain at the divisional level "running" some part of the organization, or accept promotion to the corporate headquarters organization, in which they often become a member of a complex team of peers and return to a higher-level *functional* responsibility. For example, a division general manager may become a corporate vice-president in charge of all manufacturing or marketing or administrative functions. In that job one has more formal responsibility, but one's whole style of management must change to deal with the headquarters structure. Where one was at the peak of one pyramid, one suddenly moves to the bottom of another pyramid. The most vivid example of the stress of this transition can be seen in the military, where admirals or generals used to commanding units, bases, or ships find themselves transferred into a "staff" role in the Pentagon. Suddenly they are less powerful than some of their peers (who have been around longer) and the various civil servants and politicians with whom they must deal. They also have to negotiate across interservice boundaries and accept membership in a new group, the Department of Defense.

From the point of view of career anchors, the decisions to be made about whether to move into corporate headquarters require self-insight and a clear view of what the jobs ahead entail. For those individuals anchored in technical/functional competence who may have risen to a general-management level because of interpersonal and emotional competencies, the move to a senior functional position may be a welcome relief. We have seen marketing-oriented managers struggling through the years of running a product division and then happily settling into a corporate marketing role. On the other hand, the person anchored in managerial competence will be vying for the position of group vice-president, executive vice-president, and ultimately president. From the point of view of the outside observer looking at two different division managers, it would not be possible to predict which person would want which role or to assume that everyone would want the senior "line" roles. The career-anchor concept alerts us to the fact that people do differ, even at very senior levels, in what they are seeking from their careers.

The picture I have painted of the group anchored in managerial competence may sound like a more talented or superior group than others because of the emphasis on analytical, interpersonal, and emotional competence. What I want to stress again is that this group is the one that has certain of these competencies in *combination,* but not necessarily any one of them to a greater degree than some other panelist. In other words, other alumni may have had different analytical, interpersonal, or emotional competencies, or they may have had one or two of these areas more highly developed than the managerially anchored group. But they did not have them in combination, and they were not as conscious of the need for this particular blend of skills for success in their careers.

Returning to the panel study, where are the managerially anchored people 10 to 12 years into their careers? Their titles and companies are shown below:

1. Manager of factoring systems in the corporate headquarters of a large financial corporation;

2. Sales manager and part owner of a family furniture business;

3. Sales manager in the industrial foods division of a large conglomerate;

4. Director of corporate plan administration in a large airline;

5. President and part owner of a small manufacturing firm;

6. Marketing manager in a large division of a large manufacturing company;

7. Director of administration in the insurance services division of a large financial corporation;

8. Vice-president for finance and administration in a medium-size service organization.

As can be seen, of the eight panelists in this group, only one has clearly made it to a general-manager position (no. 5). The others were in various functional-management jobs which they perceived as way stations toward general-manager responsibilities. Within the group there are two career patterns—working one's way up within a large organization and seeking larger jobs within smaller organizations after acquiring some large-company experience. Both patterns include individuals who have moved from one company to another and who have sometimes interrupted their careers with stints in management consulting, usually as a way of gaining additional experience, variety, and the opportunity to come into contact with organizations in which there may be more opportunity.

Case Illustration: Martin Mattox   When I first met Martin, I described him as an "intense, quiet type of person, self-sufficient and confident, but quite withdrawn and low key in his approach to me." He is the oldest of four boys in a local Boston family. His father is a successful salesman for a large, wholesale liquor distributor. He went to various public schools and became interested in chemistry after being invited to work in the basement lab of a friend whose father was interested in that field. For financial reasons he applied only to local schools so that he could live at home. He was accepted at MIT and came there to major in chemical engineering.

During his years as an MIT undergraduate, he came to know some other students who were advocating the value of going to business school. Martin cannot remember just what swayed him about the concept, but he began to think about it for himself, without, however, having a very clear picture of what a career in business would be all about.

In his two years in the Sloan School, Martin covered mostly production, marketing, and finance courses and did his thesis in finance because he felt that one could learn more about the guts of a business by working with financial controls and financial-planning information. He had acquired some concepts of business from his father and from having had a wide variety of summer jobs in various kinds of business organizations, but even after his master's program at MIT, he still could not articulate precisely what he was looking for in his career except possibly getting into a business of his own someday.

The value themes which emerged from the 1961 interview dealt with the importance of fairness in one's relations to others and the importance of being a dynamic go-getter who would know how to seize an opportunity. Martin clearly hoped he would have the "dynamic" qualities he associated with successful businessmen, but kept wondering out loud whether or not he had those qualities himself. He also expressed a belief that although one should be honest and have integrity and expect the same in other people, one should nonetheless be prepared for the worst. Some of his experiences, he feels, have taught him to be somewhat wary and cynical. Academically, Martin's Sloan School grades and test scores were average.

In choosing a company for his first job, Martin emphasized his need to be able to believe that the company would do things in a smart and correct fashion. He did not want to find himself in an organization that did things wrong or that used inefficient or "dumb" procedures. He also expected that he would move several times in the process of finding something that really fit his needs. He chose a large consumer and industrial products manufacturer which had a three-month rotational training program for college graduates in financial and business planning.

Martin's three months of training were followed by a series of tests, interviews, and "sales pitches" designed to get him to work in various parts of the organization which wanted his services. This process left him very unimpressed, because it seemed that management's expectations were too low for what he himself aspired to do. The one group he wanted to join was unavailable, for budget reasons. He finally ended up in an aero-space division of the company as a project administrator, checking financial data on the project and otherwise aiding the project manager. Martin's view of the job was that it could be done in one day a week and that his talents simply were not utilized properly. At this time he began to doubt whether a large company, particularly at lower organization levels, could utilize someone with a master's degree in management and reaffirmed his plan to go out on his own or get into a small business. He expressed great cynicism about how to get ahead and felt that good performance was not really appreciated.

Martin's boss had a somewhat different view of the situation. He saw Mattox as a "manager without portfolio" in having no one to supervise, but he stated that the job required considerable talent because engineers had to be kept in line, one had to know when and how to process information, and one had to know how to develop the job oneself into a full-time useful role. As the boss put it: "Mattox *should* be frustrated by his feeling of not having enough to do, but when he sees the total picture, he will realize how to restructure his job so that he will have enough. He will have to learn this for himself. Anyone who cannot do this or who is satisfied is not worth having or advancing."

Martin handled this situation by entering a period of self-education, going around to other departments to learn what all the business functions were. He did not develop within his job and said later that he "disliked both his job and his boss." In 1965, roughly two years after joining the company, he met an old friend whose father was running a small book-binding business, was invited to enter the business, and decided to do so. In explaining this decision on a questionnaire mailed in 1965, he said:

> I left_____Co. because, to be as candid as possible, they were quite pleased with work that required only two hours a day. I wasn't.

Six years in the academic environment led one to believe that a high level of competence and a fair degree of sophistication exist in the business world. The fact that they do not exist in my situation and in the company has made me slightly cynical.

The book-binding business did not turn out to meet Martin's expectations either. His friend had knowledge of the market and the business, and Martin was to bring in the managerial experience the friend lacked. They planned to make the business profitable within a year, but instead found out how "cruel the marketplace can really be." Martin spent 50% to 75% of his time out marketing and selling. In spite of this effort, he could see that it still would take at least two or three more years to develop the business. He decided that this was not the route for him to go, so he and his friend parted amicably.

Martin updated his resume, went back to the MIT placement office, used all of his contacts, and thereby landed a job in a large pharmaceutical company as a junior analyst in the cost-estimating group. Over the next two years he moved from junior to senior analyst and did capital studies, cost analyses, and most importantly, served as a liaison person in a new-plant development task force between the chemical engineers and the operations research people, who had trouble communicating with each other. He had a good boss who trained him, and he learned a good deal about the role of financial functions in a manufacturing environment. It was a good entry job, as Martin later described it, but as he moved up into the job, he again found himself underchallenged and underutilized. Not only was his salary not rising at the rate at which he thought it should, but he also said that he could do in ten hours a week what the company considered a full-time job and was praised for all of his efforts to boot. He again felt disillusioned with how large companies operated, so he decided to try his hand at management consulting.

Martin answered an ad and was accepted as a management consultant in a firm that had built a strong business in accounting and wanted to expand its services into more managerial functions. This work was very exciting because it gave Mattox a top mangement perspective which he had been lacking in his various other jobs and ventures. He met a great many managers from different industries and business functions and was able to see how all the functions of a business worked together. However, he realized after a year or so that he had made an error in going into an accounting firm because of its conservative management and its strong accounting philosophy, which made it difficult for the management consulting side of the business to grow. They wanted it merely as an ancillary service, which led to its gradual atrophy. After two years with this firm, Mattox was terminated, a personally traumatic experience which reinforced his feeling that he must eventually become financially independent.

As a result of reading advertisements and applying to various companies, Martin got a job within a few months in a large manufacturing company as the manager of facilities planning, a corporate staff position. Because of his excellent work in reviewing all major facilities expenditures, business planning, monthly reviews of operations, and various special studies, he was promoted in nine months to manager of planning. In this role he was responsible for all planning and had a staff of 11 people.

Martin describes the corporate climate during his first two years in this company as very "marginal" because of an old conservative management, but the job was interesting, so he stuck it out through a period of upheaval and found that when a new, young president came in, the climate improved sharply. The president brought in a very dynamic, young executive vice-president to head the company's group of highly diversified businesses. This man recognized Mattox's talent and offered him a much bigger job, as comptroller of one of the divisions, something he turned down as not being good enough. Mattox was then offered the position of marketing director for the entire business group, reporting directly to the group vice-president, a job which he took, has held since then, and enjoys very much. He is a kind of free-wheeling internal consultant, identifying problems in any of the divisions as they occur and then working with the managers of those divisions to solve the problems. He feels that his analytical approach has been highly successful because most of the managers he has worked with feel they need this kind of help. His own boss sets an excellent climate and is easy to learn from.

In late 1972, Martin was asked to fill in as acting general manager of one of the divisions while the general manager was off on a three-month management-development program. Martin found this highly educational, rewarding, and confidence building, because he did very well at it and learned that he could supervise people in a general-manager role. Based on this successful experience, he feels that his next step will clearly be a general-manager position in some part of the total corporation, and he sees himself as having a fairly productive general-manager career ahead. He feels that by age 33 he has achieved a good, solid, influential position and is satisfied with his career progress.*

---

*In a telephone interview in 1977 Mattox indicated that he had been promoted twice since 1973 and is now general manager of a product group and a corporate officer.

Mattox was married in 1963 and has two young children. He keeps work and family very separate and feels neither conflict nor mutual enhancement between the areas of work and family. He considers himself a good family man and is highly involved with raising his children. His wife does not work and is perceived as being basically supportive of his career goals.

In summary, what should be noted about Mattox is his preoccupation with challenging work and the full utilization of his talents, his need to get ahead, and his pursuit of a broad managerial perspective. He does not link his career to any given business function or technical area, and he does not assess potential jobs in terms of the type of work so much as the degree to which he feels fully utilized. His picture of a managerial career is not very articulated, but the drive to climb to a high level of responsibility and to achieve financial independence is obviously very strong. He has been willing to move several times, something he said he had expected from the beginning. In his final interview in 1973, he said that he felt that he had become more aggressive and dynamic in line with some of his original concerns and values and that this change was a necessary one for career advancement.

SUMMARY

In summary, the Sloan School alumni who were classified as being anchored in managerial competence differ most clearly from those anchored in technical/functional competence in being less wedded to a given area of work than to the concept of responsibility and management per se. These two groups of people are seeking very different kinds of career goals and measure their degree of success by very different criteria. Whereas the technical/functional person is concerned about the content of the work, the managerial person is much more concerned about the size of the task, the degree of challenge, and the amount of responsibility. Managerially anchored people are in what Driver (in press) calls "linear careers" as contrasted with "steady state" careers, and they measure their success by promotions, rank, and income, all of which measure "amount of responsibility."*

---

*It is not clear how the anchor groups relate to Maccoby's (1976) concepts of the "company man," the "craftsman," the "jungle fighter," and the "gamesman." The managerially anchored alumni in my sample would presumably be most like Maccoby's "gamesmen," whereas the "craftsmen" are most like my technical-functional group, and the "company men" are most like the security-anchored group, which will be discussed in the next chapter.

It should also be noted that the managerial group is highly dependent on large organizations to provide the jobs which carry high levels of responsibility with them. In a sense these people are high-level "organization men" who derive much of their own identity and feeling of success from the fortunes of their organizations. They introduce themselves in terms of their jobs, their companies' names, and the size and scope of those companies.

Organizations need both managerially oriented and technically/functionally oriented people, but they probably have to be managed quite differently, since they have fundamentally different orientations toward their careers.

11
SECURITY, AUTONOMY,
AND CREATIVITY AS CAREER ANCHORS

In the previous chapter, I discussed the concept of career anchor and the two types of anchors most common in the group of panelists—technical/functional competence and managerial competence. In this chapter, I will cover three other anchors which illustrate dramatically the variety of careers which are possible even within a somewhat homogeneous group of management school graduates.

SECURITY AND STABILITY AS A CAREER ANCHOR

Only 4 of the 44 MIT alumni clearly tied their careers to certain organizations or types of organizations providing long-run career stability, a good program of benefits, and basic job security. Though one has to infer it from the pattern of responses, the underlying concern, driving force, or set of constraints operating in these people is career stability and security.

People anchored in "security" tend to do what is required of them by their employers in order to maintain job security, a decent income, and a stable future in the form of a good retirement program, benefits, etc. By implication, such people will, more than others, accept an *organizational* definition of their careers and will have to "trust" the organization to do the right thing by them. Whatever private aspirations or competencies they may believe themselves to have, they must increasingly rely on the organization to recognize such needs and competencies and to do the best by them that is possible.

But one may lose some degree of freedom because of the unwillingness to leave a given organization should one's talents go unrecognized. Instead, one must begin to rationalize that the organization's definition of one's career is indeed the only valid definition and must accept one's dependency on the organization. It is in this group that one will probably find what has come to be labeled the "organization man," the conformist (Whyte, 1956; Schein, 1968), because in order to remain in the organization the individual must become socialized to its values and norms.

If people who are anchored in security concerns have strong technical talents, they may rise to a senior staff or functional-manager level, but if part of their psychological makeup is a degree of insecurity, that very insecurity is likely to make them unable to perform in general-manager jobs, which require a high degree of emotional security, thus limiting their career movement along the hierarchical dimension. Such people are also vulnerable to the "Peter Principle" if their talents lead them to be promoted to a level beyond their "emotional competence." They are also personally very vulnerable if economic adversity forces their employing organizations to cut back, because of lack of self-training in developing their own careers.

The four alumni in this group showed four different patterns. One person switched companies frequently, but always in the same geographical area while he consolidated his home and financial situation. He tried various ventures, including going into business for himself (a venture which failed), and ended up in a middle-management role in a fairly stable company which offered long-range security. His orientation was symbolized by the fact that he arrived at the interview and immediately pulled out a picture of his home and his family as evidences of his "success."

A second person entered the industry in which his father worked and also settled down, after several early career moves, in the geographical area in which he had grown up. He was in a middle-level functional management position at the time of his reinterview. A third panelist went back to his home town and tried working for a large consumer goods company before entering a medium-size family business in that town in a middle-level staff role. The fourth person worked in a staff role for a large corporation which ordinarily moves people frequently, but had managed to secure a commitment to be left in a single geographical area in which he had settled after graduation. None of these alumni expressed great ambitions. They were much more concerned with stability and consolidation of their total life situation.

As a final note on security as an anchor, one can distinguish both in our panelists and in other studies of managers two types of security orientation. For some people the source of stability and security rests primarily with stable membership in a given organization. For others, such as the four panelists in this study, security is more geographically based and involves a feeling of settling down, stabilizing the family, and integrating oneself into the community. One might predict that if their companies attempted to move them, they might well leave and attempt to find equivalent jobs in other companies in the same geographical areas. These people are gambling that this choice will not have to be made. Instances of the former type of security-oriented career would be people in the military or government services or in large corporations, such as the Bell System, where organizational security is very high, but the expectation exists that the person will move every few years in response to organizational needs. Such a system can work well if the supports are present for the family and if the career occupant's self-concept includes periodic travel and relocation.

In the MIT alumni group there was a definite feeling that being anchored in security represented some degree of failure, as if the person felt guilty for not having more ambition or needed to deny the lack of ambition. These conflicts and feelings reflect the degree to which the success ethic of the hierarchical career seekers, the general managers, dominates the thinking of all the alumni. Several of them found it difficult to accept the validity of their own success criterion: a stable, secure, reasonably well-integrated home and work situation.

CREATIVITY AS A CAREER ANCHOR

This career anchor is one of the most difficult to articulate because of the small number of cases we have (6 out of 44), yet it is crucial to understanding the career of the *entrepreneur*. We found in our sample that those alumni who had successfully launched ventures of their own or who were attempting to do so had a whole variety of values and motives that overlapped to a certain degree with other anchors. These people wanted to be autonomous, managerially competent, able to exercise their special talents, and build a fortune in order to be secure, but none of these seemed to be the *key* motive or value. Rather, these people seemed to have an overarching need to build or create something that was entirely their own product. It was self-extension—through the creation of a product or process that bears their name, a company of their own, a personal fortune that is a measure of their accomplishments—that seemed to be the key to these people. We observed that such people kept getting into new ventures and trying their hand at new kinds of projects. Yet as individuals they were always very central and very visible, hence the concept of creativity in the service of self-extension.

This anchor can express itself in a variety of ways, as was illustrated by the varying careers of the six entrepreneurs in our sample. One man has become a successful purchaser, restorer, and renter of town houses in a large city. While continuing in a regular job as a vice-president of an advertising agency, this man has built a real estate empire already worth a million dollars. Another man (see case illustration that follows) has built a series of new financial service organizations based on new applications of the computer in a part of the country where such services had not yet been developed. When he noticed a shortage of computer programmers, he opened a school for them in the area and brought one of his MIT alumni friends in to run the business. His own interests shifted to real estate development and land conservation, leading to the purchase of large tracts of land and a highly successful cattle ranch.

Another person has taken the gains from some early, fortunate investments in the stock market and become a venture capitalist looking for new products to develop. He tried manufacturing one such product and decided he did not have the energy to actually build an organization, preferring at this point to find the right products and people to invest in. One man has decided to work within a corporate framework, a large food and cereal company which is attempting to build overseas markets for special innovative products. He has taken a new protein product and is organizing the marketing, production, and sales of that product in several countries in South America and the Far East.

One man has built a successful planning/consulting firm which operates worldwide as a liaison between organizations, such as universities, and architects. The firm gets involved in major development projects such as the design and construction of a whole new campus. Finally, one man is operating as a free-lance consultant in marketing while looking for a product which would be worth his while to become involved with as an investor and manufacturer. In each of these six cases one senses the individual's strong need to be able to feel that whatever has come about can be clearly linked to his own creative efforts.

In putting so much emphasis on creativity in this group, I do not wish to minimize other motives such as technical/functional competence and desire for autonomy (the next anchor to be discussed). Such motives are clearly operating and visible when one talks to people in this group, but one senses that the thing which is driving them, the thing which they cannot give up, is the need to invent or create or build something on their own. And this need operates whether or not the person is successful, though I do not as yet have enough data about the effects of prolonged lack of success. What does the entrepreneurially oriented individual who does not succeed fall back on? If the creativity need is as strong as I am asserting it is, one might expect it to turn into hobbies or nonwork kinds of activities.

One may also ask whether successful entrepreneurs can settle for managerial roles as their organizations grow. Based on some 10-15 cases I have observed over the last several decades, I would assert that this is a difficult and sometimes impossible transition. The very creative talents which led to the initial building of the new organization can be dysfunctional at a time when the organization needs to stabilize itself, develop effective routines, and develop a strong professional management group for future succession.

Several patterns of handling this transition can be observed. The entrepreneur: (1) gets bored and turns the organization over to others while he or she starts up some new enterprise; (2) attempts to run the organization, has difficulty managing it, and is "forced" out by other managers or the board of directors; (3) develops a special role in the organization in order to continue with the creative impulse (e.g., Edwin Land of Polaroid continuing to invent new films and cameras as a kind of senior director of R&D); (4) learns how to play a senior-management role and exercises creative needs on special projects from time to time.

Which of these transitions will work best depends on the personalities of the people involved, the managerial talent available, and many specifics in the situation. What I wish to highlight here is that the needs to be a manager—to be analytically, interpersonally, and emotionally competent in order to exercise high levels of responsibility—are quite different from the creativity needs of the entrepreneur, and it is therefore predictable that a transition crisis of some sort will occur for either the entrepreneur or the organization or both. Since career anchors are so different, one may expect the careers of successful entrepreneurs and successful general managers to be quite different. For example, general managers may be more locked into given organizations than entrepreneurs.

Case Illustration: Cary Cresap

When I first met Cary, I described him as a handsome, pleasant articulate, warm person—full of smiles, sensitive, easy to talk to, and easy to like. Cary comes from a well-to-do family. His grandfather was a judge in a small town in Colorado and held some mining interests. Some of this family money was given to Cary by his grandmother, providing him with a $50,000 capital stake at the beginning of his career. His father was educated at Princeton and Oxford, obtaining graduate degrees in political science, but he went into investment banking in Denver because, as Cary describes him, he was very good in financial matters. After some years in investment work Cary's father took a managerial position in a Michigan firm and eventually invested in a small and dynamic electronics firm on the East Coast. He became president of this firm and has continued in this capacity. Cary's mother is a talented actress, musician, and painter and also has a college degree.

Cary was educated entirely in private schools, but he could not easily resolve whether to go into science or liberal arts. At Exeter he tried to avoid technical courses, but ended up in a chemistry course because it was the only one that fit into the schedule in such a way that he could take Friday afternoons off to go to the symphony! However, he discovered that he enjoyed chemistry. The choice of college was difficult because of a feeling of not wanting to disappoint his father. So he ended up going to Princeton, where he majored in engineering primarily because of strong advice that technical training would be good for a business career. By implication neither he nor his younger brother has ever considered anything other than some form of business for his life work.

Cary stuck with engineering and did passably at it, but was never interested enough to really do well. His interests in the liberal arts continued to be strong. He chose MIT as a graduate business school because of his technical background with its emphasis on problem solving, which he enjoyed particularly in the engineering courses. Cary's grades at Princeton were average, and his business-aptitude score for admission to MIT was slightly below average, but his grades at MIT were very high. He did his thesis in the area of organization studies, measuring organization climate. This reflects a strong theme in all of Cary's life—his concern for and preoccupation with people and good human relations. When asked "What makes a person a good person?" he answered as follows:

> Well, really a great deal of it, I would say, is being able to get along with people and relate to the group. I think everyone has his or her personal needs that have to be expressed, there is no question about that, prestige, and so on, but good people don't let these destroy more important objectives—getting things

accomplished with people. This also implies a good deal of sensitivity on the part of the individual to be able to understand what is going on and understanding others around us. One needs a certain amount of intelligence, naturally, to be able to know how to go about solving a problem that the group is trying to tackle, and to be able to steer the group back on course, and ask the right questions at the right time if things seem to be getting off base. The bad individual would probably be someone who is too authoritative, who puts his personal needs for prestige ahead of the group. He is insensitive to the operation of the group so he is unable to adjust to improve the operation of the group.

In addition to these strong people-oriented values, Cary repeatedly articulated some other values—a balanced life and harmony among career, family, and personal growth; being oneself and being natural; challenging work in which one's problem-solving skills could be exercised; and a high level of responsibility where one could relate results to one's own efforts. It is around this area that the clues to Cary's later entrepreneurial activities emerge. I asked him what his early memories were about choosing an occupation:

I had a lot of interests in my childhood. I ran a photography service and things like that. When I was in the sixth grade, I started my own newspaper. I had a printing press which I junked because it was too slow and bought a mimeograph machine. I got the kids in school to write articles for me and then set up an advertising department, soliciting parents and going around the town to local businesses. It had a pretty good circulation not only in the school but in the neighborhood where the parents of the kids lived. At the end of the year we took our earnings and gave a big party, rented a movie, and stuff like that. . . . Then the school took it over, which is one of the dirtiest tricks that ever happened [laughs] to me. They literally just took this over, saying they were starting their own newspaper and I could be editor, but you will have to give up your paper. After this it was amazing what a drop of interest there was not only on my part but on the part of all the students who had written for it . . . their contributions dropped off because they didn't feel that it was their paper anymore. . . .

Going back quite early, I had a stamp collection; at one time I was a photographer, developing my own pictures; I got interested in sailing not long after we moved east—eventually I taught sailing and ran the sailing program at camp. There was a little administrative experience too because I ran all the special activities of the camp, which gave me a good chance to be creative, which I enjoyed. I loved to rig up fantastic things for the kids to do, treasure hunts with real pirates and things like that. . . . Then I got interested in water skiing, and I ran my own school for a summer; I also was a fishing guide and boat captain one summer.

In high school and college, Cary tried various sports, but despite his talent did not engage in varsity sports because it began to take up too much of his time. He did develop his tennis game and played in tournaments for several years, however.

What strikes one about this set of memories is that whatever Cary took on, he seemed to end up running. It is as if leadership and ownership came so naturally to him that he hardly attached any special significance to them. In fact, when he talked about his future business career, he stated his ambition to be in a position of responsibility, e.g., the vice-president (not the president) of some small company. He did not talk of running his own business, though he saw his younger brother, who is also in business school, as "one of those get-rich-quick guys who is always coming up with new schemes."

Cary's major considerations in selecting his first job were that: (1) it enable him to obtain a draft deferment; (2) it be in the Denver region, where he and his new bride wanted to settle because of their love of the outdoors and the fact that the area had many opportunities for growth; and (3) the job itself provide challenge and an opportunity to learn. Cary saw his first few years in business as an "investment" in his future and imagined that he might move several times before finding his niche near the top of some small company. He rejected a good opportunity to become assistant to the president of a small company because it was located in Woodstock, N.Y., a community in which he could not image raising his future children. Instead, he took a job with a large aerospace company located in the Denver region (it also provided the needed draft deferment).

He joined the procedures section of the organization department as an associate analyst and had responsibility for analyzing and improving some of the many forms which were used for the company's administrative and control procedures. He was glad to have a job which would permit him to get around all the parts of a large organization so as to learn how such organizations work, but he also became disillusioned fairly quickly because of too much "internal politics," questionable ethical procedures in contract administration, and haphazard administration (Cary did not get a promised raise). As a result, he left the company after two years, having in the meantime established a number of valuable contacts in the Denver financial community. These contacts were established during the last six months of his work, while Cary was beginning to develop an informal financial consulting service.

Over the next ten years, Cary was involved in the founding, organizing, managing, and selling of some ten or more small companies: term insurance combined with mutual fund investment, the founding of a new mutual fund, a computer-based financial consulting service, a school for software programmers, a fresh-fish store (his only losing venture), real estate development combined with conservation work, an art gallery, and part ownership in several cattle ranches in Oregon. Cary's contribution to these enterprises was usually his ability to conceptualize, sell, and organize the new venture. He says he especially liked putting the whole package together and actually getting it off the ground, including the organization of the people who would be involved in it. Cary's brother was invited to come to Denver and join in various of these ventures, and the art gallery was a specific project for the brother and his wife because of their interest in art.

As Cary became financially successful, his interests turned increasingly to conservation work, and he was active in building an organization which combines the efforts of private interests with those of government and the environmentalists. He describes this as an uneasy alliance, but is very motivated to make the concept work. He has not been willing to take the presidency of this organization, but has become its secretary/treasurer. This work is especially important to Cary because of his continuing love of the outdoors. He spends a great deal of his time with his family going fishing, hunting, and riding. He has largely achieved his goal of a balanced life and financial independence. His various enterprises and his activities with his wife and three children occupy him happily and productively.

Most recently Cary has started some consulting jobs with an old friend, concentrating on educational institutions and an organization of Sioux Indians developing an educational program that will reduce the drop-out rate of Indian children. What seems to pervade all of these activities is the restless drive for novelty and challenge. Cary wants to use his creative skills on ever new kinds of projects, and as his business ventures are successful, he seems clearly to be turning to more public kinds of projects and organizations. Though he does not see a connection to his family background, one is also struck by the degree to which Cary's life mirrors the business dedication of his father and the artistic pursuits of his mother. Cary says that he had set as a goal for himself to make a million dollars by the time he was 35. He did not achieve this goal, setting his value at only $700,000 at the time of the interview, but he feels content with that level of success and sees himself as leveling off, working less hard, and spending more time on his family and personal pursuits.

Summary

None of the entrepreneurs in the panel talked explicitly about their creative needs. Yet it seemed obvious in reviewing their decisions and actions that they are very strong and determining. The need to be financially successful and independent is almost a measure of their accomplishment, not the primary goal. Only one of the six entrepreneurs remained in a large company. One might hypothesize that the creativity anchor almost requires the person to get into smaller ventures on his or her own in which creative accomplishment is easier to measure.

AUTONOMY AND INDEPENDENCE AS A CAREER ANCHOR

All of the seven alumni in this final group are seeking work situations in which they will be maximally free of organizational constraints to pursue their professional or technical/functional competence. They have found organizational life to be restrictive, irrational, and/or intrusive into their own private lives and have therefore left business or government organizations altogether in the search for careers that would permit more independence and autonomy. One person in this group has become a professor of business, one a free-lance writer, one a proprietor of a small retail business, and four are in various kinds of management or technical consulting, working either alone or as part of a relatively small firm.

Of course, not all consultants have autonomy as their career anchor, nor do all professors. Many of them are more anchored in technical/functional competence, and among professors one might find some who are anchored in security. It is also the case that some consultants view that job as a transition to higher-level managerial positions. What distinguishes the group under discussion here is that its members' need for autonomy is higher than their needs in other areas. They would decline opportunities to pursue their technical/functional work in organizational contexts such as government research laboratories even if such laboratories could give them better facilities or more resources to pursue their work. Autonomy is the anchor because autonomy is what they would not give up if forced to choose.

This group can be distinguished particularly from the technical/functional competence group in that the group members experience little conflict about missed opportunities for promotion and have little sense of failure or guilt about not aspiring higher. It is as if the decision to leave large organizations has been a kind of resolution of the conflict. The trade-off between status and high income versus freedom to pursue one's own life-style has been resolved to the person's satisfaction. All the members of this group appear to be happy in their work and enjoy their freedom. All have a sense of their own professional identity and can link the results of their work with their own efforts, a perception they share with the creativity group. In fact, on the surface it is not too easy to differentiate the autonomy and creativity groups, because the entrepreneurs also enjoy autonomy and freedom as they become successful. But as one listens to the entrepreneurs, it becomes obvious that they are much more preoccupied with building something, whereas the primary need of the autonomy seekers is to be on their own, setting their own pace, schedules, lifestyles, and work habits.

Case Illustration: Arthur Austin

Arthur Austin was a paradox from the start. When I first met him, he struck me as physically and intellectually different from most other management students whom I had encountered. I described him in 1961 as "small, somewhat awkward, sensitive, scholarly appearing, and clearly valuing cultural pursuits above money, power, or business success." During the interview he referred frequently to the importance of having broad interests, of being intellectual and knowledgeable, of having an in-depth grasp of one's total situation, and of having security to pursue one's personal goals. Arthur also valued analytical ability, clarity of thought, and the ability to express oneself clearly and concisely.

Yet his early career history was surprisingly conventional. After being educated in the Los Angeles public schools and developing some interests in "mechanical things" and science, Arthur applied to and was accepted by MIT. He was encouraged to try MIT by his father and liked the prospect of being able to combine engineering with business management. The interest in business dates back to junior high school, when Arthur started to subscribe to *Fortune Magazine* and read up on all kinds of businesses and industries.

Following his four years at MIT, Arthur decided he needed a period of work experience, so went to work for a large manufacturer of heavy equipment and machinery. This product and industry fascinated Arthur, who had always been interested in railroads and other transportation systems, such as the Los Angeles streetcar system. Because of his interest in economics, he went into the accounting section of one of the factories, working for the controller on various kinds of budget calculations.

The work was interesting for a while, but the community in upper New York State was rather isolated and the attitudes of management began to bother Arthur, so he decided after two and a half years to return to graduate school and invest in a management degree. He continued his interest in accounting and economics because he felt that through these subjects, one could most readily get the feel for the totality of a business. During his two years at the Sloan School, he was able to pursue another interest—his music. Arthur had played the flute in elementary and high school, had more or less given it up during college, but then played in a small symphony orchestra in the small town where he was employed. The realm of music fascinated him to the point that he wrote his master's thesis on the economics of the symphony orchestra.

Arthur was an only child. His father was a professor of physical education at a large urban university, and his mother was the assistant head of the engineering extension program in that same university. Arthur comments that his mother was in an unusual situation, since she had a master's degree in music and was strongly oriented toward music, but had begun to work as an administrative assistant in the 1940s and was now a successful academic administrator in a field far different from her own. As he looks back on the origin of his various interests, he can clearly account for the music, but not for the business or the railroad interests. He does comment that he was never interested in sports and seems to have rejected his father's occupation.

Following his MIT master's program, Arthur considered various accounting jobs and finally decided to return to the company he had originally worked for. He did not have a clear reason for this choice, though it violated several of his criteria, such as being a progressive manufacturing organization in an urban setting where cultural matters could be actively pursued. Perhaps he returned to the setting because he had acquired some experience there and was known to the people. He worked for the influential plant controller and felt quite productive at first because he knew the company's various financial systems and accounting procedures from his prior employment there. However, his work on various cost-reduction programs seemed to have no visible effects on the operation of the company, leading to frustration and a request to transfer after a year and a half.

Arthur next tried a job in data processing as a systems analyst. He had high hopes for this job, which involved systems and procedures writing, programming, straightening out of customer service operations, etc., but he found after two years that the conservative, complacent, and passive management undermined most of his efforts, so he got "disgusted and quit." Arthur stayed in upstate New York while he sent out resumes, let his friends know that he was looking, and went to various head-hunting agencies. After three months of looking, he located a job in the information systems group of a division of a large food company in the suburban New York area. He became a senior analyst with responsibilities to design cost-accounting systems, write manuals for clerical procedures, develop a planning system, and take care of various routine office administrative procedures.

The work was not very different from what he had done on his previous job, but the climate in the new company suited Arthur better, so he was initially much happier in the new situation. But within a year or so some of the same frustrations began to develop around feelings of lack of contribution, disillusionment with management, as well as a specific conflict with his boss, whom Arthur considered "unfair, devious, and manipulative."

At this point in his career Arthur faced a fundamental decision—whether to try another company or change his basic direction. After seven frustrating years in industry, he concluded that he should perhaps pursue further graduate work in economics, which had always been his main interest. He did not succeed in getting into any Ph.D. programs in economics, but he did get into the Ph.D. program in business administration at Columbia University and was able to pursue a course of study for four years involving "economics, behavioral science, conceptual and historical foundations of business, and institutional analysis." His Ph.D. thesis on the "technological innovations in the steam locomotive industry" enabled him to bring together his long-standing interests in technology, heavy machinery, and economics.

Arthur considered his four years at Columbia some of the happiest of his life. He enjoyed all the new learning and growth provided by graduate school, and he loved living in the New York City area, with all of its cultural advantages. Following graduation Arthur had two job opportunities in the New York State college system—one at Binghampton and one at Empire State College on Long Island. He chose to become an assistant professor of business at the latter in order to stay in the New York City area and because it seemed like the more challenging job. When I talked to him, he had been teaching for about a year and loving every minute of it. He sees himself as remain-

160 SECURITY, AUTONOMY, AND CREATIVITY AS CAREER ANCHORS

ing in an academic institution like the one he is in; he is totally happy there, pursuing the economics of heavy industry and music and fulfilling his various needs for cultural activities.

As I look back at Arthur's first 12 years of his career, it can best be described as a *search* to find a place where his values and talents could fit. He did not change all that much over the 12 years, but he learned a great deal about himself—what he is really like, what he values, and how he would or would not fit into various kinds of job situations. As he looked back on his industrial experience, he said that he would not give it up for anything, in spite of its frustrations, because he learned a great deal from it (albeit in a negative way).

It is not clear that Arthur would describe his own career anchor as "autonomy," but it is clear that he was not able to relax and function productively until he got himself into a situation in which he could define for himself his areas of interest and how to pursue them. The fact that he did not get his first academic job until his midthirties and had to settle for a very low salary clearly did not bother him. His success criteria are much more tied to feeling productive and pursuing his broad interests. Arthur also has remained a bachelor, which has reduced his needs for a high income. When I last talked to him, he had very much the feeling of having "gotten it all together."

SUMMARY

The Arthur Austin case illustrates a fundamental point about career anchors in general. They evolve through a process of searching, which involves testing oneself in various different kinds of settings and on different kinds of jobs until one has a clearer picture of one's talents, needs, and values. For some panelists these tests came early, and they were able to put their careers on a track early. For others, like Austin, it took almost ten years to get onto a track, and for some the search continues, even though I have already classified them. Especially in the group which is pursuing specific technical or functional competencies, one might find that further career experiences will reveal other layers of the personality.

Though it is my hypothesis that career anchors are the increasingly stable part of the person, it is clearly possible that career anchors themselves will change with new life experiences.

12
CAREER ANCHORS IN PERSPECTIVE: SOME
RELATED RESEARCH

This chapter will review a number of theoretical issues dealing with career anchors and review some related research findings which elaborate the concept.

ARE CAREER ANCHORS
APPLICABLE AT LATER CAREER STAGES?

The concept of career anchor was originally developed in the MIT panel study to make sense of the first five to ten years of alumni careers. Would one find similar kinds of anchors in midlife managers or senior managers? Though we have only limited evidence so far, efforts at the Sloan School to classify two other groups of managers have been encouraging. We gave a self-diagnostic biographical form (see Appendix 1) to 50 Sloan Fellows, a group of middle-level high-potential managers from government and industry, to determine whether a questionnaire could elicit material similar to what I had covered in my panel interviews. Each Fellow was asked to look over his pattern of answers and to classify himself into the anchor categories, based on a short lecture of what each anchor was intended to get at. It should be noted that in this group of managers there should be a strong bias toward seeing oneself in the managerial competence anchor. Since we permitted each person to rate himself, one could also give equal rating to several anchors. Table 12.1 shows the results based on 37 completed questionnaires.

Table 12.1
Self-Ratings of Career Anchors by 1975 Class of MIT Sloan Fellows

Managerial competence (MC) rated higher than other anchors	12
Technical/functional (TF) rated higher than other anchors	5
Autonomy (Au) rated higher than other anchors	3
Creativity (Cr) rated higher than other anchors	2
Security (Se) rated higher than other anchors	1
MC and TF tied for highest rating	3
MC and Cr tied for highest rating	3
MC and Au tied for highest rating	2
MC and SE tied for highest rating	2
MC, Au, and Cr in three-way tie	1
MC, TF, and SE in three-way tie	1
TF and Cr tied for highest rating	1
TF and Se tied for highest rating	1
Total number	37

Twenty-three of the 37 men who completed the questionnaire were able to give a highest rating to a single anchor category, and 12 of the 23 saw themselves, as one might expect, as higher in "managerial competence" than in other anchors. But considering that this group of middle executives was *selected* for managerial potential, there is a surprising spread of responses into the other anchor groups. Almost a third of the group sees technical/functional competence as *one* of several highest anchors, and a considerable number of people are spread across security, creativity, and even autonomy. Many respondents felt that they could not reduce their profile to a single anchor, but all felt that the given categories were sufficient to capture the major elements which preoccupied them when they thought about their careers.

To further investigate the utility of the career-anchor concept, we interviewed 20 older executives who were attending the MIT Sloan School Senior Executive Program (Hopkins, 1976). The major purpose of the interview was to study how people in this group, in the 45–55 age range, viewed the later stages of their careers, and to determine whether career anchors would discriminate among such views. Based on a short job history, aspirations for the future, and general comments about what they liked and did not like about their work, the interviewer and I were able to classify all 20 men unambiguously into a single anchor category.

Six of the men were managerially anchored; the remaining 14 were anchored in technical/functional competence. Four of these men also had strong security orientations. None was in the autonomy or creativity group, but one would not expect any in a group of senior managers from organizations. The surprising result is that even in this group, only 30 percent are clearly oriented toward general management. In both groups there was talk of early retirement and leveling off, more involvement with family, and starting up some small new ventures with their wives. Clearly a larger sample would be needed to see if differences as a function of anchors could be uncovered at this later career stage. But these two less formal studies do suggest that the concept has utility at later career stages and should be pursued.

IS THE CAREER-ANCHOR CONCEPT APPLICABLE TO OTHER OCCUPATIONS?

One can certainly see in most organizationally based occupations the kinds of people who are described in the panel study. In an attempt to extend the concept to a quite different occupation, Van Maanen analyzed police careers based on career anchors:

> If we study the careers of policemen from this perspective we find some young policemen who orient themselves toward their job such that the likelihood of career advancement is increased. For patrolmen with this *managerial competence* anchor, their goals in life center around promotions to responsible positions and the attainment of high rank in the police service. The person is perhaps attending college during off-duty hours, studying conscientiously for the various civil-service promotional examinations, and actively searching out ways to increase his opportunity to advance in rank. Interestingly . . . those patrolmen most concerned with achieving managerial responsibility were most likely to regard everyday patrol duties as unimportant and, therefore, to withdraw from them whenever possible.
>
> In contrast among policemen who are *technically/functionally* anchored, one finds here the "Cop's Cop." Whether he be a detective or patrolman, the person is seeking a role in which he can exercise his perceived police competence. Apprehending the criminal, or as the police are fond of saying, "Crook Catching" is the individual's *raison d'être* for being in the occupation. Promotion to a higher bureaucratic level holds little fascination for persons anchored here. Indeed, promotion may be viewed

with disdain, for it usually takes one away from the "action" on the street. Administrative and service duties are likely to be seen by this group as a frivolous waste of time, as can be detected in the oft-quoted motto of many officers, "We're cops, not pencil pushers or social workers."

Though it may have been overestimated as an anchor by the nonpolice public, *security* is nevertheless an identifiable anchor for some police officers. Those falling into this category will do whatever is required to maintain their job and, in fact, seek out certain organizational locations where stability, safety and routine characterizes their day-to-day tasks—communications, jail, records, etc. On the beat, these officers tend to adopt a public relations style with the public and fellow officers, valuing interpersonal dealings with people—discounting the importance of interactions with training programs, supervision and the courts, for they have little interest in career advancement.

The *creativity* anchor is the most difficult to clearly articulate in policemen, partly because of the few cases we have to deal with. However, in the police world, this anchor is crucial for understanding the so-called "rotten-apple" or "bent" policeman. Certainly, not all policemen have the situational opportunity to engage in graft, burglary, extortion, confidence games or the narcotics trade, but police do differ in regard to how far they will pursue such deviant behavior given the opportunity.

. . . Thus, the "grafter" who initiates and actively builds a parallel criminal career while engaged in police work can be seen to have a creative anchor in much the same way that the entrepreneur in the managerial world has a creative anchor.

Finally, in the police world we clearly see a category of careers that offer maximal *autonomy and independence*—the solitary radio-car officer who refuses to work with a partner, the traffic officer who values his motorcycling adventures most highly, or the undercover officer much romanticized by the popular press for his idiosyncratic, if not downright bizarre, approach to policing. Indeed, ex-policemen-turned-private-detective à la Sam Spade, Bulldog Drummond and Lew Archer are proto-types of the independent police career. Again, it is not a rejection of the technical/functional competence that marks this group, but rather it is the need for autonomy that must always be pursued. (Van Maanen and Schein, 1977, pp. 43–46)

The fact that one can categorize "careers within careers" in the manner that Van Maanen has done for policemen reinforces the point that within any given occupation or career, there are indeed very different kinds of people with different goals, life-styles, talents, and values. Sometimes these differences are masked by titles or by stereotypes of what kind of person we expect to see in any given kind of job. Yet if organizational and societal policies are to be realistic in terms of human needs, greater attention must be paid to the real differences that arise as we enter our careers. The evolution or development of career anchors early in the career is one such way to categorize these differences and to begin to understand them.

DO CAREER ANCHORS CORRELATE WITH OTHER ATTITUDE CHANGES?

In the panel study it was possible to test whether some of the attitude changes observed over the 10–12 years of the longitudinal study correlated in any way with career anchors. A comprehensive, 93-item attitude survey relating to all aspects of business was given to panelists at the beginning of the study and at the time of follow-up. The items were clustered into scales dealing with topics such as the degree to which one believes in managers as a group, the degree to which one accepts certain classical management principles such as "unity of command" or "authority must equal responsibility," the degree of belief in free enterprise, and so on (Schein, 1967). The clearest results showed up on the set of items which dealt with "classical management principles":

> "In industry there must always be unity of command so that individuals will not be subjected to conflicting authority."

> "The engineer in industry should give his primary allegiance to the company, he works for, not the engineering profession as such."

> "The human relations–group dynamics approach in industry tends to stifle the individuality of employees."

> "Responsibility should never exceed authority because the individual cannot be held responsible for what he does not control."

> "A clear-cut hierarchy of authority and responsibility is the cornerstone of the business organization."

Table 12.2 shows the scores of eight managerial and seven autonomous alumni at the time of graduate school and again at retesting. The scale went from 1 (strong agreement) to 4 (strong disagreement); the lower the score, the higher the degree of agreement.

Table 12.2
Scores of Managerial and Autonomous Alumni
On Belief in Classical Management Principles

| Managerial Anchor Alumni | | | Autonomy Anchor Alumni | | |
Person	1961	1973	Person	1961	1973
A	2.30	1.00 +	I	2.50	No data?
B	2.30	2.10 +	J	2.40	2.80 −
C	2.70	2.00 +	K	2.20	2.40 −
D	2.20	2.60 −	L	1.90	2.00 −
E	3.00	2.60 +	M	2.10	2.10 0
F	2.50	2.40 +	N	2.20	2.00 +
G	2.60	1.80 +	O	2.20	3.10 −
H	2.20	2.20 0			
Mean	2.48	2.16*		2.17	2.40

*The lower the score, the stronger the agreement with classical management principles.

As can be seen in the table, six of the eight managerial alumni be came more accepting of classical management principles, whereas four of the six autonomous alumni on whom we had complete data became *less* accepting of these principles. In other words, those alumni who moved into the organizational world changed their beliefs in the direction of the prevailing beliefs in that world; those who moved out of it moved from initial high acceptance of these beliefs toward a more neutral position.

Table 12.3 shows similar results on a set of items which reflect a generally positive attitude toward management as an occupation:

"Managers usually deal with people in a democratic manner."

"A man who is willing to work hard in industry does not need a union to protect him."

"The good manager should rely on explanation and persuasion rather than direct orders."

"To succeed in business, one must be able to take criticism without being hurt by it."

"Most managers are delightful people to know socially."

"The most important objective of a company is to manufacture and sell products which are useful to society."

Table 12.3

Scores of Managerial, Autonomous, and Creativity Alumni on Management Orientation

Managerial Anchor Alumni				Autonomous Anchor Alumni				Creativity Anchor Alumni			
Person	1961	1973		Person	1961	1973		Person	1961	1973	
A	1.83	1.83	0	I	2.25	No data	?	P	2.42	No data	?
B	2.25	2.17	+	J	2.25	2.17	+	Q	2.92	1.33	+
C	3.25	1.83	+ +	K	1.83	2.17	−	R	2.67	2.33	+
D	2.42	2.50	−	L	1.67	2.00	−	S	2.50	2.33	+
E	1.83	1.67	+	M	1.67	2.00	−	T	2.83	2.50	+
F	2.17	2.17	0	N	2.33	2.50	−	U	2.17	2.17	0
G	2.50	2.33	+	O	2.20	2.83					
H	1.83	2.33	−								
Mean	2.26	2.10*			1.99	2.28			2.58	2.12	

*The lower the score, the stronger the management orientation.

Four of the eight managerial alumni became more promanagement, two were already strongly pro and remained there, whereas two moved toward a mean position. Four of five creativity alumni moved strongly toward promanagement, as would be expected. In contrast, only one autonomous alumnus became more promanagement; five moved toward or past the mean.

The final scale, which reflects real socialization, deals with the degree to which the person feels that one can be a manager without having to compromise one's values or ethics (see Table 12.4). The items comprising this scale are:

"The good manager must be willing to compromise his own ethics and morals to some degree in order to get his job done."

"Managers often have to treat people unfairly to get their job done."

"Religious teachings cannot be strictly observed in the business setting."

"Most managerial jobs require a person to compromise his ethics or morals to some degree."

Six of eight managerial alumni changed in the promanagement direction, whereas only two of six autonomous alumni changed in that direction. On the other hand, four of the autonomous alumni and only two managerial alumni became more cynical about management. The creativity group is divided on this scale.

In summary, after 10–12 years in their careers, the managerially oriented alumni show a greater faith in management, a greater acceptance of classical management principles, and a greater belief that management as an occupation can be moral and ethical. In contrast, the "autonomy" group, which has left formal organizational life, shows a drop in faith in management, less acceptance of classical principles, and less of a belief that management can be moral. The creativity group tends to resemble the managerial group more than the autonomy group.

The numbers are too small to make statistical tests, and these kinds of results did not show up on all of the scales, but the point can be made that observed attitude changes make more sense when one looks at the group in terms of anchors than when one averages all of the alumni together. The process of socialization apparently does not operate in the same way across all business careers, but reflects the particular characteristics of that career. The career-anchor concept may be one way to classify career types so as to shed light on the per-

Table 12.4
Scores of Managerial, Autonomous, and Creativity Alumni on Management as a Moral Occupation

Managerial Anchor Alumni				Autonomy Anchor Alumni				Creativity Anchor Alumni			
Person	1961	1973		Person	1961	1973		Person	1961	1973	
A	2.13	1.00	+	I	2.38	No data	?	P	2.00	1.75	+
B	2.63	1.75	+	J	1.50	1.75	−	Q	1.88	2.38	−
C	1.63	1.25	+	K	2.50	1.75	+	R	1.75	1.00	+
D	2.13	1.75	+	L	2.25	1.75	+	S	2.75	1.75	+
E	2.50	2.25	−	M	1.67	2.25	−	T	2.25	3.00	−
F	2.00	2.25	+ +	N	2.25	2.50	−	U	2.50	2.75	−
G	3.50	1.75	−	O	2.13	3.00	− −				
H	2.75	3.00									
Mean	2.40	1.88*		Mean	2.03	2.17		Mean	2.19	2.10	

*The lower the score, the stronger the belief that management can be moral.

son's total set of attitudes and on the changes which may be expected during the socialization process.

DO THE FIVE CAREER ANCHORS
COVER ALL CAREER TYPES?

The answer to this question cannot be settled definitively until more detailed longitudinal research is done on other occupations or larger samples. The five categories used in the MIT study were sufficient to categorize all of the panelists in that study, and these same categories could be used to classify most policemen. However, one could *imagine* other anchors, as follows.

1. *Basic identity.* Especially in some lower-level occupations, one's title, uniform, and other trappings of office come to be a fundamental basis for self-definition. It may well be that for some people, just to achieve and sustain an occupational identity functions throughout their lifetime as an anchor. Such people would seek occupational situations which would clearly define their role *externally* through titles, uniforms, badges, or other highly visible means, even though such external symbols might have relatively little to do with the work they perform. Identification with a powerful or prestigious employer often serves this function. For example, when slaughterhouse employees were asked about their line of work, they said they worked for Swift and Co.; similarly, low-level civil servants say they work for the United States government, and campus custodians or janitors say they work for Harvard University or MIT, for example. This anchor would be similar to security as an anchor, but implies even a more deeply felt need for basic identity (Van Maanen and Schein, 1977).

2. *Service to others.* Social work, some aspects of medicine, some aspects of teaching, and some aspects of the ministry allow the person to express basic needs, talents, and values to work with others in a helping role; the interpersonal competence and helping are ends in themselves rather than means to an end, as in the managerial anchor group. It might be noted that all of the research so far on career anchors has been done on men, and it has been suggested that were women included, one might find that a higher percentage of them would be anchored in the more affiliative, service kinds of career pre-occupations because of their prior socialization to be more affiliative.

3. *Power, influence, and control.* It is not clear from the research done thus far whether needs for power and a talent in exercising it are a separate anchor for some people or are a portion of what we have

described as the managerial competence anchor. The people we have studied so far seem to combine power needs and talents with other needs and talents such that a general managerial orientation ends up being a better description than pure power of their concerns. However, one might find among politicians, teachers, doctors, and ministers some who find that their anchor is indeed the exercise of control and influence over others.

4. *Variety.* There may be people in all occupations who are restless spirits, but not in the same sense that the entrepreneur is one. Rather, one may find people whose talents cover a wide spectrum and whose basic needs and values are to express the full range rather than to exercise more limited talents in depth over a shorter period of time. Some professors, journeymen, tradespeople, consultants, managers, and troubleshooters say that what attracts them and keeps them in their careers is the endless variety of challenges they encounter. Flexibility of response is one of their major values, boredom one of their major fears. It is perhaps out of this group that one generates midlife career switchers who have not failed, plateaued, or otherwise "messed up." It is simply part of their life cycle to seek variety, and they may end up in what Driver (in press) has called "spiral careers."

CONCLUSION

Career anchors are *not* simply a new list of motivational constructs to be compared with those of Maslow, McClelland, or other motivational or value theorists. Career anchors clearly *reflect* the underlying needs and motives which the person brings into adulthood, but they also reflect the person's values and, most important, *discovered talents.* By definition there cannot be an anchor until there has been work experience, even though motives and values may already be present from earlier experience. It is the process of *integrating into the total self-concept what one sees oneself to be more or less competent at, wanting out of life, one's value system, and the kind of person one is that begins to determine the major life and occupational choices throughout adulthood.* The career anchor is a *learned* part of the self-image, which combines self-perceived motives, values, and talents. What one learns is not only a function of what one brings to the work situation, but also reflects the opportunities provided and the feedback obtained. Consequently, the anchor is determined to some degree by actual experiences, not only by the talents and motives latent in the person.

The main thrust of the last three chapters has been an analysis of the early career in terms of the gradual formation of career anchors.

Whether or not the anchor concept will ultimately prove to be a useful way of describing the first five to ten years of the career remains to be seen. But in any case, there is little question that this period is a time of consolidation of one's self-image, of finding out what one likes and what one is good at, and of developing a role that will be satisfying and rewarding.

The most important thing we learn from the panel study is that the road to self-discovery is a very rocky one, with many detours and choice points to be negotiated. What may look like a fairly clear path from the point of view of an organization's "bringing along its technical talent" or "developing its managers" often proves to be a very tortured process for the people negotiating the path. For many of them, one or more changes of organization are required before they find the kind of setting which matches their needs, talents, and values and in which they feel they can *be themselves* (Super, 1957). What is, from the point of view of the organization, simply a process of "turnover" may be, from the point of view of the individual, a major transition crisis involving a search for one's occupational niche. What may, from the point of view of the organization, be simply a process of learning a specialty and becoming an effective contributor prior to making the transition to management may be, from the point of view of the individual, a series of major self-confrontations around what one's technical/functional specialty is to be, how wedded one will remain to it, whether or not one likes management or is any good at it, and what to do if one's values are out of line with those of the employing organization.

Most people do negotiate the early part of the career and do establish themselves on a path, though sometimes with little insight and sometimes at the expense of some of their own needs and talents. Later career crises and how they are handled will in turn be related to how this early career establishment was accomplished, making it especially important to understand career anchors and their effects.

13
MIDCAREER: MAKING IT,
LEVELING OFF, OR STARTING OVER

Midcareer is that broad band, lasting as long as 20 years or more, between being reviewed for "tenure" and being considered for or considering early retirement. Once the period of learning and testing is over, "the die is cast"; the person is expected to make whatever contribution he or she is capable of making to the organization. Whether or not there is a *formal* process of granting tenure, midcareer begins with some messages that one has "made it" into a status of permanent member or that one is "not making it" and ought to start looking around for alternatives. The message that one has made it can carry the further implication that one has high potential, with much progress foreseen in the future toward high leadership positions, or that one is perceived as a steady contributor for the remainder of the career, with the expectation of occasional salary increments but no more promotions.

This chapter will examine first why there may be problems in this stage of the career, even a "midcareer crisis." Second, I will examine some of the underlying reasons why such problems arise, how they interact with the more general problems of "midlife," and how they can be dealt with.

WHAT ARE THE PROBLEMS OF MIDCAREER/MIDLIFE?

When we speak of "problems," we can think of several kinds of symptoms which arise in midlife and which give us clues to the fact that a problem may exist. *First,* many people in midlife report getting depressed and discouraged, running out of gas, losing motivation. Alternating with or replacing periods of depression may be periods of euphoria—bursts of energy directed toward hobbies or new social relationships and/or sexual adventures. *Second*, people report all kinds of career-related issues or problems. Their jobs no longer excite them, they feel trapped in organizations or in careers from which there is no place to go, or they make sudden, dramatic career shifts if that is economically feasible. *Third*, people report all kinds of family problems. Adolescents put new kinds of demands on their parents; they are less willing to move and are more willing to question and confront parents about their own life-style, thus forcing a reexamination of something that may never have been thoroughly examined in the first place. As wives lose their central role as mothers, they place new demands on their husbands, and this may occur at a time when the husband is emotionally least prepared to cope with such demands.

The problems of midcareer can best be delineated by first reviewing and elaborating the major *issues* which people face at this time in their careers, as outlined in Table 4.1. These issues are not presented in order of importance, and I am not implying that everyone will face all of them. Rather, I am trying to give a fairly full picture of what people *may* have to deal with as a basis for a deeper understanding of the emotional dynamics of this period.

Specializing versus Generalizing

In every career there is a kind of internal logic from being a learner to being a contributor in some special area, reflecting one's special skills which have become refined and deepened during the early career. Whether one makes one's contribution as an engineer, financial specialist, foreman, or salesperson, the early career can be seen as a time when one gets very good at what one is doing and makes one's contribution through the exercise of those highly developed skills. One major problem of midcareer is to decide whether one's long-range contribution will hinge on the continued exercise of those skills or whether one will generalize in some way or another, either by broadening one's specialist role or by getting into administration and management, which may change the role fundamentally and, possibly, irreversibly. For example, the successful engineer, salesperson, or financial analyst must decide at some point whether to: (1) accept a supervisory role if it is offered, (2) allow skills to become to some degree obsolete and move toward more of a project leader/mentor role, or (3) define the long-range career as simply becoming more and more skilled in the particular technical area of performance.

These decisions will, of course, be influenced by both internal and external factors. To the extent that one recognizes it, one's career anchor will be a major internal source of constraint and guidance, and one's accumulated experience and wisdom will enhance one's potential contribution. The organization's perception of one's talents and the value of one's experience will be a major external source of constraint and guidance. One may not perceive one's own talent for teaching others and therefore resist certain kinds of leader roles; or the organization may not perceive one's needs to be more of a generalist (or alternatively to remain a skilled technical contributor) and therefore limit our opportunities. What is important for both career occupants and managers to realize is the complexity of both the specializing and generalizing roles. There are many ways to fulfill the career anchor of technical/functional competence, and some of those ways involve becoming more of a generalist *within* one's broad area of competence. Becoming a generalist need not involve a shift in career anchor toward managerial competence; instead, one may fulfill one's needs to generalize in various kinds of advisory, mentoring roles which take advantage of one's accumulated experience and wisdom without taking on formal administrative or managerial duties.

Establishing an Organizational Identity and an Area of Contribution

Probably one of the most threatening aspects of midcareer is the feeling that one will be "lost in the shuffle" or will become a nameless "man in a gray flannel suit" not noticed by either one's employing organization or those outside it. As organizations become larger, the problem of feeling anonymous and unnoticed will probably increase, especially in careers involving fairly routine, repetitive work or work that is not clearly identifiable in terms of cultural metaphors. This lack of definition is the problem for assembly-line workers, clerks, and middle-level managers who have neither a clearly identifiable job nor a clearly identifiable rank, such as "vice-president," to fall back on. Not only does this make it hard to tell one's family and friends what one does, but at a more fundamental level it becomes difficult to identify for oneself what one's area of contribution is and whether one's efforts make any difference to anybody.

If one cannot solve this problem within the career, one consequence may well be a loss of work involvement and a shift to more concern with self-development off the job and with one's family. As Katz (1977) has pointed out, people who are in the same job for too long (five to ten years or longer) cease to be "responsive" to the job itself and therefore put more of their focus on organizational rewards such as pay, benefits, security, working conditions, and the like. Not having a clear organizational identity may be especially troubling if one is also experiencing other midlife problems which raise more general identity questions of who one really is and what one really has accomplished. For organizations, an immediate implication would be to rethink their policy of how they give "recognition" to employees and managers during midcareer, because such recognition may have special significance at this time. The need for recognition may be related not only to one's particular line of work, but to one's career stage as well.

The Dream versus the Reality

Many people in midcareer/midlife engage in self-confrontation, asking themselves the deep question of whether their career progress has been consistent with their goals, ambitions, and dreams and if not, how to resolve the discrepancy. Much of the writing on midlife emphasizes the problem of disappointment and depression when one discovers that one has not achieved what one had hoped to achieve. I think it is equally important to treat as a "problem" the case of people who find that they have risen higher than they expected to and have become locked into a success pattern which they cannot give up or of people who have found that their career anchors are quite different from what they had initially assumed, leading to the recognition that they are in fact less ambitious than they had assumed or want different things out of their career than their early ambitions had dictated. Though none of the panelists in the MIT study are yet in midcareer situations, one can already see the latent problem for those who have achieved a great deal by age 40 and for those who find themselves questioning whether they wanted to be managers in the first place. These problems will differ by career anchor—the creative or autonomous person will probably find it easier to redefine goals and switch to other career pursuits because the external constraints will be fewer; the managerial- and security-oriented people will be the most "locked in" because their pattern of success depends more heavily on organizational rewards and opportunities; the technical/functional competence people will probably show the greatest variation in adapting to midcareer problems, since their options are more variable, e.g., continued performance in an organization, consulting, or teaching.

The reassessment of one's dreams also clearly exposes the trade-offs one has made in the early career among career, family, and self-development. If one has been totally absorbed with work and spent too little time on family and personality development, will one feel that it has all been worth it, or will one feel that one has paid a price without adequate compensation? If it is possible, in terms of internal and external constraints, to redesign one's life at this point—to become more or less work involved, to become more or less accommodative to the family, to redefine career direction or change one's ambitions—midlife can be a period of high growth and personal development. For many women, this is their first opportunity to become work involved, because family pressures may be lessening. On the other hand, if one is feeling "locked in," one may simply have to maintain one's illusions, fight off depressive feelings, and adjust to the situation. One danger, however, is the assumption that one is locked in when one is *not in fact* locked in and fails to test what changes might be possible, what "small adjustments" could be made (see Chapter 6).

Accepting the Responsibilities of "Mentoring"

The problems of becoming a mentor are sometimes less visible than other problems, but for many people are a source of considerable stress. As their careers progress and they define areas of contribution, it is inevitable that others, especially younger people, will begin to look to older persons for guidance, leadership, support, help, and sponsorship of ideas. This expectation on the part of younger, less experienced employees will arise whether or not the midcareer person is in a formal supervisory role. He or she will be asked by new employees how to get things done, how things work, what the norms of the organization are, and so on, unless he or she specifically develops a reputation of being unhelpful or aloof.

The problem arising from this situation is that the older person may not want the responsibility of being a mentor and/or may not exercise it responsibly if it is accepted. Obvious examples are the older employee who (1) tells new employees all the bad things which will happen to them (usually based on personal disillusionment); (2) gives misinformation or incorrect guidance without realizing it; (3) uses the mentoring relationship to build up personal alliances and political power; (4) plays the role of the child and becomes more dependent on the younger employee; or (5) uses whatever power and experience he or she has to "put down" the new employee as some kind of initiation rite ("I had to go through it, so everyone else should also have to go through it").

From a subjective point of view, the issue is identifying one's own needs for mentoring and finding an acceptable way of meeting those needs. If they are high, how can one get into more supervisory or teaching roles; if they are low, how can one avoid getting into situations where one's impatience or lack of motivation to be mentor would become destructive? What the midcareer person must avoid is getting trapped in mentoring relationships which do not fit the person's needs or talents.

Varieties of Mentoring Roles.   The concept of mentor itself needs to be carefully analyzed so that the full range of possible work assignments which involve mentoring can be explored. Several kinds of mentoring roles can be clearly distinguished:

1. *The mentor as teacher, coach, or trainer*—a person about whom the younger person would say, "That person taught me a lot about how to do things around here."

2. *The mentor as a positive role model*—a person about whom the younger person would say, "I learned a lot from watching that person in operation; that person really set a good example of how to get things done."

3. *The mentor as a developer of talent*—a person about whom the younger person would say, "That person really gave me challenging work from which I learned a great deal; I was pushed along and forced to stretch myself."

4. *The mentor as an opener of doors*—a person who makes sure that the young person is given opportunities for challenging and growth-producing assignments, who fights "upstairs" for the young person, whether or not the younger person is aware of it.

5. *The mentor as a protector (mother hen)*—a person about whom the younger person would say, "That person watched over me and protected me while I learned; I could make mistakes and learn without risking my job."

6. *The mentor as a sponsor*—a person who gives visibility to his or her "proteges," who makes sure that they have good "press" and are given exposure to higher-level people so that they will be remembered when new opportunities come along, with or without the awareness of the younger person.

7. *The mentor as a successful leader*—a person whose own success ensures that her or his supporters will "ride along on his or her coattails," who brings those people along.

Several of these roles require the mentor to be in a position of power—opener of doors, protector, sponsor, and/or leader. Some combination of these roles is what is often referred to in organizations as a "godfather" or sponsorship system, whereby every young employee has someone older "looking out for him or her." However, it is important to recognize that the teacher, role model, and developer roles do not require high formal position or power, yet are also powerful mentoring roles. The person who has leveled off can often fulfill those latter roles very well and achieve considerable satisfaction in doing so.

Achieving a Proper Balance of Involvement in Work, Family, and Self-Development

A reappraisal of one's area of contribution, the discovery of one's career anchor, a more realistic sense of how far one is going to go in a career, and a rethinking of one's criteria for success all lead to a reassessment of how "work involved" and "accommodative" to family and self-oriented activities one is going to be in the remainder of one's life. Though the decisions made now may not be permanent, they nevertheless will represent a major commitment to the future. Facing these decisions can be a source of great stress, because trade-offs may have to be made. Pushing forward full steam in the career to achieve a high-level leadership position may mean further sacrifices in the family arena; accepting a reduced level of ambition may mean financial sacrifices and a changed life-style, which may bring new problems in the family, e.g., rethinking what kind of education one can give to one's children; deciding to pursue a second career which may be more personally fulfilling or in other ways enhancing one's self-development may mean sacrifices in both family involvement and life-style. Many people in midlife turn to highly involving hobbies, buy houses or farms to fix up, or in other ways get into very personal agendas which remove them from both family and traditional career concerns.

It is important for both the individual and the organization managing that individual to recognize that these decisions are complicated and involve work, family, and self-interaction. It is not enough to think about any one area alone in trying to resolve the problem, because the costs and benefits cut across the areas.

Maintaining a Positive Growth Orientation

The final, and perhaps most difficult, problem of midcareer and midlife to be reviewed here is that of maintaining a positive, growth-oriented attitude toward life. Many of the forces identified above are difficult to deal with, and people may be strongly tempted to become complacent and resigned to their "fate," even when clear options for further growth and development are available. LeShan, in an interesting book called *The Wonderful Crisis of Middle Age* (1973), identifies as one of the biggest reasons for such complacency what she calls "the heavy burden of our masks." We spend several decades building assumptions about ourselves, illusions which serve to maintain our self-esteem, and we define our relationships with family members, friends, and work associates in terms of these illusions or masks. As sociologists such as Goffman (1955) have pointed out, it is these presented parts of ourselves which constitute what we call "face," the claims we make for ourselves, and it is in the nature of the social order to help one another to protect and maintain "face." "Loss of face," the falling away of our masks, the destruction of our illusions, is not only a threat to the individual, but also challenges the social order in that we might find it difficult in social relationships to deal with others' realities. There are thus powerful forces operating in all relationships to maintain our own masks or facades, *and to help others maintain theirs.*

The problem of midlife growth, then, is how to establish relationships in which masks can be dropped, at least partially, to permit a realistic reexamination of one's assumptions about one's self, career, needs and values, relationships with family members and friends, and, most important, options and areas of choice. As Chapter 6 argued, we always have options and choices, but sometimes it is very difficult to locate them, and we may need the help of others in this process.

These, then, are some of the *problems* of midcareer and midlife. Let us look next at some of the *underlying dynamics* which cause them.

THE PSYCHOLOGY OF MIDLIFE

What goes on psychologically in midlife in the area of emotional dynamics, career and work issues, and family relationships? What are the psychological problems underlying some of the issues referred to above, and most importantly, what can the person do about such problems if they exist?

The problems of midlife and midcareer derive from the following:

1. The emotional realization of one's own mortality and that time is finite;

2. The rekindling of adolescent impulses and the resurfacing of adolescent conflicts;

3. The changing relationship to one's children and spouse as the children become adults;

4. The anxiety resulting from the realization of limited opportunity—the decreasing numbers of career options and opportunities because of the narrowing organizational pyramid and because of societal norms and stereotypes which work against older people.

When and how these factors come into play in any given person's's career will, of course, vary immensely. They may come in serial fashion or all at once. Some of the factors may pose no problems; others will cause crises. All we can do is to identify the problems sufficiently clearly to make it possible for each reader to diagnose his or her own situation so as to improve coping with whatever problem is at hand.

Recognition of Own Mortality

Most people are aware of death, but the emotional recognition of one's own mortality probably does not arise until midlife, because it does not become a salient emotional issue until a friend, spouse, parent, or child dies or until one contracts some illness which brings one's own frailty clearly into consciousness. Whether or not one fears death per se, its possibility brings home clearly the fact that one's life is not infinite, that one's days are numbered. This recognition in turn stimulates questions about whether or not one has accomplished in one's career and life what one set out to do and how much time remains to do it. A reassessment of one's ambitions and an assessment of one's accomplishments in comparison to one's dreams often occur as a result and often produce depression when one realizes that there may not be the time, energy, or opportunity to accomplish all one has hoped to do.

Early in the career one can ignore time and operate by the assumption that there is plenty of it to fulfill one's ambitions. By the time one reaches age 40 or 50, however, half or more of one's career is already over, and there may be little time left to do what one hoped to do. Sensing that one's energy level is not as high as it used to be, that one's physical health is not as reliable, and that one's ability to learn and adapt may be slowing down creates additional emotional burdens that must be worked through. Most people do successfully work through the feelings aroused by such circumstances and reach an adaptive solution which permits some tranquility, but the issues cannot really be avoided or swept under the rug. They must somehow be dealt with and worked through.

Feelings about mortality can be complicated by illness in one's own parents and the emotional recognition that one can no longer be dependent on them; in fact, they may become dependent, an emotional task for which one may be entirely unprepared. The financial drain of visits to parents, managing the transition of their independence to dependence—e.g., their moving in with one or having to put them into nursing homes—all can be emotionally taxing, reducing the energy and time available for career-oriented activities.

Rekindling of Adolescent Feelings and Conflicts

One of the major findings of studies of adult development is that how a person copes in later stages of life is a reflection of earlier coping styles and mechanisms. There is a kind of continuity to life. Earlier feelings do not disappear; they go underground or are transformed, but can be rekindled and can resurface. I have observed this most clearly in midlife managers whose own children are going through adolescent crises. The kinds of identity or role confusion with which their children are coping may resurface in the parent, raising doubts and anxieties about present choices. The freedom the adolescent has to choose a career and life path may be envied by the parent who experiences "wanderlust" but feels locked in; the anxieties the child experiences may restimulate anxieties about repressed impulses in the parent. The adolescent often precipitates these anxieties directly by challenging the values, accomplishments, and illusions of the parents. When the adolescent asks why the parent is working so hard, what it is all for, this can precipitate a real crisis for the family, because it challenges old assumptions which have not been rethought for years.

The consequences of all of these feelings for the career situation of the parent is that he or she may become highly preoccupied with self-concerns and self-development. Work and its requirements, organizational rules and policies—all may suddenly appear to be silly or restrictive. Just as the adolescent may view the adult world as full of inconsistencies, hypocrisies, and absurdities, so adults can suddenly find themselves seeing these same things in their own world. This recognition will not mean automatic rejection of the norms and values which are perceived, but may lead to a reexamination of them in the light of the person's own values and desires. Out of such reexamination may come new ambitions, new criteria for success, and possibly the decision to reduce career/work involvement. If the person recognizes elements of identity or needs which have not ever been dealt with, a more drastic decision to pursue a second career or a hobby may result. Most of us have unused potential, and many people find that midlife is a kind of last chance to redirect one's life to try to do something with that unused potential.

Tensions Deriving from Changing Relationship to One's Children, Spouse, and Parents

As the children grow up and leave home, several things tend to happen in the typical family: (1) the parenting role disappears, leaving unused emotional and physical energy which must be attached to new activities and roles; (2) all the daily routines around meals, recreation, vacations, etc., have to be altered; (3) the combination of (1) and (2) leads to the necessity to redistribute emotional energy among a smaller number of people in the home; where parents and one or more children were living together, the presence of only husband and wife requires a redefining of their relationship *to each other;* (4) there is a sharply reduced financial burden, since educational and support expenses are no longer in the picture, and these resources are freed up for other activities, such as travel and/or a reexamination of career goals, since financial ambitions can now be reduced.

Some of the more common effects of these circumstances are already the subject of much popular writing and TV shows. Thus, for example, the struggle of the housewife to find a new and meaningful role to replace the mothering and housekeeper role; the tension between husband and wife as they confront each other without the children as an emotional buffer or common interest between them; the efforts to define new common interests and resurrect or build new common activities (a surprisingly large number of midlife executives talk about going into business *with their wives*); the husband's scaling down of work involvement to permit the wife to go back to school and pursue a career of her own ("now its your turn"); the discovery by both partners that the one fully involved in career (typically the husband) may have developed himself more fully as a person and that the wife feels less developed and consequently discouraged and depressed (a gap may have grown between them which neither really noticed until the children were physically gone); more drastic adaptations such as separation, divorce, extramarital adventures, or more drastic psychological consequences such as severe depression and various forms of illness.

The feelings which arise with children and spouse can be complicated by further feelings deriving from changed relationships to one's own parents. The death or illness of parents, their possible dependence on one, and other demands they may make may have

184 MIDCAREER: MAKING IT, LEVELING OFF, OR STARTING OVER

effects for which one is not prepared. Long-repressed feelings toward one's parents may now resurface and have to be dealt with—anger for having been controlled, guilt about having failed to meet parental standards, pity, or resentment. In addition to having to physically take care of and become reinvolved with one's parents, one may also have to relive and deal with inner turmoil stimulated by that reinvolvement.

Anxiety Resulting from Realization
of Increasingly Limited Opportunities

One of the most difficult psychological issues of midlife is the realization that career opportunities are in fact becoming more limited as one ages and that social norms operate to make it more and more difficult for the older person to exercise various vocational options. Even if one is on a success path climbing to the higher levels of a company or achieving higher status in a technical/functional career, there is the reality of the narrowing pyramid and the realization that the available slots become fewer and fewer as one nears the top of an organization or a profession. For those who feel they have leveled off or, worse, feel they are not making it, this anxiety may become severe. To be laid off in midlife is a traumatic event even if one's job was boring and going nowhere, because of the real possibility that one might not find anything else.

How to take such a potentially traumatic situation and turn it around into a growth-producing situation is one of the major challenges confronting human resource management. Some companies are exploring more systematic counseling to aid "outplacement," some volunteer or self-help organizations are springing up to provide services for midlife managers or engineers who have been laid off, some educational institutions have begun to provide specific courses to help midlife people rethink their career options and redefine themselves in more positive terms, and some government-sponsored projects are providing money for counseling centers, educational programs, and half-way houses to help tide over the person between jobs. Whenever I have talked to people who have attended such programs or to those who manage them, I have been told that the biggest problem is the psychological one of dealing with anxiety and destroyed illusions. The person has to be helped to build a new self-image and possibly new skills to reenter the labor market with a positive orientation. Such rebuilding often involves rethinking the issues: Am I a specialist or a generalist? Do I want to be an administrator? What are my special areas of contribution? What is my career anchor? Do I want to be an individual contributor or identify with an organization? How much do I need security and "tenure"? How much am I willing to be mobile? What kinds of mentoring needs do I have, and how can they best be played out?

The mentoring needs are especially important to think through clearly, because some of the most radical yet productive shifts in career hinge on a clear recognition of one's needs to be a mentor. For example, I have recently met a number of successful managers who chose in midlife to become either teachers or career counselors and reported that in the new role they were able to use much of their acquired knowledge and skill but in a setting that was free of many of the constraints of their former organizational settings.

CONCLUSION

The underlying psychological problems dealing with recognition of mortality, rekindling of adolescent conflicts, changed relationships with family members, and anxiety around limited future opportunities fuel the issues and problems of midcareer and midlife. There is much going on in both midcareer and midlife which creates stress and provides opportunities for growth. Crises can be viewed as opportunities if people can find ways of getting in touch with their feelings and working through them to new resolutions. Sometimes this process will require professional help from counselors and psychiatrists; sometimes it will be enough to work things through with spouses, family members, and close friends. What should be avoided is denial. Growth is unlikely to occur if the person suppresses and denies whatever feelings have been generated by the various forces reviewed above. Self-confrontation may lead to a conscious decision not to rock the boat, not to make major changes. Such a conscious decision to accept the status quo is probably much better than drifting along without any insight into why one is drifting.

In Chapter 15, I will make some comments about how organizations can respond from a human resource management point of view to some of the issues of mid- and late career. The intention here has been to identify these issues from the individual's point of view and to show that they are normal and "predictable" crises of adulthood which we all share (Sheehy, 1976).

A Comment on Late-Career Issues

The problems of the later career, retirement, and postretirement could fill a whole volume, but basically they are extensions of the problems identified in this chapter. In the outline in Chapter 6 they are reviewed in minimum detail, and in Chapter 15 some comments are made on how organizations can think about and manage these issues. For the present, I wish simply to note that the key to an understanding of this period, as for any other life period, is to take a developmental view, i.e., identifying the developmental tasks of the late career and treating this stage too as one in which further growth can and does take place. The goal for both the individual and the organization must be to maintain a proactive growth orientation throughout all of the stages of the career and life.

MANAGING HUMAN RESOURCE PLANNING AND DEVELOPMENT

In Part 3 the perspective shifts to that of the manager. From the point of view of the total organization and its needs for human resources, how can one think about and generate a total system which will identify, develop, and manage human resources throughout the entire career cycle? How can one create an HRPD system which will remain responsive to changing organizational and individual needs? What role do individual managers have in such a system, and how should that system be organized overall?

14
HUMAN RESOURCE PLANNING
AND DEVELOPMENT: A TOTAL SYSTEM

INTRODUCTION

When viewed from the managerial perspective, human resource planning and development is a highly complex process:

1. Human resources are not the only ones which have to be managed in the total process of creating an effective organization. Human resources have to be meshed with other resources, such as money, technology, space, and information.

2. Human resources are not passive or stable. People both react to how they are managed and, as I have tried to argue throughout this book, change over time. What may work for a young subordinate may not work for that same person in midlife.

3. Human resources can make the difference between organizational failure and success. If the organization has the wrong people for the job, or if people work below their potential or fail to learn new skills as organizational needs change, the organization is less likely to be effective in achieving its goals.

4. The complexity of most organizational tasks requires a wide variety of people to get the job done. Thus no one approach to human resource management can be applied to everyone. People's needs vary, requiring managers to develop more flexible approaches to the development and management of their various categories of subordinates.

We will look at this complexity from two points of view. First, it is necessary to show how a total HRPD system should be conceived of as a set of interacting components. Then we will return to our developmental perspective and look specifically at some of the planning components as might be applied to a career-development approach to human resource management.

THE COMPONENTS OF AN HRPD SYSTEM

The components of an HRPD system and their sequential interrelationships are shown in Fig. 14.1. Organizational activities are shown on the left side, individual activities on the right, and the various matching processes in the middle column. I will discuss the various components sequentially, recognizing from the outset that the system has many feedback loops and is typically engaged in all of the activities simultaneously.

Organizational and Human Resource Planning (Boxes A and B)

An effective HRPD system must explicitly link its organizational planning to its human resource planning (A and B). The long-run strategic direction in which the organization is headed has tremendous implications for the kind of work that might have to be performed at some future time, and it is not safe to assume that somehow the human resources will then be available to do that work. As work becomes more complex and as certain kinds of specialists become scarcer, it becomes more essential for all organizations to think through in long-range terms what kinds of skills they will need.

The short-run tactical or operational plans of the organization provide the most immediate input to the human resource plan in specifying what kinds of *jobs* need to be filled and in what *numbers*. It should be noted that such input cannot be a one-way link. Rather, both the long- and short-range organizational plans should be provisionally checked against human resource plans to determine how realistic they are in terms of the immediate availability of people, the chances of developing the talent which may be needed, and the possibility of recruiting such talent if it is not available. In many planning processes I have observed, it was the constraint on human resources which in the end determined critical decisions such as growth rate, acquisitions policy, decentralization, etc. The question that must inform the planning process is: Do we have the people to manage and run the kind of organization we envision in the next one to five years,

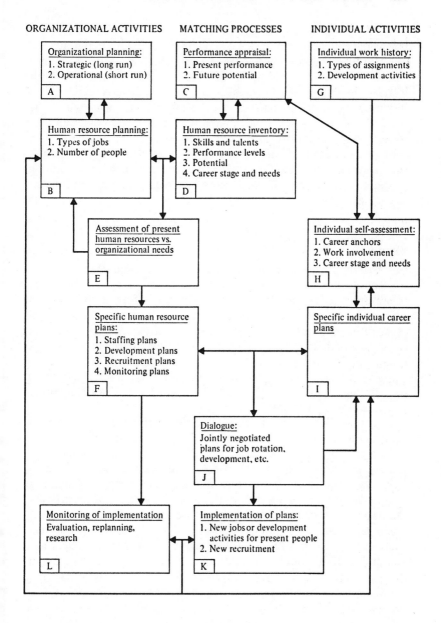

Fig. 14.1 The components and interrelationships of a Human Resource Planning and Development system.

and if not, how do we get them? If those questions cannot be answered explicitly, the strategic decision needs to be rethought.

Strategic planners often argue that human resource planning is too difficult or vague to be taken seriously as a consideration in the total planning process. One reason for this argument is that organizations have not developed some of the other components which Fig. 14.1 shows and which would make the process less vague and less difficult. In other words, effective human resource planning also implies the presence, among other things, of an effective performance-appraisal system which feeds relevant and useful information into an inventory on the basis of which more informed planning decisions can be made.

Performance Appraisal and the Human Resource Inventory (Boxes C and D)

In order to plan effectively, one must have valid and useful information on the present state of the human resources. Any HRPD system, therefore, needs to develop a way of collecting information on present levels of skills and talent, present levels of performance, potential for growth in technical/functional areas and various categories of management, and the career stages of present employees (and by implication their career-related needs and motives). Such information is usually collected as a by-product of the performance-appraisal system or through a portion of that system designed specifically to provide organizationally relevant information.

A real dilemma in this area is initially determining what information should be collected and then developing a method of collecting it which will produce valid information without creating undesirable side effects. For example, from the organizational point of view it may be highly desirable to rate or rank each person's long-range potential for higher-level managerial jobs. But two problems arise: (1) how to make such estimates of the future reasonably valid, especially when the rating or ranking may be made by supervisors who themselves do not know what the future requirements for a manager may be; and (2) how to make such ratings or rankings without revealing to the people rated that they have been classified in this manner. There is evidence that if the ratings are treated as open and to be shared with the employee, they will be less valid, because supervisors will not be willing to make negative judgments which might in some way harm the careers of their immediate subordinates; on the other hand, keeping the ratings completely secret creates tension in the system, because everyone knows that the ratings exist and must wonder where they fall. A further complication may be the new privacy laws, which will make it difficult for the organization to keep any information of a personal nature secret from any employee who requests such information.

Furthermore, the other basic purpose of performance appraisal—to stimulate open communication between a boss and a subordinate for purposes of improving performance—is undermined to varying degrees by global ratings designed to go into centralized files and inventories. One solution is to separate the two processes in time or to use different procedures and forms for each. For performance *improvement*, the process should emphasize detailed behavioral descriptions and incidents which facilitate a dialogue on a day-to-day basis and which maximize feedback from which the subordinate can learn. For purposes of building the human resource *inventory*, the process should emphasize more careful review of the various skill areas in which the employee has had experience, more details of the work history, more information about the employee's own career aspiration, and more global estimates of potential by the supervisor. Such estimates of potential should be reviewed by the next level supervisor to ensure that they are based on more than stereotypes or vague impressions, and only if there is agreement by two or three people should such information be treated as "valid" and entered into the system.

When and how such information is fed back to the subordinate is a complex issue. At a later stage in the dialogue on development planning (box J) it is often necessary to give some feedback, but it can be global and general rather than specific and detailed. Organizations vary in the kinds of cultural norms which grow up around "openness," and individual supervisors vary in the degree to which they feel comfortable giving generalized feedback. What I am trying to draw attention to here, however, is that whether or not feedback occurs and how it occurs does not influence the "needs" of the HRPD system for some kind of valid information on human resources which is stored for planning purposes. Such information then serves as essential input to the human resource planning process (box B), which in turn serves as input to basic organization planning (box A).

Assessment of Resources versus Needs (Box E)

Once the planning process has specified a set of organization "needs" and the human resource inventory has specified what is available, some assessment can be made by comparing the plan with the inventory. Such an assessment will either identify critical constraints, which will force a more fundamental replanning of strategic or operational goals, or will lead forward to more specific human resource plans. The issue here is organizational linkage. Who is to be involved in making these assessments, and by what process should they be made? Is it sufficient to have an inventory on paper for planners to use, or is it necessary to have a dialogue between the planners and those concerned primarily about inventorying? Since the processes of both planning and "measuring" people are relatively imprecise, it is probably essential to bring the people involved into explicit dialogue. Though it may be more time consuming, it seems essential to have this dialogue in order to check assumptions, perspectives, and points of view before drawing conclusions about what is or is not possible with a given set of people who represent the organization's "human resources."

Specific Human Resource Plans (Box F)

Specific human resource plans involve the actual jobs and actual people of the organization, in contrast to the generalized planning for job families and categories of people in box B. If the general plans hold up following the assessment activity (box E), specific plans have to be made to fill certain jobs, create development programs for certain people, launch recruiting activities in areas where new skills are involved or where it would take too long to develop people inside the organization, and create monitoring systems to ensure that the activities above are producing the desired results.

Several comments need to be made about the linkage of this activity to others in the total system. First, in many organizations this specific planning activity is the *only* piece of the system which the organization has in operation. As jobs open up or as people need to be promoted or moved, representatives from the personnel department meet with line managers on an ad hoc basis and decide how to juggle the pieces of the puzzle. Some organizations have "management development committees" which worry about position planning (how future openings will be filled) and people planning (how high-potential people will be moved in an optimal fashion). The information used comes directly from individual supervisors, often in an ad hoc, unsystematic fashion. The process may or may not use any input from the individual and is often a political process reflecting the relative power of different managers. Whether or not longer-range organization plans are taken into account is a function of whether the managers who are working on a particular move are themselves oriented to those longer-range plans. Positions are filled and people are moved, but little monitoring is done to determine whether the moves were of benefit to either the individual or the organization.

If the organization needs no more than such a process of position and people planning because it is in a fairly stable environment, there is in fact no reason to worry about the other components. But it is dangerous to assume that such a process is a complete system and that it could meet organizational needs in a more dynamic environment. And it is certain that such a process will *not* produce optimal development of the human resources, because it will be insufficiently linked to the individual issues such as career stages, career anchors, work-family conflicts, dual careers, etc.

A second general point about the activities in box F is that they can come into conflict *with each other*. For example, a common problem I have encountered is a conflict between staffing plans and development plans. In order to fill a position, it is proposed that a given person should be moved into it. However, that move may not be the best move for that person from a developmental point of view. What, then, is more important in the long run—fill the position or create a developmental opportunity for a person who may represent an importation *future* resource? A decision in favor of keeping the person on a development plan and recruiting for the open position outside may run into another conflict in that the recruiting budget may now be over-run. Without a more centralized human resource policy or plan (at the box B level), it is difficult for the organization even to determine what its recruiting and development budget should be. The danger is that decisions get made in terms of *short-run* costs and benefits without ever assessing the longer-range costs and benefits, a policy which usually favors staffing policies which move people simply by where the organization needs them in the short run, undermining both development and recruitment activities in the long run.

If specific human resource plans are to remain responsive to changes in both organizational and individual needs, they must remain linked to both the more general organizational planning activities and the needs of the individual. Those individual needs can be partly represented through the human resource inventory, but a better matching system would ensure that some dialogue actually take the place between the individual and the manager who is making a specific plan for that individual before the plan is implemented. If such a dialogue is to occur, the individual also must be prepared for it, focusing us on the next portion of the total system, the "individual activities."

Individual Work History, Self-Assessment,
and Career Planning (Boxes G, H, and I)

Many managers who sit down with a subordinate to discuss the latter's "future career with the company" have found that the subordinate becomes virtually nonverbal or utters platitudes like wanting to "get ahead" or receive a "couple more promotions." If a dialogue is to occur between a manager and a subordinate, both parties must be prepared, must have thought about career issues, and must have some information about themselves and the organizations. Therefore, a total HRPD system must include some support for each and every employee's becoming more career conscious and must provide guidelines, workshops, training materials, or whatever else seems suitable to aid this process. And by "every employee" I mean here everyone up to the top management of the organization, because only a boss who has thought about his or her own career can have a useful dialogue with a subordinate about career matters.

Organizations have various means for stimulating individuals to think through their work histories, gain insight into their own career anchors, and think through their work, family, and self-development needs. Such means include company-sponsored career-development workshops, inside or outside testing and counseling, the use of assessment centers to help individuals gain a better self-assessment, the use of self-administering work books or training manuals which help the person do a self-assessment, and encouragement of the use of the performance-appraisal feedback session as a career-exploration device. Externally stimulated activities such as job posting also serve a critical function in helping individuals think through what they want to do next and provide feedback opportunities during the internal job-application interviews.

Probably the most important activity in this regard is supervisory encouragement. If the organization signals to all of its people a concern for career-development issues and backs up this concern with self-assessment opportunities, people will find ways to get a better insight into their own needs. What managers in the organization must come to realize is that such a positive climate for career development right through to the top of the organization is not merely of value to the individual, but is also a crucial component of the total HRPD system, because it facilitates optimal long-range human resource development.

Dialogue Between Managers and Career Occupants (Box J)

The dialogue between manager and career occupant is, in a sense, the critical juncture in the total HRPD system. Here individual and organizational needs meet, and some kind of ultimate matching must take place. If the organization has done its homework in the form of adequate planning and inventorying and if the individual has done his or her homework in the sense of getting some self-insight into needs, goals, and aspirations, a real dialogue can occur. Such a dialogue is not necessarily a single meeting between a boss and a subordinate. It may be a process which occurs over a period of weeks or months during which both individual and organizational needs are explored. A management development committee trying to fill some important positions may talk to people, their supervisors, personnel representatives, and even outsiders to see what the recruiting possibilities are, but the conversations take place with a mutual exchange of information as the goal.

The trigger for such a dialogue usually occurs when a position opens up and some moves of people have to be made, or when a person is clearly ready for a promotion or a rotational assignment. What is important at this point is to avoid the process becoming a "monologue" in which managers or personnel specialists make up their own minds on what would be "best for everyone" and then simply sell the decision to the individual and various other managers who may be involved. Any job rotation, major change in assignment, movement from technical to supervisory work, special development activity such as attending a university program or in-house training program requires a balanced discussion in which the individual has a chance to express his or her needs and in which there is an opportunity to determine whether or not the projected move will be mutually beneficial to both the organization and the individual. Out of such dialogue there should come a *jointly negotiated plan* for future career moves which match the needs of the organization and the needs of the individual.

To provide a clear example, one need only look at the growing tendency of multinational companies to involve not only the manager who is being considered for an overseas assignment, but his or her family as well in a totally negotiated decision to ensure that the new assignment will be compatible with personal and family needs. What is currently done for such major moves should, in principle, be done for any move across any organizational boundary. What I have said earlier (Chapter 5) about work-family interaction and the growth of dual-career families will make it even more important to have a real dialogue and to build the HRPD components that will prepare both the manager and the subordinate for such dialogue.

Implementation of Plans (Box K)

Once a decision has been made to move an individual, send someone to a development program, or launch a recruiting drive to fill a job, some system must exist to implement the plan. This point may seem trivial, but many personnel development systems stop with a jointly negotiated decision which is written down on an appraisal form and sent to the personnel department, where it dies. For example, a supervisor and a given subordinate may agree that a move from one function such as engineering to another function such as marketing may be in the best interests of both the individual and the organization. But this agreement alone will not make it happen unless some mechanisms exist in the HRPD system to pick up such information and launch an implementation plan. Similarly, the decision may be made that a person should attend a university management development program, but no mechanism or budget may exist to implement that plan, nor may there be any provision for replacing the person while he or she is attending the program.

There is no one best way to organize the implementation function, but it should probably combine some segment of the personnel or development activity where information is centralized and can be analyzed in terms of total organization implications and some line-management committee which has the power to allocate funds and initiate moves. Many organizations use personnel development committees consisting of senior line managers and staff from personnel development as a joint group reviewing development plans, recruitment plans, and other staffing activities, deciding how to integrate these various plans, and implementing them. If such a group includes or has the backing of top management, it not only ensures better implementation, but also validates the entire HRPD function and thereby increases the quality of all of its components.

Monitoring, Evaluation, and Replanning (Box L)

The total HRPD cycle ends with some activites which systematically monitor whatever has been done, evaluate the outcomes of these activities against the goals set for them, and feed back this evaluation information into the basic planning process. For example, if a person was moved from engineering to marketing or attended a university development program, someone in the organization (often that person's supervisor) should assess how the move or the program worked out and feed that information back into the system. Not only the organization but also the individual will be evaluating any given activity, so the feedback information will go back into the individual's self-assessment as well.

Probably the best way to organize the monitoring and evaluation activities is to have a centralized monitoring system in the personnel development organization which identifies what needs to be monitored, who should do the evaluation, and who should get the results of the evaluation. But the actual work of evaluation is obviously the job of the individual, various supervisors, and possibly members of the personnel development committee. The development of *procedures* for evaluation, the schedule, and the monitoring is the job of a centralized staff organization. The work, the assessment of implications, and the replanning must be returned to the line organization. Ultimately the information must end up as an input to the planning process (box B), to the human resource inventory (box D), and to the individual (box G).

If this total process is working well, it should not only improve human resource planning, but also provide information on how to improve development activities themselves. From the evaluation of present activities the organization can learn something about optimal career paths, what kinds of rotational moves do and do not work well, what sorts of development programs are beneficial to whom and how they should be timed, the optimum lengths of time for assignments, and so on. Most organizations have much information about their own career-development system ready for analysis, but someone must see the value of such analysis, pull the information together, and begin to make inferences from it. All too often every individual manager has his or her own theory about development, and these theories never get checked against facts which might be readily available within the organization. As part of the monitoring and evaluation activity, one might consider a small personnel research unit which focuses specifically on human resource development so that the organization can learn better from its own experience.

SUMMARY AND CONCLUSIONS

In this chaper I have tried to depict all of the necessary components of an HRPD system and the linkages that should ideally exist between them. The actual organization of such a system will vary from organization to organization, and such variation is entirely appropriate, since different organizations need different things. What is important is to view the components as a kind of minimum checklist of activities which must be present in some form or another and to ensure that the organizational and individual activities remain in some kind of balance. As organizations become more vulnerable to environmental turbulence and to the vicissitudes of their people, it becomes increasingly important to maintain a healthy balance in the system between activities which serve the needs of the organization and those which serve the needs of individuals.

15
HUMAN RESOURCE PLANNING
AND CAREER STAGES

This chapter relates the human resource planning activities more explicitly to the stages of the organizational career, focusing on how the planning components in particular are affected by the developmental perspective. In other words, how can one rethink the planning activities in the light of the fact that every person in the organization will go through career stages, from being a recruit to ultimately retiring? This perspective takes us back to Fig. 1.2, which is expanded in Fig. 15.1. The figure focuses us clearly on the need to relate various different kinds of matching activities to different stages of the organizational career.

Breaking down the planning activities by the stages of the career reveals four different kinds of planning which must be carried out. With each of these planning activities come certain kinds of matching activities which take into account the needs of the individual as well as the organization.

1. *Planning for staffing*—deciding what kind of work needs to be done and how to get the human resources to do it;

2. *Planning for growth and development*—deciding how best to utilize the human resources in the organization, how to ensure their optimal level of growth and development, and how to ensure continued high levels of performance throughout the active career of all employees and managers;

ORGANIZATIONAL NEEDS   MATCHING PROCESSES   INDIVIDUAL NEEDS

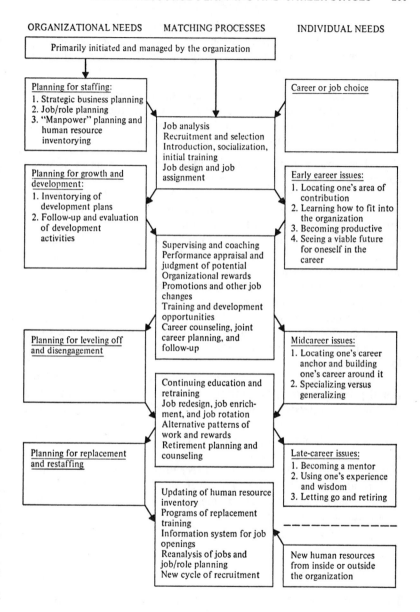

Fig. 15.1 Human Resource Planning and Development: A temporal development model.

3. *Planning for leveling off and disengagement*—deciding how best to deal with loss of motivation, declining energy levels and skills, changing employee needs with age, lack of promotional opportunities, and ultimately retirement;

4. *Planning for replacement*—deciding on an optimum system from the point of view of both the organization and the employee of replacing that employee when that decision is warranted and ensuring that an adequate replacement is available.

These four planning activities make up a planning cycle which covers the history of any given organizational career. It is important to note that the primary focus of these activities is the *organization* and its needs—ensuring that jobs at all levels are filled and that performance in those jobs will continue at a high level over a defined period of time. Obviously one cannot make such determinations without considering the needs and characteristics of the individuals in the jobs, but it is important to recognize that those individual needs, etc., are, from the point of view of the organizational perspective, *not* the primary concern. In fact, too much human resource planning fails because it becomes overconcerned with planning for the needs of the present employees in the system rather than being concerned with the needs of the *organization* to function effectively in terms of its own long-range goals.

Each of the planning activities generates a number of organizational processes which become the vehicles by which organizational and individual needs are matched (the middle column in Fig. 15.1). Some of these activities were shown in Fig. 14.1 and are elaborated here in a developmental perspective. The emphasis in this discussion will be the *planning activities* and the *information required for such planning*, not the actual processes of recruitment, placement, training, performance appraisal, etc. To cover those matching activities in detail would require another volume, and for our purposes it is more important to highlight the *planning*, because how that is done will determine the ultimate effectiveness of the matching activities.

PLANNING FOR STAFFING

The responsibility for staffing typically starts at the top of the organization in terms of the basic goals or organizational plans, but then shifts to various lower levels of management, where jobs are actually to be filled, and to various staff or support groups which become involved in the details of human resource planning, recruiting, selection, training, and job placement. In order for these activities to be carried out effectively, several kinds of *information* are necessary as input to the planning process.

1. *Job analysis—specific information about jobs to be filled and the characteristics needed in the person who would fill that job*, e.g., skills, attitudes, motives, past experience, etc.;

2. *Career analysis—general information about the careers in the organization or in that type of industry*, e.g., types of career paths or typical job sequences over a period of time, general patterns of occupational distributions within the organization, typical rates of promotion, typical or possible sequences of rotational moves, etc.;

3. *Labor-market analysis—information about the characteristics of the labor market, both internal and external, from which job candidates are to be recruited*, i.e., knowledge of the needs, values, motives, skills, and potential of recruits (derived from human resource inventory for internal people);

4. *Job/role planning—projections into the future in relation to how jobs or organizational roles may change as the nature of the business and its environment change* (job/role planning will be covered in some detail in the next chapter).

Job Analysis

What the job requires is typically the main focus of the staffing activity. Job analyses are carried out and translated into recruiting requirements. Most organizations have learned to do this fairly effectively for lower-level jobs and highly specialized jobs at all levels, but have not developed tools for effective descriptions of managerial jobs. The job/role planning process to be described in the next chapter is intended to be a beginning step toward improving the process of *managerial* staffing.

The ability of the organization to forecast how jobs will change and what new mixes of skills will be needed in the future at all levels, up to and including top management, will become more crucial as the various environments within which the organization operates change. It is this planning activity especially which must be linked to the organization's strategic planning so that decisions about new products, new markets, acquisitions, diversifications, and changing rates of growth can be translated sensibly into staffing plans.

Career Analysis

Information about organizational careers, typical career paths, and promotional or rotational patterns is necessary in order to make accurate estimates of long-range needs and resources. For example, if an organization knows that it will need five new plant managers over the next ten years based on its growth projection, it becomes important to know how long it takes to develop and train such managers, where to look for them in terms of present job levels, and what kinds of experience or skill mixes to look for based on *knowledge* of who has been more or less successful in such jobs in the past. It may be that if the organization studies the career histories of its past plant managers, it will find that there are systematic differences between those that have been more or less effective in that job. Such internal "research" may reveal that effective plant managers have had rotational assignments outside of manufacturing, or it may serve to test assumptions on the part of managers that "only people with an engineering background" can make it into plant management, and the like.

Most organizations have a wealth of information about the career paths of their own employees and managers, but such information is often unanalyzed, yielding instead to stereotypes or untested beliefs on the part of senior managers who trust their own background, experience, or intuition more than the available data. As jobs become more complex and as certain categories of specialists and managers become more scarce, it will become more important for organizations to allocate resources to the *empirical* analysis of organizational careers and to make information of this sort more available to all levels of management.

Case Illustration: Engineering Managers.   An example from a recent consultation project will illustrate the potential importance of such information. I was involved by the manager of an engineering group in the analysis of why his organization was having trouble completing projects on time and within budgets. This group had always been very effective and quick, but was showing signs of slowing down, of excessive formalization, of "complacency" and indifference to the company's needs for new-product development, and of unresponsiveness to some of the pressures from top management. Many managers complained that the old company way of doing things was no longer working, that people had lost motivation, and that creeping bureaucracy was taking over.

In order to plan a sensible interview program in this large engineering organization, I asked to see a print-out listing all of the people, their age, rank, and length of time with the company. Such information was readily available from personnel records. It was also possible to print out the data in several "cross-tabulations" so as to correlate length of service with age and rank. Several pieces of information almost jumped out of the data once we began to inspect the print-outs: (1) 87 percent of the people in the department had been in the company less than five years, and 33 percent had been hired within the last two years; (2) of the recent hires, almost a third were in supervisory positions, implying that they had been hired in as supervisors rather than being promoted from within; (3) the *senior* managers of this group were all "old timers," having spent ten years or more in the company.

An obvious conclusion was that there simply had not been enough time for large numbers of engineers and their supervisors to absorb the company culture, to learn the way in which projects were supposed to be carried out, to learn whether it was more important to adhere to formal procedures or to get the job done if procedures came into conflict with one another, and so on. Once it was recognized that the department was functioning with a group of very recently hired people, it was easy to make a decision to launch a major program of supervisory training and project management, during which the company's philosophy and system would be taught.

Discussions of the supervisory training program revealed another category of information which bears on job/role planning. The senior managers of the group asked themselves what the resource constraints were—the scarce kinds of abilities and skills which crucially determined success in projects. This question revealed that the crucial skills of the effective project engineer in this company were abilities to work at various interfaces: (1) the ability to talk to top management and sense what they wanted in the way of products; (2) the ability to sense the marketplace and its needs either through direct contact with customers or effective conversation with marketing and salespeople (this also meant the ability to *reject* marketing ideas when those ideas did not make sense to engineering); and (3) the ability to be "smart" in the face of multiple inputs on design (this meant that the engineers had to learn when to trust their own judgment and to reject various inputs which would slow the projects down).

Once these particular abilities had been articulated, it became possible to do two further things: (1) review the career histories of engineers and supervisors who clearly had these abilities in order to determine what experiences may have contributed to their learning or what prior background was involved; (2) based on such further analysis, decide what kind of training or developmental experiences should be planned to speed up the process by which the young engineer recently hired by the company could acquire these abilities.

As might have been expected, a scarcity of project managers and project engineers with the requisite abilities was revealed. The discovery made it clear that senior managers had to straighten out their own priorities on the various projects and had to decide how to deploy the existing resources across the crucial projects while training and development activities were launched to increase the size of the talent pool. A full-time person was hired into the personnel department of the engineering group to concentrate on "career development," which now includes a special training program for new supervisors and new hires, a career counseling program to help engineers plan their own career paths in the light of what is needed and wanted in the total group, an interview program of existing managers and engineers to bring out further information on how the career path in this company works out and the important developmental experiences as one progresses, and a program addressed to changing career motivations, technical obsolescence, and other problems which will develop as this total group "ages."

The important lesson from this case is that the planning process requires information, and such information is usually available and ready for analysis if its relevance is recognized. Such recognition in this case came from senior management, from staff people in the personnel department, and from the consultant working as a team on the project-overrun problem.

Labor-Market Analysis

Information about the characteristics of the labor market is crucial in order to avoid stereotyping the needs and goals of present and future employees. We have seen dramatic changes in the last decade or two in what people's concepts of work are, what they regard as success, what degree or level of ambition they have, how they balance the requirements of their careers with those of their family and self, and so on. It is simply not safe for managers or recruiters to assume that they know what the internal or external job candidate wants or has to offer. It is becoming more critical to take the time and make the effort to find out and to use information rationally as part of a planning process.

A clear-cut example is the growth of the dual-career family. Many married employees want to balance their own career needs with those of their spouses, which means new attitudes toward geographical movement, time off, and organizational loyalty. From the point of view of the employing organization, such considerations may mean a more explicit policy of considering individual needs in relation to a projected geographical move, allowing more time off when needed by the employee because of family constraints, periods of part-time work, paternity as well as maternity leaves, etc. Beyond these kinds of considerations, it may become necessary for organizations *to plan for higher rates of turnover*, with the recognition that such turnover is not a failure of the career management system of that organization, but simply a fact of life in a dynamic labor market of the future. More explicit programs of hiring high-talent people at midlife to replace those who leave, combined with explicit developmental activities geared to teaching the company's way of doing things quickly, will then be required as routine parts of the staffing process.

Job-posting systems and other devices which involve employees much more in managing their own careers will also become more important as employee needs, motives, and skills become more diverse. Organizations will find themselves in a more genuine negotiation with internal or external job applicants as work becomes more specialized and human resources of the kind needed become more scarce. Rather than letting these problems arise and then coping with them, it is possible to develop information and use it explicitly in the planning process. Managers will have to recognize that the allocation of resources to such information-gathering activities is a good investment on a par with market research or R&D investments.

Job/Role Planning

Projecting into the future and trying to determine the implications of organizational changes for the human resources which will be needed in the future is a difficult but necessary task. In my experience, it is difficult to convince managers to put time into forecasting, because such activities are abstract, have long time horizons, and cannot be readily checked out against results. To most managers I have encountered, day-to-day crises are normally more compelling than "crystal ball gazing." However, if the activity itself is recognized as important, it is possible to develop a climate of "brainstorming" around the future, especially if the managers are involved in off-site meetings, where a more relaxed, pensive atmosphere can be developed. At such times it is important to link conceptually the general business planning activity with the question of "what does this mean for our future needs in the human resource area" and to go beyond the numbers game of simply trying to project *how many* of each type of person will be needed. The key is to focus on jobs and roles, to ask how managerial work will change, what kinds of organizational structures may be envisioned, and what kinds of people will be needed to function effectively in such structures.

As ideas come out, someone in the group should record them as if they were developing a job description, circulate such descriptions to others, and build up some group history around the planning activity so that it does not always seem as though one is starting from scratch. A planning specialist or organization development consultant can fulfill a key role here by serving as an internal recorder, clarifyer, and articulator of the sometimes only partially formed ideas of line managers. The planner/consultant may provide a process, but the ideas should come primarily from line managers themselves. Once they have thought about the issues, they can then be given the thoughts of futurists and professional planners as additional food for thought, but in my view it is line managers who must ultimately wrestle with these ideas and develop their own view of the future.

In summary, I have argued that planning for staffing requires several kinds of information input dealing with jobs, careers and career paths, the internal and external labor market, and the future. Only if such information is developed can one set about to do a realistic job of recruiting, selecting, training, and placing. As was brought out in previous chapters, it is difficult for the individual and the organization to come to terms with each other effectively without a good exchange of valid information. What I have focused on so far is the organizational side of this. Companies need to know more about themselves and need to learn to share such information more effectively. Such sharing is at the heart of the next set of activities, which grow out of development planning.

PLANNING FOR GROWTH AND DEVELOPMENT

A true understanding of how to plan for the growth and development of human resources rests ultimately on a better understanding of the growth and development process itself. The very language we use—"we must develop our people"—reflects an erroneous model, in that it implies that some external force can develop a person. Instead, we must start with the recognition that the process of growth and development occurs from *within* the person and is controlled and limited by inner forces. What the environment can do is to provide opportunities and challenges on the one hand and accurate feedback or knowledge of results on the other hand. But in between, it is only the person who can accept the challenge, try out a new response, succeed or fail, learn something new, and thereby grow and develop. The focus of developmental planning therefore must be on the challenge to be provided and the system of feedback, the two components that are under the control of the organization.

In most cases the development planner is the supervisor whose decisions on how to allocate work, supervise, appraise, give feedback, etc., will create the environment within which the subordinate will or will not develop. The kind of information the supervisor needs as the basis for such planning is illustrated by the chapters in Part 1 of this book. The more supervisors know about human development, especially in the adult years, the better the chances that they will know how to create optimal challenges and optimal systems of feedback for subordinates. The effective management of human resources and the creation of a climate of growth and development are, in a sense, the same thing, because the factors which tend to lead to high performance are usually the same as those which lead to growth and development.

Key to these processes is a valid model of growth. McGregor (1960) pointed out many years ago how a manager's behavior is ultimately a function of that person's world view or set of assumptions about human behavior. He observed that when managers thought about the development of their subordinates, they often talk about a kind of *engineering model*—how to take the human raw material and fashion it with various tools into the kind of person needed by the organization. McGregor observed that an alternative and more appropriate model in terms of what we know about human nature is an *agricultural model*—how to take the various kinds of "seeds" which are available, plant them in the appropriate kind of soil, provide fertilizer, water, correct amounts of sunshine, transplant when needed, and so on. The potential of the seed is within the seed, but the organization can play a big role in creating the environment and providing the conditions necessary for optimal growth.

The actual planning activities which would go into effective *development* planning are a logical extension of the staffing ones. The kinds of information needed for staffing also directly impact on development planning. The more managers know about jobs, organizational careers, the labor market, and the future of the organization, the better they can plan for the optimal growth of their subordinates. The more such information is available, the better the process of performances appraisal and feedback, because managers will have a better context within which to appraise subordinates' performance. Only if managers have such information can they ensure that the developmental opportunities they are creating for their subordinates will in fact lead to learning which is relevant to the future needs of the organization. The important point to recognize from the point of view of an HRPD system is that how work is assigned and how performance is appraised are integral components of the system and must be linked with other parts of the system and coordinated across the organization.

Role of Staff and Line in Development Planning

If the basic responsibility for creating a climate of growth is the manager's and if the basic growth can come only from within the individual, what role is there for coordinating and integrating activities on the part of top management or specialist groups within the organization? The role of top management is clearly to establish the importance of development planning, to ensure that managers at all levels receive the training necessary to do it effectively, to ensure that the activities are coordinated across the various parts of the organization, and to monitor the process. The role of specialists is to generate the information necessary for effective development planning, to ensure that such information gets to all managers and employees, and to monitor the process for purposes of giving top management information on how it is going in various parts of the organization. Clearly the specialist also has to function as an effective internal consultant, working closely with all levels of managers and employees in providing information, expert counsel, and process help as needed.

An additional developmental function which is becoming more and more necessary is *career counseling*. Such counseling would have several functions: (1) helping people to become more proactive in the management of their own careers by providing opportunities to do personal planning; (2) providing information to people on their strengths, weaknesses, and developmental needs; and (3) providing information to people about career options inside and outside the organization, possible career paths (how one gets ahead in the organization), and what the person would have to do in the way of self-development to qualify for future positions which may be desired. Such information and thinking through of options would prepare people to negotiate more effectively with their organizations on career development, which would, in the long run, be of benefit to both the organization and the individual.

While it seems clear that some form of counseling would be very helpful, it is less clear *who* should do the counseling—the person's line manager, a staff specialist working for a corporate or central group, a staff specialist outside the organization whose services are paid for by either the organization or the employee, or some combination of these. Let us look at some of the advantages and disadvantages of each alternative.

On the matter of the *insider* versus the *outsider*, the insider is likely to possess more relevant information about the career options available within the organization; the outsider can do a more thorough appraisal of the individual seeking the counseling and give more objective feedback. The *line* boss may be in the best position to evaluate the specific strengths and weaknesses of the person being counseled relative to known career options, but may be least trained in conducting an effective counseling session (and may find it awkard to get into such a session with a subordinate). The *staff specialist* (either inside or outside the organization) may be an excellent counselor by training, but may not have good information about the person being counseled or may have incomplete information on career options in that organization.

Clearly what is needed for effective career counseling is: (1) counseling skill; (2) information about the person being counseled—aptitudes, motives, experience, specific strengths and weaknesses; and (3) information about the career options and paths available within and outside the organization. This list suggests that *no one person may be in a position to do the whole job*—it may take some combination of performance appraisal, assessment, and information sharing by several parties before the individual is in a good position to make valid judgments about future career choices and options. Each organization will have to work out its own optimal system for accomplishing these tasks by training line managers to provide valid feedback on performance and on career options, while at same time providing either inside or outside career counseling specialists to aid the employee in thinking through the options and forming a valid self-assessment. To aid this process many companies have also offered at their own expense the opportunity for the employee to go through assessment centers or psychological testing with outside specialists.

In summary, planning for growth and development requires a clear understanding of how growth occurs and the role which the organizational environment plays in that process. The critical foci for the planner and manager become the design of work to be optimally challenging, the process by which employees are assigned work to match their needs for challenge with the opportunities afforded in the job, and the process by which feedback or knowledge of results comes back to the person. This cycle of challenge, trial, and feedback is the core of the development process. In order to aid individuals in their own career planning, it is also desirable for the organization to provide or encourage some form of counseling which would emphasize information about individual strengths, weaknesses, and development needs, and would provide data about career options, career paths, and other information about the opportunity structure which the person faces. Such information is not only valuable to the individual, but also essential for the manager so that developmental opportunities created for subordinates will be more likely to provide the kinds of learning which will be of ultimate value to the organization.

PLANNING FOR LEVELING OFF AND DISENGAGEMENT

Planning for staffing and development is growth-oriented, but a reality of life is that growth stops, people level off, lose motivation, energy, and/or skill, promotional opportunities dry up, jobs cease to be challenging, skills become obsolete, and both the individual and the organization are eventually faced with the prospect of disengagement. Surprisingly little has been written about disengagement, or "breaking out" of organizations. Much more attention has been given to "breaking in." Yet people do quit or get laid off, people do retire, and people do lose their energy or motivation for work and "retire on the job," creating a period of disengagement that may last for years. What is involved in this process, and how can the organization plan for it?

The most important thing for the manager and the planning specialist to have is a full understanding of the dynamics of the career in mid- and late adulthood and how those career dynamics interact with other adult-development issues. As this book has tried to emphasize, the person does not live by work alone—work, family, and self interact, and the nature of this interaction changes throughout the course of the adult life. It is essential, therefore, to understand some of the possible forces which may act on the individual to cause loss of energy or motivation and to assess whether the organization can or *should* do anything about those forces.

There are a number of possible reasons for potential disengagement:

1. The person's level of knowledge and skills has become obsolete;

2. The person's existing talents and skills are no longer needed by the organization because the nature of the work has changed;

3. The person still has potential for promotion, but there are no slots available because of the narrowing pyramid;

4. The person has been doing the same job for too long and has become unresponsive to this job as such;

5. The person's needs and motives (ambitions) have become less career-oriented and more self- or family-oriented, or the person's criteria for success have changed in the direction of accepting a lower level or rank in the organization—the person has developed lower work involvement.

Having identified the possible cause of loss of motivation or disengagement, it is then important to find out for any given employee or manager which causes are the major ones operating. Without knowing precisely *why* people are behaving the way they are, it is not possible to design preventive, ameliorative, or remedial policies and programs. For example, in highly technical organizations, there are probably at least two major patterns operating among engineers and scientists —some have become technically obsolete but are still highly motivated toward technical contribution (for this group a program of continuing education would be a potential remedy); some have become less interested in climbing a technical ladder, having settled for a lower level of ambition and having become more involved with family and community. For this latter group technical retraining is a waste of time; instead, people in this group might benefit from work which encourages more mentoring, less demanding time schedules, etc. (Bailyn, 1977).

To give another example, there is growing evidence (Katz, 1977) that the sources of job satisfaction across a wide variety of employees change systematically with the actual length of time a person has had a given job (job longevity). Using the job factors developed by Hackman and Oldham (1975), Katz showed that during the first six months or so on a job the person needs to have a feeling of *task significance* as well as feedback, or *knowledge of results.* During the first one to five years the factors of *autonomy* (being able to influence how the work is done), task *identity* (having a clearly defined job), and *variety* become relatively more important. If a person stays on the job for five years or more, all of the "intrinsic" factors, such as the nature of the work itself, seem to become less important. On the other hand, contextual, or "extrinsic," factors, such as the nature of supervision, pleasant social relations at the place of work, working conditions, good pay, benefits, and a good retirement program, which have been important throughout, now become relatively much *more* important.

The implications are clear—job enrichment, job redesign, and other programs dealing with the work itself may be relevant only for people who are in the first few years of a given job, a period Katz calls the "responsive" period. If job longevity gets to be five years or more, the employee becomes unresponsive to job redesign, and either remedial emphasis has to shift to a program of job rotation (which may be resisted if people have become used to a given job), or, more likely, the organization has to accept the fact that the only remedies lie in improving the job context, pay, and benefits. For more personal growth experiences the employee will turn more to family and off-the-job activities.

If the organization recognizes the potential danger of loss of job motivation with increasing job longevity, it may decide on an explicit program of job rotation, as a *preventive* measure. For example, a number of companies have instituted the policy of reviewing the personnel file of every employee (including managers) who has held the same job for five consecutive years, investigating carefully what the reasons are, and then deciding explicitly what should be done. If the reason is discovered to be that the person can no longer contribute, and there is no training or continuing education possibility, layoff or termination may be the only solution. More likely, it will be discovered that the person has talents or aspirations which are still of value to the organization if that person is moved into another type of work. Such movement must obviously be a joint decision between the employee and the organization and may require assessment and counseling as part of the process, but the organization may have to take the initiative in stimulating such a career move precisely because the employee may have become complacent and unresponsive as a result of job longevity. If it is discovered that the employee's needs have changed but that his or her contribution is still worthwhile, the organization may continue the person in his or her present assignment if it does not block others, or create a special assignment that takes advantage of whatever level of motivation is present.

In diagnosing the causes of loss of motivation, special emphasis should be given to what we are learning about career stages and their attendant psychological dynamics. For example, the Dalton, Thompson, and Price (1977) studies of engineering careers bring out clearly that in mid- and late adulthood there is an increase in people's needs to become mentors to others and to use their *general* experience and wisdom. If the organization recognizes this changing pattern of needs, it can often provide career opportunities which respond to such needs. For example, a senior engineer can be put in charge of an orientation or training program for junior engineers; older, technically obsolescent engineers can be attached to project teams in liaison roles to manufacturing or marketing, where their past experience would help the project to handle the interfaces more effectively; older engineers can be given temporary assignments as group leaders of task forces without implying commitment to a permanent supervisory position, and so on. For any of these solutions to work, it is essential that the manager and the human resource planner recognize the underlying needs which are operating so that the solution can be responsive to those particular needs.

For those employees whose work involvement has genuinely declined and whose needs to be involved in family, community, personal hobbies, etc., have increased, it may make sense to permit part-time work, sabbaticals, semiretirement, and other solutions which acknowledge the fact that although the *quality* of the work is still acceptable, the person does not have the energy to produce at former levels. In fact, it is very important that the quantity and quality issues be distinguished very carefully. It is easy to make the erroneous assumption that if a person is working less hard or has "retired on the job," the quality of what that person is doing has gone down too. It may be that the quality has remained high while the quantity has declined. If so, some version of part-time work makes much more sense than termination.

As a final note to this section, it should be mentioned that the process of retirement itself should be planned for and managed carefully. There is ample evidence that retirement can be very traumatic to the employee. Many companies are finding that such trauma can be ameliorated by providing counseling, seminars, and information sessions on how to handle finances, etc., well before the actual retirement date. For many categories of employees, capacity to contribute does not cease with formal retirement age; retaining them on part-time status, as consultants, or in some other advisory role may be a far better solution for both them and the organization than complete termination.

Sources of Resistance

The thrust of this discussion has been to broaden the diagnosis of the possible causes underlying disengagement and to broaden the range of options available to an organization for dealing with the problem. Some of these options imply the acceptance of lateral career growth, part-time work, temporary assignments, or training assignments as valid and valuable career moves. However, the implementation of such moves may run head-on into two major obstacles with which the human resource planning process must deal explicitly:

1. Prevailing norms in organizations that success can be measured only by promotion;

2. The need to move older people out of organizational slots in order to open up those slots for younger people, i.e., the need to keep younger people motivated by the promise of promotion.

The single biggest reason why an older person may not accept a temporary assignment, a lateral rotational move, or part-time work is that she or he does not view it as *forward* movement in some kind of career path. The single biggest reason why an organization pushes people toward early retirement or lays them off rather than finding a way to utilize their remaining talents is the belief that it must create openings for younger people "on the way up." Both of these forces are real, and organizations will have to learn how to deal with them creatively. Legislation or union pressure toward concepts of life-time employment will force some of this creativity, because organizations will have fewer options to get rid of people.

To deal with success norms may be more difficult, because they reflect the norms of the total society. New ways of providing recognition and status will probably have to be found. Here again some information gathering as part of the planning process may be crucial—what is it that the older, partially disengaged person really does value if promotion is clearly no longer an option? I suspect that most organizations have *insufficient* information about the needs and values of their older employees and therefore may be designing personnel programs on the basis of assumptions and stereotypes rather than hard facts. Analyses of survey data by age and job longevity, such as those done by Katz and Van Maanen (1976), may reveal patterns of what older employees are seeking that will be useful inputs to the human resource planning process.

Summary

I have tried to highlight that planning for disengagement requires a high level of understanding of the causes of loss of motivation or the ability to contribute and that one cannot design preventive, ameliorative, or remedial programs without a clear picture of the underlying causes. When such information is gathered, it will likely be found that there are a number of different patterns operating which will require different kinds of solutions. Special emphasis was given to the mentor role as one such solution. Finally, it was emphasized that prevailing success norms and policies to move older employees in order to make room for younger ones will have to be dealt with as major sources of difficulty in implementing some of the obvious solutions.

PLANNING FOR REPLACEMENT

Planning for replacement has many of the same elements as planning for staffing, thus completing the whole cycle of career development and planning. As information is developed that certain employees will retire or move or be promoted, the organization must have a system for staffing those jobs. Most organizations use some combination of (1) a centralized personnel-records system or inventory which lists employees' career histories, skill areas, and appraisals, and (2) some system of requiring all managers to train their own replacements.

Some companies have very elaborate systems of gathering and storing information about all levels of management. These systems may include detailed appraisals of present skills, potential for growth, ranking of the individual relative to others on present performance or growth potential, and so on. Such information would normally be a part of the human resource inventory previously referred to.

When a position opens up because of a promotion or termination, one or two levels of management above that position typically become involved in reviewing all of the candidates. If the organization emphasizes training one's own replacement, less attention will be paid to formal records and more will be given to the supervisor's estimate of the readiness of a given subordinate for promotion. If a supervisor has not trained his or her own replacement, that supervisor may not be moved or promoted unless the organization is then willing to look outside for a replacement. Norms may develop that promotion must be from within, but such norms may be violated as soon as the growth rate makes it impossible to find enough people inside. The staffing and replacement processes then become one and the same.

As was pointed out in Chapter 14, it is important to make the replacement process something more than an immediate firefighting operation. The human resource inventory should become the basis for longer-range planning—examining rates of movement, patterns of promotion, and career-path sequences. On the other hand, the presence of an inventory does not guarantee that it will aid long-range planning or restaffing, because the kind of information which may have been gathered about people may not be valid or may not be relevant to future kinds of jobs. Appraisals based on present types of work may not provide information on how a given person might perform in some new kind of work. Ratings of potential for growth may be based on what present managers imagine higher levels of management to be like, but such projections on their part may be quite unrealistic.

I have encountered a number of organizations that have put most of the emphasis on the actual data-gathering system and have paid relatively little attention to the content or the validity of the data. When a question is posed about the validity of the information or whether it is the right kind of information for planning purposes, I have encountered blank stares, defensiveness, or "we never thought of that" kinds of responses. Such responses are paradoxical, because the same manager who will defend the overall system will admit to inflating ratings of subordinates rather than taking a chance on hurting their careers, because he or she "knows that *other* managers are pushing their own candidates along." Similarly, that same manager will often point out that the candidates "the system" identifies for a given job are not as competent as others whom she or he "knows personally." Each manager assumes that the system probably helps "others," and no one gets motivated to redesign the system so that it will be genuinely helpful and perceived as valid by all. Such overall redesign will probably not occur in organizations until the replacement process gets too complex to be handled "informally" or until top management recognizes that a valid human inventory system is really needed for long-range planning and becomes willing to devote the managerial energy to creating it.

An inventory that does contain relevant and valid information can not only lend itself to replacement staffing, but also become a genuine source of a variety of information needed for all planning and career development activities. For example, some efforts to analyze such inventories by means of mathematical models may reveal patterns of career progression that would enable planners to make more precise estimates of where surpluses or shortages will occur under different assumptions about growth of the organization (Burack, 1975). Transitional probabilities can be calculated to reveal the likelihood of a manager's moving from one function to another. Such data may reveal what have been called "sources and sinks" —functions or departments which provide managers for other parts of the organization (sources) and functions or departments which are dead ends, i.e., no one ever moves out of them (sinks). Such analyses can be an extremely useful way of understanding career patterns within a given organization.

Summary

I have emphasized that replacement planning completes the career planning cycle and overlaps with planning for staffing; thus all of the kinds of information needed for staffing also become relevant for replacement. Beyond this, the replacement process usually emphasizes some kind of human resource inventory and some process of supervisory training of their own replacements. The main issues around the inventory have to do with the relevance and validity of the information gathered. If such inventories are to be useful as planning tools, they must emphasize information about people which reflects the realities of the kind of work the organization will have to do in the future.

CONCLUSION

Each of the four planning processes which must be carried out if the HRPD system is to take a developmental perspective is linked to matching activities such as recruitment, training, job placement, performance appraisal, rotation, compensation, job design, etc. The planning is highly dependent on various kinds of information which can now be highlighted.

1. Effective staffing cannot be done without information about job requirements and the skill and experience levels of employees presently in the system. Therefore, some kind of human resource inventory and some kind of job/role analysis are prerequisites for any staffing or replacement process.

2. A human resource inventory cannot be created without obtaining valid and relevant information from supervisors on their subordinates. Consequently, one of the major functions of a performance-appraisal system is to generate such valid and relevant information. But the supervisor cannot know what information is relevant without knowing more about the nature of the work for which he or she is appraising subordinates. The performance-appraisal system, therefore, must be based on a process of job analysis and job/role planning which takes into account the future directions of the organization.

3. Supervisory ratings, rankings, or descriptions entering the performance-appraisal system will not be valid unless norms are developed that valid information is in the long run more important than protecting the interests of one's immediate subordinates. Such norms cannot develop if top management is insufficiently involved in the judgment of what information is really needed and how valid it is. Such involvement will not occur unless top management itself gets concerned about job analysis and job/role planning as a means of understanding better what skills, values, experiences, and competencies are relevant for future performance in the organization.

4. Employee development cannot occur without job challenge and feedback. Many of the "development systems" in use emphasize the *identification* of development needs and even record such needs in the human resource inventory, but fail to give feedback to the employee of what those needs are and how they might be met.

5. The development of information about career paths, career dynamics, future directions of the organizations, the changing nature of work, and so on, must be widely disseminated to managers to order to aid them in creating developmental opportunities which are valid and relevant to the organization. If managers do not understand career dynamics and do not know where their organizations are headed, they cannot create the right kinds of developmental opportunities for their subordinates.

Underlying all of the planning and development activities discussed above is the need for valid information about the needs of the organization—the kind of work that must be done today and that will have to be done in the future. In the next chapter I will underline this point by presenting some ideas for job/role planning, particularly for managerial jobs.

16
JOB/ROLE PLANNING

One of the most difficult activities in any HRPD system is to focus on *jobs* and their evolution, independent of the particular people who may be occupying such jobs. There is ample evidence that with growing technological complexity, economically and politically more turbulent environments, and more rapid social changes, the job of the manager, in particular, is changing in various ways. Managers are having to deal with more varied people and more varied jobs as growing technological complexity creates wider interdependences in organizations. New concepts of social responsibility make managers accountable to a wider variety of constituencies both inside and outside the organization and even legally liable not only for their own actions, but for those of their subordinates as well. More work now gets done in groups and meetings, and so on.

It is my argument that some portion of the total HRPD system must be devoted to a systematic analysis of such changes, whatever they are, so that future staffing of such jobs ensures that the necessary skills, motives, and values will be represented in the job incumbents. What has been lacking in this area is any kind of vehicle or tool for doing such planning. It is the purpose of this chapter to suggest an approach to the development of such a tool and to exemplify its use for the job of "general manager." I deliberately chose the general-nanager job because it is in a sense the most complex and also the one where planning mistakes can be the most costly if the person and job are mismatched.

The job/role planning process can be laid out as a set of steps, each of which will be reviewed and illustrated in this chapter:

Step 1—projecting into the future some of the major changes which will be occurring in the organization and its various environments;

Step 2—developing a list of the key dimensions presently characterizing the *job* of general manager;

Step 3—identifying those dimensions which will be most affected by the changes projected in Step 1, including the adding of new dimensions which may not have been thought of in Step 2;

Step 4—identifying the personal characteristics (motives, talents, and values) which will be most relevant to effective performance on the key dimensions identified in Step 3;

Step 5—determining the degree to which the present candidates for future openings possess the personal characteristics identified in Step 4;

Step 6—generating a plan for development of the personal char acteristics needed or for recruitment of new individuals with those skills if development seems impractical.

STEP 1—PROJECTING INTO THE FUTURE

There is ample evidence from our own day-to-day experience that our society and its component institutions and organizations are changing in a number of important ways.* These changes are related to more fundamental changes in the state of the whole world with respect to four elements which for most organizations make up their basic environment: (1) technology; (2) economic conditions; (3) political-legal conditions; and (4) sociocultural conditions and values. I will focus the discussion on the effects of technological complexity and changing social values.

Effects of Technological Complexity

The first set of trends to be described is related primarily to the rapid growth of technology in the last several decades and the growing seg-

---

*For good examples, *see* Bennis and Slater (1968), Michael (1968), and Roeber (1973).

mentation of the marketplace. Not only are more different products and services available, but the world, as it becomes more affluent, is also demanding more of these products and services. As a consequence, several important changes can be observed in organizations.

1. Organizations Are Becoming More Differentiated and Complex.   One of the major consequences of the technological explosion is that products and services are more sophisticated than they used to be, and in turn the organizations which make these products and/or deliver the services therefore have to be more differentiated and complex. Whatever our example—the multiplicities of "new math" or reading programs in elementary school education, the proliferation of majors available to college students today, the growing variety of consumer products, or the sophistication implied in supersonic aircraft, nuclear-powered weapons systems, or space exploration—the trend is clearly toward much more complex, differentiated organizations.

This trend means that there will be more different kinds of occupational specialists who must be managed and whose efforts must somehow be tied together into a coherent organizational whole (Gruber and Niles, 1976). Many of these specialists are neither motivated nor able to talk to one another, creating special problems of integration of effort. The highly specialized design engineer or computer programmer working in the research and development end of the company or in manufacturing often has little in common with the financial analyst whose specialty is the management of the company's investment portfolio or the personnel specialist concerned with the most recent interpretation of the affirmative action legislation. Yet all of these and many other specialists contribute in major ways to the welfare of the total organization, and their efforts have to be integrated. Beyond this, senior management must begin to worry about and plan for the specific career development of such specialists in that many of them would be neither able nor willing to go into managerial positions.

2. The Subunits of Organizations Are Becoming More Interdependent.   In order to produce a complex product or service effectively over a period of time, the many subspecialities of the organization need to be coordinated and integrated, because they are simultaneously and sequentially interdependent in a variety of ways. For example, if the financial department does not manage the company's cash supply adequately, there is less opportunity for capital expansion or R&D; on the other hand, if an engineering design sacrifices some elements of quality for low cost, the result may be customer complaints, a lowered company reputation, and a subsequent decreased ability of the company to borrow money for capital expansion. In this sense, engineering and finance are in fact highly interdependent, even though each may be highly specialized and neither may interact with the other directly.

Sequential interdependence is the more common situation. The engineering department cannot get its work done properly if R&D has not done a proper job; in turn, manufacturing cannot get its job done properly if engineering has produced unbuildable designs; and sales and marketing cannot get their job done if they have poor products to sell. These types of interdependence have always existed within organizations. But as specialization increases, interdependence also increases, because the final product or service is more complex and more vulnerable to any of its parts' malfunctioning. Nowhere is this clearer than in computer products or services. The hardware and software have to be designed properly in the first place and then implemented by a variety of specialists who serve as the interface between the final user and the computer system. If any of the specialists fails to do his or her job, the entire service or product may fail.

3. Organizational Climates Are Becoming More Collaborative/Cooperative.   One major effect of increased specialization and interdependence is that competition between organizational units or individuals is coming to be recognized as potentially more destructive, and the organization climate is becoming more supportive of collaborative /cooperative relations. This trend runs counter to the external marketplace philosophy that competition is a good thing, but is increasingly seen to be a necessary adaptation within organizations, even if *inter*organizational relations continue to be competitive.*

This trend poses a particular dilemma for managers whose own careers have developed in very dog-eat-dog, competitive environments and who simply do not have the interpersonal competence to redesign their organizational processes to be more supportive of collaborative relations. I have met many a manager who pays lip service to "teamwork," but whose day-to-day style sends clear signals of not really understanding or supporting the concept, with the predictable consequence that this person's "team" does not function as a team at all. Unfortunately, both the manager and the subordinates may draw the erroneous conclusion that it is the teamwork *concept* which is at fault

---

*If this trend is worldwide, one will begin to see more evidence of interorganizational collaboration as well, not for political reasons of communism versus capitalism, but for practical reasons of technological necessity. Centralized planning and industrywide coordination may become necessary simply to keep systems functioning at all.

rather than locating the problem in their failure to *implement* the concept.

4. Organizations Are Becoming More Dependent on Lateral Communicating Channels.   Closely connected with the need for more collaborative, teamwork relations is the need for information to flow laterally between technical specialists rather than going through a hierarchy, with concomitant loss of time and probable distortion of the message. For example, some companies are putting the R&D and marketing departments closer to each other geographically and stimulating direct contact between them rather than having higher levels of management attempt to translate marketing issues for the R&D people. The customer, the salesperson, and the marketing specialist in a complex industry such as electronics all probably know more about the technical side of the business than the general manager does and therefore must be brought into direct interaction with the designer and engineer if a viable product or service is to result. Jay Galbraith (1973) has argued very convincingly that the information-processing needs of organizations based on task complexity and environmental uncertainty are, in fact, the major determinants of organization structure and that hierarchical structures work only so long as task complexity and uncertainty are fairly low. Lateral structures such as project teams, task forces, ad hoc committees, and cross-functional organizational units become more common with increased complexity and uncertainty.

Here again, managers face a novel situation because of the likelihood that their own careers have been spent in organizational settings dedicated to principles of hierarchy and chains of command. In such "traditional" organizations the tendency to communicate with people outside the chain of command is actually discouraged and punished. Not only will the organizational reward system and climate have to shift to encourage lateral communication, but in addition managers will have to be trained to create lateral structures and to make them work.

5. Power Is Coming to be Based More on Information than Formal Position and Is Becoming More Decentralized.   With increasing specialization and complexity, it becomes more and more difficult for the general managers to retain power, because they will not possess sufficient information-processing capacity to integrate all the technical information needed to make a decision. Managers still retain responsibility, accountability, and control over organizational processes, but their tasks increasingly shift from making private, solitary decisions to *creating decision processes* which bring together the various specialists whose information must be integrated. Furthermore, these specialists are ultimately the only ones who know whether or not they are contributing all they know to a particular problem, so general managers are increasingly dependent on the motivation and goodwill of the various subordinates and specialists in areas outside of their direct control. What this means on a practical level is that the general manager will have to become more skillful in eliciting information, creating a climate in which people will feel like sharing information, judging the validity and relevance of information, ensuring that the right lateral communications are occurring so that information from several specialists is integrated, and then ensuring that a sensible decision is reached out of all of these processes. The manager becomes less powerful in controlling the *content* of decisions and must become more skillful in using formal power to produce the right decision-making *processes*. Managers must also become more skilled in influencing the behavior of peers, people above them, and people below them who have key items of information or key skills, but over whom they have no direct control. As I have argued, one of the best ways to develop such influence is to become more knowledgeable about the career motivations of various specialists and to create reward and development systems which are congruent with such motivations.

6. Organizations Are Relying More Heavily on Groups, Meetings, and Other "Temporary Systems."   This phenomenon flows directly from the ones discussed above in that interdependence, wide distribution of information, and task complexity all require more simultaneous processing of information which can be done only in some form of face-to-face meeting. If the organization is large enough and has enough of each type of specialist to allocate one to each major product or project area, this form of organization becomes equivalent to "divisionalization" and is generally not viewed as temporary. But even within divisions the further specialization and differentiation of skills have necessitated that the same specialists work on more than one project at a time, creating some form of what has been called a "matrix" organization in which the daily work is done in a variety of project teams, task forces, or other temporary groupings (Galbraith, 1973; Davis and Lawrence, 1977).

This form of organization poses two major *new* management tasks: (1) how to allocate the time and effort of a given specialist across a range of projects or tasks, and (2) how to design and run teams or meetings for effective task performance. Most managers who have developed in traditional organizations are not only inexperienced in either of these tasks, but may also have strong value biases against the use of groups or teams. Such managers tend to call meetings because they have no choice, but then often mismanage them and prove to themselves that the meeting was a poor tool in the first place. Obviously the answer lies in enlarging the interpersonal competence of managers.

In summary, technological changes which have produced much greater product and service complexity and a much greater rate of change in all aspects of society have had a visible impact on organizational functioning. So far we have concentrated on those trends which affect the structure and basic organizational processes of the organization in focusing on differentiation, specialization, interdependence, and power decentralization, resulting in a greater need for innovative integrative structures and various forms of group interaction.

Effects of Sociocultural Value Changes

In order to understand the kinds of value changes I will be describing, it is necessary to first outline some of the sociocultural conditions which have changed in the last several decades (Roeber, 1973). It is difficult in this complex area to decide what is cause and what is effect, and I do not pretend to be a historian. But certain observable trends are worth isolating, even while acknowledging that we do not fully know how they are interconnected.

1. Western society's fairly prolonged period of economic security and overall increase in wealth have made it possible for more and more people to take the time to obtain an education and to observe, analyze, and question the world around them.

2. The incredible growth of the mass media has made it possible to identify problems and issues more quickly, disseminate them more widely, and thereby get a greater variety of views of these problems. Problems of race discrimination, injustices, political corruption, urban squalor, and political intervention in other nations become not only more visible, but also subject to much closer scrutiny from more points of view (and in some cases magnify problems by drawing attention to them). The mass media also serve as powerful sources of education for even those who could not afford the luxury of a special period of education such as college.

3. The growth of large, technologically complex organizations has produced, at one extreme, many meaningless jobs, creating a concern with "quality of working life" and, at the other extreme, a demand for more specialists and managers. Large organizations and tech-

nological complexity have also been seen by many as the source of loss of community, loss of individual identity, and loss of control over one's destiny.

4. We are living in a period when there is no longer a clear-cut frontier. Instead, we are experiencing the effects of population crowding and the potential destruction of our own habitat. Both of these factors have necessitated more restrictions of individual freedom and more government intervention to ensure the conservation of the environment, all of which exacerbates the above-mentioned effects of large organizations.

One can summarize these trends by noting that they pose a real dilemma—one set of forces is opening up our choices, while another ʳet of forces is reducing our choices. The dilemma of life in today's world is how to take advantage of our wealth and education, which are giving us more choices, in a world which is so complex, so incomprehensible, and in many ways so intractable as to make choice almost meaningless.

It is clear which way the dilemma is being resolved at the level of social value. We are becoming more and more what Roeber calls a "voluntary society":

> The greatest change is coming from the massive accumulation of small elements of free choice throughout the population. The leading characteristic of the move toward voluntarism is its lack of structure and pervasiveness. There are many manifestations: the growing dissatisfaction of workers; the impossibility of getting people to do certain jobs or, if workers are hired, of being able to ensure that jobs are done well; the loss of an agreed moral base in society and the rejection of authority; the questioning of such basic assumptions as the relative roles of men and women; the rejection of the blind workings of the marketplace and, specifically, the attacks on market mechanisms by consumer and environmental movements; the more political movements like Black Power and Women's Lib; the dissatisfaction with a democratic process that provides no means for the will of the population to be effective in large decisions. These are the manifestations of a willingness to choose. . . . (Roeber, 1973, p. 50)

To articulate these changes in the specific context of the relationship between individuals and their employing organizations, we can list the following *specific kinds of value shifts* which are becoming increasingly clear to managers, at least in North America and Western Europe:

1. *People are placing less value on traditional concepts of organizational loyalty and the acceptance of authority based on formal position, age, or seniority and are placing more value on individualism, individual rights vis-à-vis the large organization, and "rational" authority based only on expertise and knowledge.* Increasingly, people are demanding that the tasks they are asked to perform make sense and provide them with some challenge and opportunity to express their talents. Increasingly, people are demanding that the rights of individuals be protected, especially if they are members of minority groups or are in danger of being discriminated against on some arbitrary basis such as sex or age. Increasingly, people are demanding some voice in decisions which affect them, leading to the growth of various forms of industrial democracy, participative management, and worker involvement in job design and even corporate decision making. From the point of view of the employing organization, worker involvement also makes sense to the extent that the trend toward specialization of tasks is occurring. For many kinds of decisions, it is the worker who has the key items of information and therefore *must* be involved if the decision is to be a sound one.

2. *People are placing less value on work or career as a total life concern and less value on promotion or hierarchical movement within the organization as the sole measure of "success" in life.* Instead, more value is being placed on leading a balanced life in which work, career, family, and self-development all receive their fair share of attention, and "success" is increasingly being defined in terms of the full use of all one's talents and contributing not only to one's work organization, but to family, community, and self as well.

3. *People are placing less value on traditional concepts of male and female sex roles with respect to both work and family roles.* Thus in the career and work area we are seeing a growing trend toward equal employment opportunities for men and women, a breaking down of sex-role stereotypes in regard to work (e.g., more women are going into engineering and more men are going into nursing), and a similar breaking down of sex-role stereotypes in regard to the proper family roles (more women are becoming the primary "breadwinner," and more men are staying home to take care of children, do the cooking, and clean the house). Our society is opening up the range of choices for both men and women to pursue new kinds of work, family roles,

and life-styles. One of the major consequences is the "dual-career" family; both husband and wife work, and both are equally committed to career development, thus forcing organizations to develop new personnel policies and forcing social institutions to develop new alternatives for childcare.

4. *People are placing less value on technological progress and economic growth and are placing relatively more value on conserving and protecting the quality of the environment in which they live.* Assessing the impact of technology is becoming a major activity in our society, and we see growing evidence of a willingness to stop progress—e.g., reluctance to build the supersonic transport or even allow our airports to use existing SSTs; highway construction which comes to an abrupt halt in the middle of a city; refusal to build oil refineries, even in economically depressed areas, if the environment would be endangered; serious debate of books such as *The Limits to Growth* (Meadows *et al.*, 1972), which argue against the automatic acceptance of the proposition that economic growth is good.

These value changes in combination have created a situation in which the incentives and rewards offered by the different parts of our society have become much more diverse and consequently much less integrated. We see this most clearly in the organizational "generation gap"—older managers or employees who are still operating from a "Protestant ethic" attitude toward work versus young employees who question arbitrary authority, meaningless work, organization loyalty, restrictive personnel policies, and even fundamental corporate goals and prerogatives. Middle managers in executive programs such as the Sloan Fellows program at MIT complain that they cannot resolve the conflicts they observe between their older bosses and their younger subordinates. They feel caught in the middle, without the necessary insight or skills to ameliorate the problems.

Many of the problems and "crises" of midcareer cited in recent books and newspapers (Beckhard, 1972; Pearse and Pelzer, 1975; Tarnowieski, 1973; Sheehy, 1974, 1976; Chew, 1976; Davitz and Davitz, 1976; LeShan, 1973) can also be viewed as products of these value shifts. As options and choices have opened up and as managers have begun to question the traditional success ethic, they have become more ready to refuse promotions or geographical moves, more willing to "retire on the job" while pursuing family activities or off-the-job hobbies more actively, and have even resigned from high-potential careers to pursue various kinds of "second careers" seen to be more challenging and/or rewarding by criteria other than formal hierarchical position or amount of pay. From the point of view of the employing organization, this represents lost productivity at the man-

agerial level, which is as or more serious than the lost productivity of
the engineer whose talents are obsolete or the plateaued, unmotivated
hourly employee at lower levels.

Implications for Managers.   What all this means for the managers of
tomorrow is that they will have to manage in a much more "plural-
istic" society, one in which employees at all levels will have more
choices and will exercise those choices.* Managers will not only have
to exhibit more personal flexibility in dealing with the range and
variety of individual needs they encounter in subordinates, peers, and
superiors, but will also have to learn how to influence organizational
policies with respect to recruitment, work assignment, pay and benefit
systems, working hours and length of working week, attitudes toward
dual employment of husband and wife, support of educational activities at a much higher scale, development of child-care facilities, etc.

With respect to all of these issues, the manager will indeed be
caught in the middle among: (1) the legal pressure from government
agencies around sex, age, racial, and any other form of discrimination; (2) community pressures from various interest groups concerned
with equal rights, protection of the environment, product quality and
safety, and other forms of consumerism; (3) pressures from corporate
policies to maintain an efficient and profitable operation and a fair return to stockholders; (4) pressures from the marketplace in the form
of ever more severe competition and the need to continue to operate
with ever smaller profit margins; (5) pressures from employees,
whether unionized or not, to improve the quality of working life,
create flexible corporate policies, provide challenging and meaningful
work, and be a responsible "corporate citizen" (Schein, 1966).

The particular trends outlined may, of course, be incorrect or incomplete. The important point, however, is that any job/role planning process should start with some kind of forecast, some attempt to
look into the future or to project out the implications of the present.

STEP 2—IDENTIFYING KEY JOB DIMENSIONS

Based on the kinds of projections outlined above, I have developed
the following dimensions as being most relevant to the analysis of the
general manager's job.† Again it needs to be said that these dimen-

---

*The concept of the management of pluralism was contributed by my col-
league Lotte Bailyn and captures nicely the essence of what is happening in
our organizations.

†Past efforts in this area are well reviewed in the chapter on job analysis in
Pigors and Myeis (1977).

sions could be different in any given organization at any given time. The ones I present below are my best guess based on what I have observed and on surveys of managers—1300 MIT alumni of the 1950s, of whom approximately 50 had reached positions as presidents, executive vice-presidents, or division general managers, 500 alumni of the Sloan School of Management, the previously described panel study (*see* Schein, 1972; Bailyn and Schein, 1974, 1975). The dimensions are laid out so that the reader can rate his or her own job against them (see Table 16.1), as to both the actual job and how it should be performed.

Dimension 1 relates to the degree to which managers must integrate the efforts of others who are technically more knowledgeable than they are. Dimension 2 refers to the degree to which managers must rely on information which is supplied to them by their subordinates. Because the subordinates will know more, managers will have to develop processes of monitoring the thinking and decision making of their subordinates rather than doing the decision making themselves (dimensions 3 and 4). This circumstance tends to go against the grain for most managers. Because they are accountable for the *consequences* of the decisions, they tend to see themselves as having to also *make* the decisions. What I have observed in many situations is that managers continue to feel accountable, but if they do not have enough information, they closely monitor the thinking of their subordinates, test alternative decisions with them, get proposals from them, and make the final decision themselves when the alternatives are completely clear. As one manager whom I have observed for many years puts it:

> I am not very smart in a one-to-one situation. Any one of my subordinates can always sell me on anything. But when I get a group of my subordinates talking to each other and examining alternatives, I get smart awfully fast just listening to all the different facts and points of view. After we have debated and discussed an issue for a while, it becomes pretty obvious to all of us what our decision should be.

In effect, then, this manager *ratifies* the decision which came out of an interpersonal process between himself and his subordinates. The important issue is that the manager has created the process which permits subordinates to communicate and think clearly and which permits the manager to monitor the quality of that thinking.

Dimension 5 refers to the fact that as managers become integrators rather than doers, they become *identifiers* of problems rather than "firefighters." In other words, managers increasingly have to take a broad perspective, to figure out which things are really impor-

Table 16.1
Managerial Job/Role Profile

Each of the following dimensions expresses a key element of the managerial role.

1. Think about your present job/role. Rate your *present behavior* in your job by placing an *X* through the number that best describes your present behavior.

2. Now go back over the items and decide *ideally* what your present role requires of a manager. Rate each of the items on how the job role *should* be performed by putting a *circle* around the number that best expresses your opinion.

	Low				*High*
1. Degree to which I *integrate the efforts of others* who are technically more competent than I am.	1	2	3	4	5
2. Degree to which I have to rely on *second-hand information* which is gathered by my subordinates.	1	2	3	4	5
3. Degree to which I have to *monitor the thinking and decision making* of my subordinates rather than doing the thinking and decision making myself.	1	2	3	4	5
4. Degree to which I *facilitate the "processes" of management and decision making* rather than make day-to-day decisions.	1	2	3	4	5
5. Degree to which I identify problems and ensure that the right problems are worked on by others rather than solve the problems *brought to me* by others.	1	2	3	4	5
6. Degree to which I work with and in groups of various sorts (committees, meetings, task forces, etc.).	1	2	3	4	5
7. Degree to which I operate as a consultant/ catalyst in my day-to-day managerial role.	1	2	3	4	5
8. Degree to which I am *dependent on my subordinates* for total performance rather than it being within my own control.	1	2	3	4	5
9. Degree to which my level of *responsibility* (accountability) *is greater than* my direct degree of control.	1	2	3	4	5
10. Degree to which I *actively manage the selection and development of my key subordinates.*	1	2	3	4	5
11. Degree to which I spend time considering the *long-range health of the organization* rather than the day-to-day performance of it.	1	2	3	4	5

tant, and state them in such a way that they can be worked on. This requires a high level of analytical skill because as the environment and organizational tasks become more complex, managers will find it easier and easier to be seduced by the day-to-day problems brought to them by others instead of attempting to take a broader view and identifying what is really important for the long-range health of the organization.

If managers work increasingly in groups with subordinates and others who have more information than they do, they will have to begin to see themselves in a consultant/catalyst role vis-a-vis the group members (dimension 7) and to develop the kinds of skills needed to perform in that role. Some of these skills are the ones implied in dimensions 3, 4, and 5 relevant to problem identification and problem solution. In addition, managers will need interpersonal and group skills so as to make groups and meetings effective vehicles for problem solving.

Dimensions 8 and 9 state in another way the consequences of having one's subordinates be technically more competent—in a real sense the manager becomes dependent on their performance, and in an equally real sense the manager becomes accountable for decisions made with and by people who may fall outside the sphere of the manager's direct control. Some of these people will be direct subordinates, but will be highly professionalized technical people who are self-motivated and not easily controlled; some of them will be technical resources in other departments assigned on a temporary basis to a project for which the manager is responsible; some of them will be in service groups entirely outside the control of the manager; and some of them will be peers in other groups which are highly interdependent with the manager's own group.

Dimension 10 refers to the critical function of being able to select one's own subordinates if one is as dependent on them as the discussion above implies, and dimension 11 refers to the general perspective the manager takes toward his or her job and organization.*

When various groups have filled out this questionnaire, some fairly consistent trends have emerged. As expected, the higher ranking and more "general" the managers are, the more likely they are to describe both the requirements of their jobs and their actual on-the-job

---

*If the dimensions are now understood, the managerial reader should rate his or her present job on each of them. Having completed the ratings in terms of present behavior and ideally how the job *should* be performed, the reader can analyze more closely which of the dimensions were rated high (4 or 5) and which of them were rated low (1, 2, or 3).

behavior in terms of the high end of the scales. As one gets into middle-level management, one finds a general drop in how managers describe their present behavior, but only certain dimensions drop in terms of what these managers perceive to be the requirements of their jobs. Specifically, they give lower rating to dimensions 2, 3, 8, 9, and 11, which implies less of a feeling of being dependent on subordinates, more direct involvement in decision making, and less concern for long-range organizational issues.

STEP 3—IDENTIFYING CHANGE-SENSITIVE DIMENSIONS

Once the relevant dimensions have been identified (and this is the most difficult part of the analysis), one can ask various people to rate "how they feel the job will change in the future," based on their perceptions of organizational changes. Such future projections can be obtained from higher-level managers, planners, consultants, and any others who may have knowledge of the future directions of the organization. At this point, one may also wish to add other job dimensions, such as "degree to which I deal with outside groups such as consumer advocates or government regulatory agencies," "degree to which my job requires careful compliance with various laws," etc.

The next step in the use of the instrument as a planning tool would be to identify those dimensions showing the greatest amount of change from present job description to future job projection. For example, a group of managers may agree that the biggest difference between their present job and their job projection will be the need to function more as a consultant to various groups of subordinates. Once such a change-sensitive dimension has been identified, it should be thoroughly discussed by the planning team to ensure clear understanding of the nature of the perceived change. Such an analysis or discussion should be undertaken for each change dimension identified before the next step, analyzing what new kinds of competencies, skills, motives, values, and attitudes may be needed for future general managers to perform effectively in the new role, can be taken.

STEP 4—IDENTIFYING RELEVANT
MOTIVES, VALUES, AND SKILLS

Given the new characteristics of the managerial job outlined above, what skills, abilities, motives, and attitudes will be required to perform it successfully? To begin to answer this question, I first constructed a list of all kinds of traits, motives, and abilities which could conceivably be related to performing the managerial job and asked various groups to rate themselves as they presently saw their behavior and as they ideally wanted to be. The 45 dimensions we derived are shown in Table 16.2, again laid out in a fashion suitable for readers to rate themselves. The total list is broken down into four basic categories: (1) motives and values; (2) general abilities and analytical skills; (3) interpersonal and group skills; and (4) emotional skills.

1. Motives and Values.   Most of these items are self-explanatory and are included because they showed up strongly as characteristics which differentiated general managers from other categories of managers (Schein, 1972). They highlight the motivational side of the managerial job and in a sense test the degree to which the person really wants to be manager, is involved with the managerial career, and is comfortable in performing some of the duties and responsibilities of management.

2. Analytical Abilities and Skills.   The items listed in this category are an attempt to list the various abilities required to analyze a problem and reach a decision, particularly in situations of increasing complexity and uncertainty. Thus items 15 and 16 deal specifically with the situation in which managers must rely on others and sometimes must ratify a course of action which they might not even pursue themselves.

3. Interpersonal and Group Skills.   This area is sometimes oversimplified to just communication and leadership skills. I have tried to spell out as specifically as possible all of the different skills involved in selecting subordinates, creating good relationships with them, communicating with others, creating a climate of collaboration, dealing with conflict constructively, and becoming generally more competent in managing interpersonal processes. Item 35 could probably be expanded to include abilities to set up and run meetings of various sorts, to conduct negotiations, and to manage intergroup conflict situations which may arise.

4. Emotional Skills.   This area attempts to delineate the particular emotional skills associated with the managerial role. Again the effort is not to oversimplify into global categories such as "toughness" or "ability to work under pressure," but rather to pinpoint as specifically as possible the separate components of this general characteristic. If we were rating some other occupation, such as physician, we would have quite different dimensions, such as "making immediate decisions of life or death" or, in the case of a pilot, "functioning under condi-

Table 16.2
Managerial Characteristics Profile

---

1. Rate yourself as you are now on each characteristic by putting an *X* through the appropriate number.

2. Rate where you *would like to be* by *circling* the appropriate number on the scales to the right of the items.

A. Motives and Values	*Low*			*High*	
1. My desire to get a job done, my need for accomplishment.	1	2	3	4	5
2. My commitment to my organization and its mission.	1	2	3	4	5
3. My desire to work with and through people.	1	2	3	4	5
4. My career aspirations, ambitions.	1	2	3	4	5
5. My degree of involvement with my career.	1	2	3	4	5
6. My desire to function as a general manager free of functional and technical concerns.	1	2	3	4	5
7. The degree to which I feel comfortable about exercising power and authority.	1	2	3	4	5
8. My desire for a high level of responsibility.	1	2	3	4	5
9. My desire to take risks in making tough decisions.	1	2	3	4	5
10. My desire to monitor and supervise the activities of subordinates.	1	2	3	4	5
B. Analytical Abilities—Skills					
11. My ability to identify problems in complex, ambiguous situations.	1	2	3	4	5
12. My degree of insight into myself—my motives.	1	2	3	4	5
13. My degree of insight into myself—my strengths.	1	2	3	4	5
14. My degree of insight into myself—my weaknesses.	1	2	3	4	5
15. My ability to sense quickly what information is needed and how to get it in relation to any given problem.	1	2	3	4	5
16. My ability to assess the validity of information I have not gathered myself.	1	2	3	4	5
17. My ability to learn quickly from experience.	1	2	3	4	5
18. My flexibility, my ability to think of and implement different solutions for different kinds of problems.	1	2	3	4	5

B. Analytical Abilities—Skills (cont.)	Low				High
19. My breadth of perspective—insight into a wide variety of situations.	1	2	3	4	5
20. My creativity, my ingenuity.	1	2	3	4	5

C. Interpersonal and Group Skills

21. My ability to select effective key subordinates.	1	2	3	4	5
22. My ability to develop open and trusting relationships with subordinates;	1	2	3	4	5
23. with peers;	1	2	3	4	5
24. with superiors.	1	2	3	4	5
25. My ability to listen to others in an understanding way.	1	2	3	4	5
26. My ability to develop a climate of collaboration and team work among my subordinates;	1	2	3	4	5
27. among my peers;	1	2	3	4	5
28. among my superiors.	1	2	3	4	5
29. My ability to develop managerial processes which ensure high-quality decisions without my having to make the decisions myself.	1	2	3	4	5
30. My ability to create a climate of growth and development for my subordinates.	1	2	3	4	5
31. My ability to communicate my own thoughts and ideas clearly and persuasively.	1	2	3	4	5
32. My ability to communicate my feelings clearly.	1	2	3	4	5
33. My ability to diagnose complex interpersonal or group situations.	1	2	3	4	5
34. My ability to influence people over whom I have no direct control.	1	2	3	4	5
35. My ability to design management processes for intergroup and interfunction coordination.	1	2	3	4	5

D. Emotional Skills

36. The degree to which 1 am able to make up my own mind versus relying on the opinions of others.	1	2	3	4	5
37. My degree of tolerance for ambiguity.	1	2	3	4	5
38. My ability to assess the wisdom of proposed courses of action without having first-hand knowledge of the situation.	1	2	3	4	5

D. *Emotional Skills (cont.)*	*Low*			*High*	
39. My ability to pursue a course of action even if it makes me uncomfortable.	1	2	3	4	5
40. My ability to take risks, to make a decision even if it may produce strong negative consequences.	1	2	3	4	5
41. My ability to confront and work through conflict situations (versus avoiding or suppressing them).	1	2	3	4	5
42. My ability to keep going after an experience of failure (losing a negotiation, a product failure, the loss of a good subordinate, etc.).	1	2	3	4	5
43. My ability to confront painful issues of social responsibility (EEO, product safety, environmental impact, etc.).	1	2	3	4	5
44. My ability to fire someone.	1	2	3	4	5
45. My ability to continue to function, to make decisions with incomplete information and in the face of continued environmental turbulence.	1	2	3	4	5

tions of high anxiety," and so on. The particular dimensions listed come from observations of managers, interviews with panel members, and what managers themselves say about some of the more stressful aspects of their job.

In constructing such an instrument, one should leave room under each major category for the planning team or individuals who may be doing the rating to write in additional dimensions. Though I have tried to cover the majority that may be involved, there are no doubt others which will immediately occur to the reader and which should be added if the tool is to be a useful one.

Relating Job Dimensions to Personal Dimensions

Once the master list of dimensions has been identified by a planning group, the next step is to relate this set of personal motives, values, and skills to the managerial job dimensions identified as most likely to change in the future. For each of the managerial dimensions identified in step 3, it is now necessary to go through the whole list in Table 16.2 and determine which of the motives, values, and skills will be most critical for effective performance in that piece of the managerial job. For example, if it has been decided that the general manager of the future will have to operate more as a consultant and rely more on subordinates, it is immediately apparent that "desire to work with and through people" (item 3), "ability to identify problems" (item 11), "ability to assess second-hand information," (item 16), "ability to select subordinates" (item 21), "ability to develop open and trusting relationships" (item 22), "ability to listen" (item 25), "process orientation" (item 29), "wisdom" (item 38), and "ability to pursue courses of action even though uncomfortable" (item 39) become some of the critical motives and skills which would be needed.

Similarly, if some other managerial dimension is identified, such as the need to deal with more external pressure groups, other kinds of motives and skills would then be seen as relevant to effective performance of that part of the job. The important point is to *systematically identify first the job dimension and then go through the list of motives and skills to identify those most relevant to the performance of that job dimension.* For each key dimension identified, a new list of relevant skills can then be constructed as the preliminary to step 5.

STEP 5—ASSESSMENT OF PRESENT CANDIDATES

Once the relevant personal dimensions (motives, values, and skills) have been identified, there are various ways of assessing present candidates in terms of future needs:

1. *Self-ratings* by present managers in the system. In those areas considered important for future performance and for which self-ratings tend to be low, one could launch training and development activities to ensure an increase in those areas. On the other hand, some of those areas may be ones judged not to be susceptible to training. In this instance the self-ratings could become a basis for not being selected for a future job. If the management development or planning group did not wish to impose a situation in which candidates were asked to rate themselves under the pressure of "eliminating themselves" from consideration, the concept of self-rating could be replaced by supervisory ratings, assessment centers, or some other external criterion.

2. *Ratings by supervisors* overcome the obvious problems of biased self-ratings, but introduce the problem of supervisory bias and possibly an inability on the part of the supervisor to judge a given subordinate on a given dimension. On complex dimensions it may be desirable to have both self-ratings and supervisory ratings before attempting to reach a conclusion about a person's level of motivation or skill. Because of the difficulty inherent in both self- and supervisory

ratings, organizations have introduced assessment centers or psychological testing even at very high levels of the organization.

3. *Assessment centers,* with or without psychological testing, are designed to provide insight on a job candidate's skills and motivation in complex areas. Many of the dimensions listed in Table 16.2 are difficult to observe unless one puts the person into a special simulation which tests that particular skill. Overt performance in the simulation is observed both by trained psychologists and managers trained to be observers, thus providing multiple input to the final judgment of the degree to which the candidate possesses a given skill or motive (Bray and Grant, 1966).

4. *Global judgment* by everyone who knows the candidate is often the final criterion used to assess a given area, and in complex areas such as the person's ability to make "wise" judgments, the global composite judgment of many who know the person may be the most valid. Such global judgments often benefit from a detailed knowledge of the candidate's job history, record of performance in various kinds of prior situations, and ability to handle various kinds of situations.

By whatever means the judgments are made, at some point in the job/role planning process a decision must be reached as to whether the motives, values, and skills deemed necessary for future performance in the job being analyzed are (1) already present in some candidates; (2) developable in some candidates in a reasonable time frame; or (3) neither present nor developable, in which case a decision must be made to recruit from outside the organization or look for another source of candidates.

STEP 6—IMPLEMENTATION OF THE SELECTION, DEVELOPMENT, OR RECRUITMENT PLAN

The final step in the job/role planning process is to implement the decisions reached at the end of Step 5. The organization must: (1) set about to select the candidates who are seen to have the requisite skills into the jobs when they open up; (2) launch the right development plans to have candidates ready when the jobs open up; or (3) plan to do whatever internal or external recruiting is necessary to generate qualified candidates. All too often the process of planning stops short of this final implementation step. I have seen organizations conclude that they would need several general managers within five years, that they had no candidates ready for such jobs, yet would launch neither a development nor a recruitment program to deal with the future need.

Instead, they seemed to operate by the vague hope that in five years the problem would somehow take care of itself, that some "cream would rise to the top from somewhere."

It is my hunch that when such nonaction occurs, it is because no one in the organization quite knows how to go about developing the skills needed. For example, it is becoming clearer that the general manager of the future will have to be especially skilled in various interpersonal areas, be able to manage intergroup conflicts, be able to deal with various outside pressure groups, and have all kinds of emotional stamina to function in a continuously turbulent environment. How does one develop someone for those skills if they are not already there? The answer is not simple. It probably lies in a very carefully thought-out program which *combines* careful selection of people with talent, carefully planned sequences of challenging assignments negotiated with the person so that they meet internal as well as organizational needs, and carefully timed outside development activities such as sensitivity training workshops, university development programs, and the like. The person's own initiative and desire to learn is key at every step, which underlines the point I stressed in reviewing the overall HRPD model, namely, that a genuine negotiation must take place between the individual and the organization based on self-knowledge in both parties.

SUMMARY AND CONCLUSIONS

This chapter has provided a detailed outline of the process of job/role planning. Though the illustration used throughout was geared to high-level "general manager" jobs, the six steps outlined can just as easily be applied to any job. The steps are to project some kind of organizational future, develop a list of dimensions of the job to be analyzed, identify those dimensions most likely to be affected by the changes projected; identify the personal characteristics which will be most relevant to performing on those particular dimensions, assess candidates on those dimensions, and then select, develop, or recruit according to the outcome of the assessment process.

The focus of this entire process is the identification of organizational needs. In a total HRPD system of the kind described in Chapter 14, it is essential that some attention be given to the analysis of job changes, quite apart from whatever attention is given to the developmental needs of present employees in the organization. The ultimate challenge is to be able to match the future needs of the organization with the future needs of the individual, so that as organizations and careers evolve, they remain in some kind of synchrony.

17
TOWARD AN INTEGRATED VIEW OF HUMAN RESOURCE PLANNING AND DEVELOPMENT

This chapter will bring together the various themes and issues explored throughout this book. I have been approaching the problem of individuals and organizations from a career-development perspective and have argued that only by considering explicitly the dynamics of careers can one get a full understanding of how individual and organizational needs can be matched. In this chapter, I will review some of the major conclusions which flow from this kind of perspective and then comment on some wider implications for the management of human resources.

BASIC CONCLUSIONS

1. Neither organizational effectiveness nor individual satisfa·tion can be achieved unless there is a better matching of what the organization needs and what the individuals who spend their working lives in those organizations need. Any HRPD system must be simultaneously concerned about organizational effectiveness, both short- and long-run, and individual effectiveness and satisfaction, both short· and long-run.

2. Both the organization and the individuals within it are dynamic, evolving systems whose needs change because of changing environments and changing internal factors deriving from age, life experiences, and family circumstances. The matching of needs is thereiore a

dynamic process which must be periodically monitored and managed.

3. Both the organization and the individual should take a proactive rather than reactive stance toward career planning and management. The key to effective matching will be an effective planning process on the part of both the organization and the individual to ensure that the dialogue on career moves and development activities is based on good information, self-insight, and clearly thought-out intentions.

4. The dynamics of this matching process cannot be managed without more knowledge about: (a) individual life cycles and how self, career, and family development interact throughout those cycles; (b) the nature of organizational career dynamics, career paths, career stages, and other aspects of how organizations recruit, utilize, and manage their human resources; (c) the reciprocal interaction of individual and organization, the processes of organizational socialization, and the process of individual innovation.

5. The particular dynamics of the early career must be carefully assessed to ensure that the manner in which people are brought into organizations, socialized, and launched on their careers creates an optimal psychological contract which permits matching of the organization's needs for a high level of contribution and/or innovation with the individual's needs for locating his or her particular area of specialization and contribution.

6. The dynamics of finding one's career anchor must be understood so that a sufficient range of job challenges and feedback maximizes the opportunity of every individual to discover what his or her career anchor is. Without insight into one's career anchor, the problems of mid- and late career are much more likely to be severe, with neither individual nor organization having a good basis for matching each other's needs.

7. The dynamics of the middle and, by implication, late career must be understood and sympathetically managed so that people can level off and disengage without becoming a source of difficulty to the organization. Lower levels of contribution and job involvement and more concern with mentoring and using acquired "wisdom" can all be turned into resources if both individual and organization understand that there is a natural career evolution here for many people. It is the minority who will climb the narrowing pyramid and occupy positions of leadership and senior management. The need to identify and develop this group is equally important, but its needs are different, requiring different developmental plans.

8. Human resource planning and development must be viewed as a total system involving planning components on the part of the organization, individual planning, a joint negotiation of career-development moves, and an implementation and monitoring system to ensure that goals are achieved. A special portion of this planning process must be devoted to job/role planning to determine how various key jobs in the organization will change as the organization evolves and various environmental changes take place.

9. A total HRPD system consists of many separate components which must be linked. Some of these components are primarily planning activities; others are the various matching activities which create the development system. Such matching activities reflect the various phases of the career and can be listed in summary form as follows:

Planning Activities	*Matching Activities*
1. Planning for *staffing*	1. Job analysis and job/role planning
	2. Recruitment
	3. Selection
	4. Training
	5. Job assignment and job design
2. Planning for *growth and development*	6. Supervision, guidance, coaching
	7. Performance appraisal and judgment of potential
	8. Feedback, provision of knowledge of results, pay, and benefits
	9. Challenging job assignments, developmental job rotation, job posting, job enrichment
	10. Training and development programs
	11. Career counseling and joint target setting and negotiation
3. Planning for *leveling off and disengagement*	12. Continuing education and retraining
	13. Job redesign
	14. Lateral job rotation to reduce job longevity

Planning Activities	*Matching Activities*
	15. Alternative systems of payment, benefits, and recognition
	16. Alternative work patterns— part-time, time off, split jobs, special assignment, etc.
	17. Seminars and counseling for retirement
4. Planning for *replacement*	18. Human resource inventorying
	19. Replacement training
	20. Job/role planning and analysis

This list of activities or components is intended to highlight the complexity of any HRPD system and to illustrate how many activities have to be coordinated and integrated if the total system is to function effectively for either the organization or the individual.

10. Special attention must be given in any HRPD system to key career transitions where important organizational boundaries are passed: (a) initial entry into the organization; (b) the transition from being a specialist to a generalist; (c) the transition from technical/functional work to administration and management; (d) the transition from provisional member to permanent member of the organization; (e) the transition from functional manager to general manager; (f) the transition from fully work-involved to being more accommodative to family and self concerns; (g) the transition from being "on the way up" to "leveling off"; (h) the transition from group member to individual contributor; (i) the transition from maximum concern with own contribution to greater concern with being a mentor to others; and (j) the transition from being employed to being retired.

These transitions involve different issues, as I have tried to point out throughout this book. But it is important that some group in the organization view all of them as part of a common HRPD system so that they get managed in a coordinated fashion. As we learn more about the career and life cycle, it should be possible to take a more coordinated approach to managing all phases of it.

The ultimate accountability for the management of the total HRPD system must rest with line management. The personnel function, where many of these activities often end up, must be the staff specialty *helping* line managers to manage the entire human resource function effectively by providing tools, information, training, and support. But the personnel department by itself cannot integrate these functions, because many of them, such as planning, supervision, performance appraisal, and job assignment, fall outside the function altogether. If line management does not see a given problem or dilemma, it may be the personnel specialist who will bring it to management's attention, but ultimately the problem can be solved only within the line function itself.

HOW CAN HUMAN RESOURCE PLANNING AND DEVELOPMENT SYSTEMS BE IMPROVED?

Based on this analysis and on observations of how HRPD systems work in many of today's organizations, what can we do differently? What can the organization do differently to facilitate its own effectiveness and the growth and satisfaction of its people? How can those individuals work more effectively on their own behalf so that the matching process is based on a more genuine negotiation between the individual and the employer? When this matching process fails to work, how can educational and other institutions help? Let us examine each of the major factors with this normative view in mind, recognizing that what is being called for here is to some extent a projection into the future and therefore only as valid as our vision of that future.

What the Organization Can Do

Organizations can undertake three types of activities in terms of their basic goals: (1) activities designed to produce greater *self-insight* on the part of the organization (insight on the part of managers into how their own organization functions with respect to HRPD and career dynamics); (2) activities designed to increase the *involvement of employees* at all levels in their own career planning and development; and (3) activities which increase the *range and flexibility of organizational (managerial) responses* to various kinds of individual needs and life situations. Let us examine each set in turn.

1. Activities designed to increase organizational self-insight. First, the link between strategic planning and job/role planning should be strengthened in order to increase managerial understanding of what is ahead and how it will influence the work of the organization. Such information must be not only gathered by a systematic planning process, but, even more important, *disseminated* to as many levels of management as is feasible. Many organizations do the planning but then fail to reveal the results to all but a small number of top managers. For such information to be useful, ways will have to be found to disseminate it without managers' feeling that they are giving away secrets or making unchangeable commitments.

Second, *systematic study of the career dynamics operating in the organization must be undertaken.* Through analyses of job histories of senior managers, specialist staff, and individual contributors, some attempt should be made to identify typical promotional sequences, patterns of job rotation, average length of time on a given job, when transitions from functional work to management or functional management to general management are made, etc. Again, such information may be viewed as "private" or, if revealed may be viewed by some as constituting a commitment to people lower down in the organization. Ways must be found around those objections so that managers at all levels can become more knowledgeable of career dynamics in their organization.

Third, *systematic study of the career-related and personal/family needs and values of employees at all levels, including senior levels of management, should be carried out at regular intervals.* If there is one thing that is becoming evident in organizations, it is that needs and values vary with age, type of work, job longevity, rank, sex, past experience, and family situation. Organizations could well use interview programs or attitude surveys to systematically monitor those needs and values as basic input to any HRPD system.

These three activities would produce the kind of information needed for other activities, such as performance appraisal, judgment of potential of employees, career counseling, replacement staffing, and planning for development and disengagement. The more complex organizations become, the more essential it will be for them to replace intuition and the beliefs and stereotypes of a few managers with systematic data. It makes little sense to launch expensive HRPD programs on an insufficient data base.

2. *Activities designed to increase employee involvement in career planning and development.   First, information about organizational career dynamics and career options should be shared with employees.* If employees (and again we include all levels of management here) do not have information on the basis of which to plan their own career development, they cannot become involved in it and are likely to leave

or become passive. Such information can be probabilistic and uncertain—that is, managers can say that they do not know the options or that there are no clear patterns. But such negative information still makes it easier to plan than to have no information at all (or, worse, have incorrect beliefs about what happens and what is available). Therefore, whatever is known should be shared.

Second, employees should be counseled and encouraged to become proactive in regard to their careers. It is likely that most members of organizations have learned to be somewhat passive about their careers and need active encouragement to think about, plan for, and implement their own developmental activities.

Third, career-development workshops should be made available. As part of any training and development program, organizations should make available two- to three-day workshops so that groups of interested employees could meet to learn about career dynamics, engage in self-assessment activities, and practice planning their own career development. Such workshops could be integrated with existing programs of assessment.

Fourth, employees should receive systematic encouragement and financial support for education and training. It is likely that any counseling, assessment, or workshop activity will reveal needs for further education and training. As such needs are identified, the organization should have a clear policy of giving partial or full support to such activities in terms of finanial help, time off, etc.

Fifth, job posting should be instituted and employees should be encouraged to seek new assignments. The best way to encourage their involvement in career development is to make it possible for employees to apply for jobs internally, to be encouraged to think through what kinds of work they want, and to seek positions which would allow such work. For lower levels of employees, encouraging participation in job redesign serves this same critical function.

Finally, opportunities to negotiate around work-family conflicts or around career crises should be increased. In other words, managers should set a climate that encourages subordinates to feel free to bring up crises, conflicts, or personal issues which are interfering with work, so that accommodations can be worked out. The important prerequisite is that the employee should feel that it is legitimate to bring up such issues and to negotiate with the organization to find some optimal solution.

All of the activities suggested would have the effect of activating employees toward being more responsible for themselves and their careers. It is my assumption that in the long run, this will be in the best interests of both the employee and the organization. However, there is no point encouraging such participation if the organization is not willing to make accommodations of the sort which will be described below. It is not enough for the organization to understand itself and the needs of its employees and to encourage them to become more proactive. The organization must also develop the capacity to respond.

3. More flexible management policies and practices to facilitate matching are needed.   More flexibility is needed in the design of work to ensure optimal challenge and opportunities for growth. Job enlargement, job enrichment, job redesign and other activities dealing with the actual work should be encouraged so that at all levels in the organization, some optimal challenge can be maintained. It must be remembered that human growth will not occur without some challenge; hence the design of work should explicitly consider how much challenge there is in it. Attention should also be given to managerial jobs, which can become as stultifying as some forms of hourly work.

Flexibility is also needed in the kind of work assigned to create variety, relief from monotony, and developmental opportunities. What I have in mind here is special projects, task forces, and other forms of *temporary assignments* which permit the employee to try out new talents and challenges without having to make an irreversible commitment. Such temporary jobs should be used especially around key transitions, such as that into management, to make it easier for people to give up kinds of work for which they are not suited or which they may not like.

Third, more flexibility is needed in the giving of performance feedback. Managers should learn more about when, how, and around what issues to give subordinates knowledge of how they are doing. One key to improving this whole process is to learn how to solicit feedback or to encourage one's own subordinates to solicit feedback when they need it or are ready for it. For feedback to be helpful in the growth and development process, it must be relevant, timely, accurate, valid, and related to what the subordinate is specifically attempting to learn.

Fourth, more flexibility is needed in regard to working arrangements. As we discover that people have different kinds of needs and that these needs change during their life cycle, organizations should become more responsive and flexible around working hours (flex time), length of the working week, patterns and lengths of vacations or unpaid leave, part-time work, split jobs, and so on. What may be from the point of view of the organization a small accommodation, such as permitting a person to work for a few weeks at half-time, could be enough to save a difficult family situation for that person. It should be noted that for such accommodations to occur, it is necessary for the organization to not only be willing to be flexible, but also create a climate which will lead to employees' asking for such accommodations.

More flexibility is also needed in reward, benefit, and recognition systems. To the extent that employee needs differ and change, it can be predicted that people will want different things at different times and that not everyone will want the same things in the first place. Different forms of payment, the use of stock options, bonuses, hourly rates versus salaries, different kinds of benefits, etc.—all have been found to be relevant in some situations and for some people. Creating more options in this area and giving employees genuine choices will be increasingly necessary if individual and organizational needs are to be matched. The important thing to recognize is that different forms of reward should be linked to different kinds of work, age levels, family situations, and other factors not directly related to rank. For the senior manager the stock option may be critical; for the young engineer, paid trips to engineering society meetings may be critical; for the young clerk or production worker, a good insurance and medical benefits policy combined with good vacation options may be critical; for the dual-career employee, opportunities for time off may be critical, and so on.

More flexible promotion and career advancement systems are needed in recognition of different kinds of career anchors. Not everyone wants to climb the hierarchy, so ways must be found to "promote" people along other dimensions—bigger projects, more autonomy, greater variety of work, more opportunities for job rotation, more access to the policy-making and leadership functions through membership in key groups or committees, more formal recognition or the granting of valued privileges, more mentoring opportunities, etc. Obviously these systems relate closely to the reward systems mentioned above and will have to be coordinated with them. The most important priority here is to find viable career ladders for specialists and individual contributors because of the likelihood that they will be playing a bigger part in the organization of the future.

Finally, more flexible policies will be needed in regard to geographical movement as employees are increasingly limited in mobility by employed spouses, personal relationships and needs, and their children's needs. Data are accumulating that if people's families do not adjust well in a new situation, they do not perform at a very high level. It is therefore clearly in the organization's interest to check out total family attitudes and not to move people who do not wish to be moved. I have recently encountered a number of companies that report that single people are even harder to move than married ones, because they form attachments in the community which are not as transferrable as spouse and children. The important point is that organizations should negotiate genuinely around these issues and cease to regard people as disloyal if they refuse to move.

All of the points above imply a degree of sophistication and skill on the part of individual managers, which may be possessed by only a few in today's typical organization. If these activities are to be implemented, therefore, it is also necessary to start training and development programs for managers in how to do it—how to plan, to gather information about people's needs and values, design challenging work assignments, give effective performance feedback, deal flexibly and creatively with the variety of needs which will be revealed among their subordinates, and fit all of this into the limits imposed by the typical organizational policy structure. It will not be easy. In effect, managers will be asked to pay far more attention to *people management* than ever before and will need training in how to do this effectively. And the issues will be just as salient between executive vice-presidents and their group vice-presidents in corporate headquarters as it will be between first-line supervisors and their shop-floor employees. If HRPD systems are to be fully effective, line managers at *all* levels will have to be more effective in managing people.

What the Individual Can Do

The biggest danger to the individual in tomorrow's world is that he or she will feel increasingly powerless in the face of a complex society, monolithic organizations, and unpredictable labor markets. As I indicated in Chapter 16, our affluent society is creating more options, but at the same time it is getting more and more difficult for people to decipher what is going on in the organizational world. Hence more people are opting out of large organizations altogether. However, if viable career opportunities do exist in organizations, it should be possible for individuals to manage their organizational careers more effectively, even if their employing organizations do relatively few of the things suggested above.

The key to this effective career management, like the key to coping with any life task, is to become proactive and an *effective diagnostician*—able to identify the problem, operate with a maximum of self-insight, build up a repertory of possible responses, and know how to select the appropriate response (Miller, 1977). The key to coping effectively is self-insight into what one wants out of one's career, one's talents and limitations, one's values and how they will fit in with the organizational values, and so on. Too many people never ask, much less attempt to answer, these kinds of questions. It was shocking to me when I conducted the interviews for the MIT panel study and discovered how many respondents said that they had never in ten years of their careers asked themselves the kinds of questions which I was asking just to fill in the details of their job histories.

People should seek responsible career counseling; they should get themselves assessed if they are not sure of what their talents and values are; they should review their own biographies with the aid of some of the many self-diagnostic books now available (e.g., Ford and Lippitt, 1972; Miller, 1977). People should talk to their friends and should cope with career-development problems just as they would with any other life task. None of us should become complacent and assume that even the most benign or humanistic employer will, in fact, manage our careers in our own best interests. If the employer is enlightened enough to negotiate with us, we must have ourselves in hand in order to have a position from which to negotiate. I have known many managers who, when called into a career-counseling session by their own boss, were at an absolute loss for words. They had no questions or issues; they had simply not thought about it.

What Outside Institutions Can Do

We cannot assume that even if the organization is doing its best to take into account individual needs, it will always be possible to reach an accommodation—to match those individual needs with organizational ones. People will find that their needs are incompatible with what the employer has to offer, and organizations will find that they have to terminate employees because no present and future matching seems possible. In many such situations the individual may find that some outside help is needed to reconstruct the career, to get it back on track, to find a viable path. Such help must come from various educational, community, and other institutions such as unions, professional associations, etc.

The essential role of government and educational institutions will vary with the stages of the career. It is obvious that the incentives and constraints which can be created by government through support of research, scholarship programs, dissemination of information about occupations, and so on, can influence to a considerable degree *entry* into a career. It is also fairly clear how social security policies and legislation about retirement, medical insurance for the aged, and other programs can influence the stage of retirement. What is less obvious is how government, educational, and community and professional orga-

nizations can help midcareer and midlife issues. Is there even a need
for such influence and help, or can the individual and the organization
manage the matching process without intervention?

The evidence is piling up that in a rapidly changing society, there
is indeed a crucial role for a "third party," because the matching process does break down in ways that cannot be ameliorated by either the
individual or the employer. For example, a major change in technology is likely to lead to such a substantial number of employees whose
skills are now obsolete that no single employer will be able to bear the
cost of retraining. Without legislation forcing life-time employment,
we will see an increase in layoffs or "outplacements" in a wide variety
of organizations and at all rank levels. If economic conditions worsen
in some industries, even high-level managers will be forced out of organizations to seek new careers. Career switching will, of course, result not only from organizational pressures, but also from an increasing number of individuals' exercising some of the options which are
increasingly becoming available. In many cases the switch for women
will be from housewifing and mothering to paid employment and full
career involvement. In all of these moves government and other institutions will probably have an essential role to play.

The essense of this role will be to facilitate career switching by
providing:

1. *Mechanisms whereby individuals can obtain a better insight into
their strengths, weaknesses, career anchors, and future potential so
that they can make wiser choices.* Such mechanisms might be better information dissemination about career options and financial support
for participation in testing, assessment centers, and career counseling.
Such services might be provided by government agencies, local educational institutions, professional associations, or community service
agencies, but the expenses of such services will clearly be higher than
what either the present employer or the individual employee might be
able to manage alone.

2. *Financial support for a period of retraining is a second key element to facilitating career switching or entry into a career at midlife.*
Just as there are scholarships available for needy students entering
college, support must be found for midlife adults who are mismatched
in their present careers to take time off to study or train in preparation
for entering a new career. If the person has not been fortunate enough
to save a fair amount of money in the early career years, it is unlikely
that he or she could afford in midlife to enter the kind of educational
program that would make real career switching possible. Whether

such money comes from government, consortia of employers, local educational institutions, or professional associations is less of an issue than the basic recognition that it must come from somewhere other than the employer or the individual.

3. *Educational and training programs geared to midlife career entrants or career switchers will have to be developed in greater numbers.* We are only beginning to see how to create programs to serve the needs of the adult learner to enter new occupations and professions. Existing educational programs are only beginning to explore the pros and cons of taking in students in their thirties and forties. Learning theories are only beginning to acknowledge the fact that adult learning may be possible but different from childhood and adolescent learning (Knowles, 1970). Adult education centers sponsored by local communities, university extension programs, and courses offered by community colleges are already available in many areas, but the admission of midlife adults into full-fledged professional training programs which grant higher degrees is not yet widespread. For example, many universities run executive development programs for mid- and late-career managers, but only a few, such as the Sloan Fellows Program at MIT, run for 12 months and grant a Masters degree at the end of the program. Admission of midlife adults into law schools, medical schools, divinity schools, engineering schools, and so on, is not as yet widespread, but will have to become more so as more adults exercise the option to switch careers. Government agencies will probably have to provide some of the financial incentives, but only by a real involvement of the educational sector and the local community will real change take place in this area.

The ultimate role of government and educational institutions will be to monitor the process of human resource planning and development and to intervene intelligently only where there is evidence of mismatching. For such monitoring, diagnosis, and intervention to occur in an optimal fashion, government agencies must set up their own planning activities, diagnostic mechanisms, and systems for intervening through legislation, financial incentives, special programs, and the like. But the important point is not to intervene where it is not needed and not to overplan. The individual career occupant and the employing organization must take primary responsibility for those things which they can control. Government and other institutions should step in only where there is clear evidence of mismatching and where it is clear that the problem is beyond the coping capacity of the other two actors in the situation.

SUMMARY AND CONCLUSION

This chapter has reviewed the major conclusions about human resource planning and development as viewed from a career perspective. I have outlined what organizations, individual career occupants, and outside institutions such as government agencies, schools, community groups, and professional associations can do to facilitate an optimal matching of individual and organizational needs. It is my hope that by spelling out the various components which have to be considered, highlighting the dynamics of the career, and indicating what the various actors can do, both organizations and individual career occupants will become more proactive, diagnostic, and sophisticated in this difficult process of matching individual and organizational needs.

Appendix 1
CAREER ANCHOR SELF-ANALYSIS FORM*

In the questionnaire you are asked to give objective information in the left-hand column and reasons for your choices, decisions, etc., in the right-hand column. Be spontaneous in your answers. The main purpose is to give you information about yourself which will help you to determine your own career anchor.

External Factors and Events	*Internal Reasons and Feelings*
1. What was your major area of concentration in college?	Why did you choose that area? How did you feel about it?
2. Did you go to graduate school? If yes, what was your area of concentration; what degree did you get?	Why did you go or not go?

External Factors and Events	*Internal Reasons and Feelings*

3. What was your first job after school? (Include military if relevant)

What were you looking for in your first job?

_____   _____

_____   _____

_____   _____

4. What were your ambitions or long-range goals when you started your career? Have they changed? When? Why?

_____

_____

_____

5. What was your first major change of job or company?

Did you or the company initiate it? Why did you initiate it or accept it?

_____   _____

_____   _____

_____   _____

_____

What were you looking for in your next job?

_____

_____

_____

_____

_____

Continue to list what *you* consider to be the major job, company, career changes *you* see in your career. List each step and answer the questions *for each* step.

External Factors and Events	*Internal Reasons and Feelings*

6. Change _____   Why did you initiate or accept it?

_____

_____

_____

_____

What were you looking for?

_____

_____

_____

_____

7. Change _____   Why did you initiate or accept it?

_____

_____

_____

_____

What were you looking for?

_____

_____

_____

_____

_____

External Factors and Events   *Internal Reasons and Feelings*

8. Change _____   Why did you initiate or accept it?

                                                           What were you looking for?

9. Change _____   Why did you initiate or accept it?

10. As you look back over your   What about those times did you
    career, identify some times   enjoy?
    you have especially enjoyed
    it.

    _____   _____

    _____   _____

    _____   _____

    _____   _____

External Factors and Events	*Internal Reasons and Feelings*
11. As you look back, identify some times you have not especially enjoyed it.	What about those times did you *not* enjoy?
12. Have you ever refused a job move or promotion?	Why?
13. How would you describe your occupation to others?	What do you see yourself to be?
14. Do you see any major transition points in your career? Describe the transition objectively.	How did you feel about it?

External Factors and Events	*Internal Reasons and Feelings*
	Why did you initiate or accept it?
	_____
	_____
	_____
	_____
	Review all of your answers in this column and look for the pattern in the answers. Do you see any anchor in the answers?
	_____
	_____
	_____
	_____
	Rate each of the anchors below based on your answers above, from 1 to 5; 1 = low importance, 5 = high importance.
	Managerial competence _____
	Technical/functional competence _____
	Security _____
	Creativity _____
	Autonomy _____

Appendix 2
CASE EXAMPLE: DIAMOND
PRODUCTS CORPORATION

My original contact with Diamond Products stemmed from a request by its president to help the top-management team become more effective as a group in managing a rapidly changing business. Diamond had grown by geographic expansion, some diversification, and some acquisitions of related businesses.

For the past ten years, the company had operated on the assumption that the best way to make the total business effective was to keep divisions separate and to let each division become as autonomous as possible. Division managers who really wanted to run their own show were put in charge of the divisions and were measured strictly on their own divisional performance. Corporate headquarters stimulated and rewarded competitiveness among the divisions, even though some of them were dependent on others (some divisions were involved in supplying raw materials for the whole corporation, some were manufacturing parts used by all of the other divisions, etc.). Internal transfer pricing, common marketing strategies, and other total-company activities were negotiated in heated, competitive, frustrating meetings or were legislated by corporate management.

Some symptoms began to surface suggesting that this form of organization and the total company climate were not building long-range effectiveness:

1. There was a high attrition in division managers, some of whom quit in frustration and some of whom were fired for not making their

divisions profitable even in the face of evidence that they could not, by themselves, achieve profitability without the cooperation of some of the other divisions;

2. There was considerable circulation of *mis*information about people; i.e., each division was deliberately hoarding its own good people and not making them available for promotion into better jobs in other divisions, often by lying about the quality of their people;

3. Rigidities were identified at the division-management level, e.g., ineffective middle managers were pin-pointed, but nothing could be done to remove them because the division general manager refused to have anyone dictate to him how he should run his division;

4. Squabbles arose over the use of common corporate services such as personnel and labor relations, public relations, legal, data processing, etc., with divisions expressing their dissatisfactions by duplicating the services at great cost rather than working together to improve the corporate services;

5. Meetings of division general managers were unproductive shouting matches or political negotiation sessions, leaving corporate management with the feeling that the common corporate good was persistently being subverted.

Some members of corporate management and some division general managers recognized that: (1) the nature of the business had changed; (2) it had become more complex, with environmental pressures in key areas such as labor relations increasing and affecting the entire organization, making centralized and common positions more important; (3) a good management-development program had to be interdivisional, since not enough challenging, growth-producing jobs were available within given divisions for high-potential managers; and (4) too much key information was lost through the interdivisional competition. In particular, it was recognized that top management itself had grown up in and fostered the climate of autonomy and competitiveness and would itself have to change and send new signals to the rest of the organization.

A series of discussions at the top of the organization revealed that the company's long-range growth plan required the development of more general managers and that the present climate and form of organization were working against an effective program of identifying and developing such managers. "Management development" became the vehicle for several major organizational changes, because it was recognized that the long-range health and continued growth of the organization would depend to a large extent on its ability to develop a different kind of manager in large numbers. This different type of manager would have to be more collaborative in orientation, less concerned about autonomy, more concerned about how to work effectively in a highly interdependent set of organizational structures, and more concerned about the total health of the company than with the specific unit or division performance (e.g., willing to see some of the best unit/division people promoted into higher-level jobs in other divisions).

To help to launch this organizational change, the company decided first to attempt to identify its key managerial resources across all of its divisions. In order to do this, a top-management team had to begin to work on a brand new and somewhat unfamiliar task—the description of an effective manager and the production of a set of criteria for each of the divisions to use in identifying its high-potential people. This activity, in turn, required them to think through more clearly the nature of their business, its long-range strategic goals, and its rate of diversification and growth.

All of this was possible only because top management now saw the connection between: (1) a strategic plan couched in terms of products, markets, and financial goals; and (2) the necessity to plan for human resources. Top management recognized that the strategic goals could not be accomplished without certain kinds of human resources and that those resources did not then exist in sufficient quantity within the organization. Furthermore, top management could see how the present organization structure and climate were actually working to the detriment of the identification and development of the right kinds of managers and, therefore, were undermining the possibility of reaching their own strategic goals.

Top managers undertook a series of meetings in which they first thrashed out in some detail what kind of manager was needed in the future, based on their more general vision of the future of the corporation. In my role as outside consultant, I supplied several inputs:

1. Constant reminders that the basic corporate strategic plan and the human resource plan were highly interdependent—that the development activities they might undertake were ultimately for the sake of the basic health of the company and only secondarily for the sake of the individuals who would be developed;

2. Conceptual models of what a manager does and what kinds of skills, attitudes, and values she or he must exhibit in order to be effec-

tive in certain kinds of organizational forms (e.g., if the divisions were to become more interdependent, the manager would have to be willing and able to work collaboratively with peers from other divisions);

3. Process consultation on the team building within the top group itself, since they were attempting to function differently than they had in the past and had little experience on how to be an effective group or how to run an effective meeting; i.e., they had to learn right in their own meeting some of the skills they were putting down as necessary in their own managers of the future, since they did not themselves possess some of those skills (Schein, 1969).

The *building of this top management team* can be described as a new adaptive process created in response to obtaining various kinds of information on changes which were occurring in their internal and external environments. The results of this process some months later were: (1) a *clear directive to division managers* to identify their high-potential managerial resources according to a set of criteria which top management had worked out, and (2) the setting up of a series of *review meetings* where division managers would share with top management their assessments of their key people.

I attended these review meetings and found that both the corporate group and the division managers had to learn how to hold such meetings. In spite of the existence of the criteria, division managers would come to the meeting with a list of names of high-potential people based only on global stereotypes and backed up only by vague statements such as "has always done a good job, has gotten good performance reviews, has a good attitude, etc." In other words, the reviews were highly judgmental, general, and lacking in any specific information which could give top management any sense of the individual being discussed. Yet the culture of the organization was so strong that no one in the group recognized the problem; everyone was dissatisfied, but no one could identify the source of the problem as a lack of relevant information about the people being discussed.

What broke the ice was, in a sense, an accident. Someone asked a very simple question about one of the high-potential managers: "When did he first enter the company?" The division manager did not know the answer, reached into his briefcase, and pulled out the personnel records of the individual being discussed to obtain the answer. On a hunch, I inquired what was in those records. It turned out to be a detailed *performance* history of the man, what projects he had actually worked on in his various jobs, and *how he had done on those specific projects*. The whole group instantly recognized that this kind of information was precisely what they wanted to know about each individual. The division manager had compiled it, gone over it, drawn very general conclusions, and *only reported those conclusions.* What the group needed to know was the actual basis for the conclusion so that some common criteria of who had done what could be established.

Parenthetically, this insight ultimately led to a rethinking of the performance-appraisal system and the decision to record actual work and projects completed along with general evaluation on the appraisal forms. Furthermore, the group gradually became aware of how performance appraisal can become a planning tool in that it can generate the kind of information needed by the human resource planner. At the same time, the dilemma was recognized that if information about individuals becomes a basis for planning which requires *centralized information in personnel records,* that very centralization of information might undermine the use of performance appraisal as a basis for a very open and frank discussion with employees of their own career plans. At a later time we delved into this issue more deeply, and the company decided that it needed more than one system of performance appraisal—one for the purpose of human resource planning and one for the purpose of performance improvement and career counseling. Such a dual system was then developed and a series of training workshops held to institutionalize it.

The top-management group gradually learned how to conduct effective review meetings with each of the division managers and built up a file of its high-potential managers. This process revealed two further things: (1) the company might be facing a shortage of key managers in the future if its rate of growth continued, and (2) the high-potential managers needed to become involved in a much more focused development program to learn many of the specific skills which they would need in their future jobs. The top corporate group and the division managers jointly decided at this point that the process of creating a program of development on a total companywide scale required professional expertise which they did not presently have in the organization. Issues surrounding the assessment of people, performance appraisal, sending people to outside development programs, etc., were recognized as involving complex psychological and moral issues which top management felt should be handled in a maximally professional manner.

To ensure that such professionalism would be available and to implement a companywide development program around the criteria which had been established for future managers, the company decided to hire a full-time director of management development who would also be professionally trained and capable of dealing with the psychological and moral issues identified. For example, the company decided to extend the use of the assessment-center concept (which had been developed earlier at lower levels of management) to the development of higher-level managers, but no clear criteria existed about degree of voluntarism that should be built in, who should see the results of the assessment, and so on. The new director of management development worked with me in developing viable procedures and criteria which would, on the one hand, provide the company with the kind of information it needed and, on the other hand, would stimulate the development it sought without violating the privacy of the individual by revealing to the company assessment center data which it neither needed nor should have.

The process of adaptation described so far focused on the new activities which were specifically created to ensure that the right kinds of managers in the right numbers would be available for the company's future needs. The top corporate group recognized at the same time that the climate of competition between "autonomous" divisions was ultimately destructive to the management-development program it was attempting to create. The group could also see how the competition between divisions was leading to concealment of information, duplication of services, and unnecessary fighting even in areas of genuine interdependence.

In order to deal with these problems directly, top management decided to create a new operating group which would consist of the key division managers and their boss, the executive vice-president in charge of operations. This group would attempt to build a set of norms of collaboration and teamwork and try to reverse the traditional company culture of autonomy and competition. The group would meet regularly (once a week), the members would be encouraged to get to know one another very well, and the agenda would focus on common problem areas.

It was recognized that the success of this group would depend to a large extent on: (1) the personality of the executive vice-president; and (2) his ability to set up a reward system which would favor collaboration over competition and which would stimuiate teamwork and group problem solving. Individual members of the group, including the executive vice-president, had gone to various group dynamics workshops over a number of years and were intellectually clear about what they were trying to do. It remained a difficult task, however, to put the intellectual insights into operation in a corporate culture that had grown up around autonomy and competitiveness. After two years of working together, this group is still struggling to become more collaborative. It has succeeded in some areas and not in others. As acquaintance level and trust have increased among the division managers themselves, collaboration has become a more natural way for them to operate. The group's common commitment to management development serves as one of the continuing forces toward collaboration because of the obvious degree of interdependence which the members feel around this task. Of most importance in this activity has been the group's recognition that planning for the development of others also necessitated some planning for its own development so that an appropriate organization structure and climate would be built for the future managers who were being developed. Underlying this insight was the fundamental assumption that the total organization's health and effectiveness would continue to hinge on the group's capacity to link strategic plans to human resource plans and to continue to cope with a rapidly changing internal and external environment.

The existence of this group and its new way of operating has improved not only operations but business planning as well. Product and market decisions have been more carefully thought through, and a number of key reorganizations have occurred at lower levels, creating, in some cases, cross-divisional groups or matrix structures where common resources were involved and interdependence was high.

SUMMARY AND CONCLUSIONS

The Diamond Corporation is at this point in midstream. It has undergone a number of significant changes which have improved its total "health," but much remains to be done. What the case illustrates best is the interplay among: (1) *strategic business planning* (the decision to continue to grow and diversify); (2) *human resource planning* (the recognition that the absence of the right kind of manager was the major constraint on further growth); (3) *human resource development* activities (the creation of a program to identify high-potential managers, the creation of an interdivisional team to facilitate developmental moves across divisions, the redesign of the performance-appraisal system, the hiring of a full-time director of management development); and (4) *operational decisions* (the creation of the new operational group, the attempt to create a new corporate climate and reward system, and the restructuring of some parts of the organization to be more cross-divisional). One would be hard pressed to identify where business/organizational issues left off and human resource issues began. Only by treating them together was it possible for Diamond to move forward more effectively.

BIBLIOGRAPHY

(Items preceded by an asterisk (*) are workbooks for self-diagnosis.)

Allen, R. F., and S. Silverzweig, "Changing the Corporate Culture," *Sloan Management Review* 17 (1976): 33-49.

Avery, R., "Enculturation in Industrial Research," *IRE Transactions on Engineering Management* 7 (1960): 20-24.

Bailyn, L., "Career and Family Orientations of Husbands and Wives in Relation to Marital Happiness," *Human Relations* 23 (1970): 97-113.

Bailyn, L., "Involvement and Accommodation in Technical Careers: An Inquiry into the Relation to Work at Mid-Career," in J. Van Maanen, ed, *Organizational Careers: Some New Perspectives*, New York: Wiley, 1977.

_____. "Accommodation of Work to Family," in R. Rapoport and R. N. Rapoport, *Working Couples*, London: Rutledge and Keagan Paul; New York: Harper & Row, 1978.

Bailyn, L. and E. H. Schein, "Where Are They Now, and How Are They Doing?" *Technology Review* 74 (1972): 3-11.

_____, "Life/Career Considerations as Indicators of Quality of Employment," in A. D. Biderman and T. F. Drury, *Measuring Work Quality for Social Reporting*, New York: Wiley (Sage Publications), 1976.

Baltes, P. B., and K. W. Schaie, *Life-Span Developmental Psychology: Personality and Socialization*, New York: Academic Press, 1973.

Barnard C. I., *The Functions of the Executive*, Cambridge, Mass.: Harvard University Press, 1938.

Beckhard, R., *Organization Development: Strategies and Models,* Reading, Mass.: Addison-Wesley, 1969.

_____, "The Executive You're Counting on May Be Ready to Mutiny," *Innovation* (May 1972): 31.

Bennis, W. G., *Organization Development: Its Nature, Origins, and Prospects,* Reading, Mass.: Addison-Wesley, 1969.

Bennis, W. G., and P. E. Slater, *The Temporary Society,* New York: Harper & Row, 1968.

Berlew, D., and D. T. Hall, "The Socialization of Managers," *Administrative Science Quarterly* 11 (1966): 207–223.

Bischof, L. *Adult Psychology,* New York: Harper & Row, 1976.

Blake, R. R., and J. S. Mouton, *Building a Dynamic Corporation through Grid Organization Development,* Reading, Mass.: Addison-Wesley, 1969.

Blau, P. M., J. W. Gustad, R. Jenson, H. S. Parnes, and R. C. Wilcox, "Occupational Choices: A Conceptual Framework," *Industrial and Labor Relations Review* 9 (1956): 531–543.

*Bolles, R. N., *What Color Is Your Parachute,* Berkeley, Calif.: Ten Speed Press, 1972.

Bray, D. W., and D. E. Grant, "The Assessment Center in the Measurement of Potential Business Management," *Psychol. Monog.* (1966): 80.

Bray, D. W., R. J. Campbell, and D. E. Grant, *Formative Years in Business,* New York: Wiley, 1974.

Burack, E., *Organization Analysis,* Hinsdale, Ill.: Dryden, 1975.

Chew, P. *The Inner World of the Middle Aged Man,* New York: Macmillan, 1976.

*Crystal, J. C., and R. N. Bolles, *Where Do I Go from Here with My Life,* New York: Seabury Press, 1974.

Dalton, G. W., P. H. Thompson, and R. Price, "Career Stages: A Model of Professional Careers in Organizations," *Organization Dynamics* (Summer 1977): 19–42.

Dalton, M., *Men Who Manage,* New York: Wiley, 1959.

Datan, N., and L. H. Ginsberg, *Life-Span Developmental Psychology: Normative Life Crises,* New York: Academic Press, 1975.

Davis, S., and P. R. Lawrence, *Matrix,* Reading, Mass.: Addison-Wesley, 1977.

Davitz, J., and L. Davitz, *Making It From 40 to 50,* New York: Random House, 1976.

Dill, W. R., T. L. Hilton, and W. R. Reitman, *The New Managers,* Englewood Cliffs, N.J.: Prentice-Hall, 1962.

Driver, M., "Career Concepts—A New Approach to Career Research," in J. Paap, ed., *New Dimensions in Human Resource Management,* Englewood Cliffs, N.J.: Prentice-Hall, in press.

Erickson, E. H., "Identity and the Life Cycle," *Psychological Issues* **1** (1959): 1–171.

Fogarty, M. P., R. Rapoport, and R. N. Rapoport, *Sex, Career, and Family,* Beverly Hills, Calif.: Sage, 1971.

*Ford, G. A., and G. L. Lippitt, *A Life Planning Workbook,* Fairfax, Va.: NTL Learning Resources Corp., 1972.

Galbraith, J., *Designing Complex Organizations,* Reading, Mass.: Addison-Wesley, 1973.

Gellerman, S. W., *People, Problems, and Profits,* New York: McGraw-Hill, 1960.

Ginzberg, E., S. W. Ginsburg, S. Axelrad, and J. L. Herma, *Occupational Choice: An Approach to a General Theory,* New York: Columbia University Press, 1951.

Goffman, E., "On Face-Work," *Psychiatry* **18** (1955): 213–231.

Gould, R. L., "The Phases of Adult Life: A Study in Developmental Psychology," *American Journal of Psychiatry* **129** (1972): 521–531.

_____, "Adult Life Stages: Growth toward Self-Tolerance," *Psychology Today,* (February 1975).

Gruber, W. H., and J. S. Niles, *The New Management,* New York: McGraw-Hill, 1976.

Hackman, J. R., and G. R. Oldham, "Development of the Job Diagnostic Survey," *Journal of Applied Psychology* **60** (1975): 159–170.

Hall, D. T., *Careers in Organizations,* Pacific Palisades, Calif.: Goodyear, 1976.

_____, "A Theoretical Model of Career Sub-identity Development in Organizational Settings," *Organizational Behavior and Human Performance* **6** (1971): 50–76.

Hall, D. T., and K. Nougaim, "An Examination of Maslow's Need Hierarchy in an Organizational Setting," *Organizational Behavior and Human Performance* **3** (1968): 12–35.

Havighurst, R. J., "Youth in Exploration and Man Emergent," in H. Borow, ed., *Man in a World at Work,* Boston: Houghton Mifflin, 1964.

Hopkins, A. D., "Managers at Mid-Career: Where Are They Going?" master's thesis, M.I.T., Sloan School of Management, June 1976.

Horvath, L., "Career Development System in a Socialist Country: A Case Study of Hungary," *Career Planning and Development,* International Labor Office, Management Development Series Number 12, 1976, pp. 49–76.

Hughes, E. C. *Men and Their Work,* Glencoe, Ill.: Free Press, 1958.

Jacobson, R. C., "The Socialization of Technically Trained College Hires in a Computer Company," master's thesis, M.I.T., Sloan School of Management, June 1977.

Jacques, E., "Death and the Mid-Life Crisis," *International Journal of Psychoanalysis* **46** (1965): 502–514.

Kahn, R. L., D. M. Wolfe, R. P. Quinn, J. D. Snoek, and R. A. Rosenthal, *Organizational Stress: Studies in Role Conflict and Ambiguity,* New York: Wiley, 1964.

Kalish, R. A., *Late Adulthood: Perspectives on Aging,* Monterey, Calif.: Brooks-Cole, 1975.

Kanter, R. M., *Work and Family in the United States,* New York: Russell Sage, 1977.

Katz, R., "Job Enrichment: Some Career Considerations," in J. Van Maanen, ed., *Organizational Careers,* New York: Wiley, 1977.

Katz, R., and J. Van Maanen, "The Loci of Work Satisfaction," in P. Warr, ed, *Personal Goals and Work Design,* New York: Wiley, 1976.

Keen, P. G. W., "Cognitive Style and Career Specialization," in J. Van Maanen, ed., *Organizational Careers,* New York: Wiley, 1977.

Kimmel, D. C., *Adulthood and Aging,* New York: Wiley, 1974.

*Kirn, A. G., *Lifework Planning,* Hartford, Conn.: Arthur G. Kirn & Assocs., 1974.

Knowles, M. S., *The Modern Practice of Adult Education,* New York: Association Press, 1970.

*_____, *Self-Directed Learning,* New York: Association Press, 1975.

Kolb, D., and R. E. Fry, "Toward an Applied Theory of Experiential Learning," in C. Cooper, ed., *Theories of Group Learning,* London: Wiley International, 1975.

Kotter, J., "Managing the Joining-Up Process," *Personnel* (July–August 1972): 46–52.

_____, "The Psychological Contract: Managing the Joining-Up Process," *California Management Review* **15** (1973): 91-99.

Lawrence, P. R., and J. W. Lorsch, *Developing Organizations: Diagnosis and Action,* Reading: Mass.: Addison-Wesley, 1969.

LeShan, E., *The Wonderful Crisis of Middle Age,* New York: David McKay, 1973.

Levinson, D. J., C. M. Darrow, E. B. Klein, M. H. Levinson, and B. McKee, "The Psycho-Social Development of Men in Early Adulthood and the Mid-Life Transition," in D. F. Ricks, A. Thomas, and M. Roof, eds., *Life History Research,* Vol. 3, Minneapolis: University of Minnesota Press, 1974.

Levinson, H., *Organizational Diagnosis,* Cambridge, Mass.: Harvard University Press, 1972.

Maas, H. S., and J. A. Kuypers, *From Thirty to Seventy*, San Francisco: Jossey-Bass, 1974.

Maccoby, M., *The Gamesman*, New York: Simon & Schuster, 1976.

McGregor, D., *The Human Side of Enterprise*, New York: McGraw-Hill, 1960.

Meadows, D., D. Meadows, J. Renders, and W. Behrens, *The Limits to Growth*, New York: Universe Books, 1972.

Michael, D. N., *The Unprepared Society*, New York: Harper & Row, 1968.

Miller, D. B., *Personal Vitality*, Reading, Mass.: Addison-Wesley, 1977.

*_____, *Personal Vitality Workbook*, Reading Mass.: Addison-Wesley, 1977.

Miller, D. C., and W. H. Form, *Industrial Sociology*, New York: Harper, 1951.

Neugarten, B. L., *Middle Age and Aging: A Reader in Social Psychology*, Chicago: University of Chicago Press, 1968.

Osipow, S. H., *Theories of Career Development*, 2d ed., New York: Appleton-Century-Crofts, 1973.

*Pearse, R. F., and B. P. Pelzer, *Self-Directed Change for the Mid-Career Manager*, New York: AMACON, 1975.

Pietrofesa, J., and H. Splete, *Career Development: Theory and Research*, New York: Grune and Stratton, 1975.

Pigors, P., and C. A. Myers, *Personnel Administration*, 8th ed., New York: McGraw-Hill, 1977.

Plovnick, M. S., "Primary Care Careers and Medical Student Learning Styles," *Journal of Medical Education* (September 1975): 849–855

Powers, M. E., "Top Management in Boston Area Banking Industry: Career Paths, Promotion Practices and Socialization," master's thesis, M.I.T. Sloan School of Management, 1977.

Rapoport, R., and R. N. Rapoport, *Dual Career Families Re-examined*, New York: Harper & Row, 1976.

_____, eds., *Working Couples*, London: Rutledge and Kegan Paul; New York: Harper & Row, in press.

Rapoport, R. N., *Mid-Career Development*, London: Tavistock, 1970.

Roe, A., *The Psychology of Occupations*, New York: Wiley, 1956.

Roeber, R. J. C., *The Organization in a Changing Environment*, Reading, Mass.: Addison-Wesley, 1973.

Rogers, K., "Crisis at the Mid-Point of Life," *New Society*, August 15, 1974, pp. 413–415.

Schein, E. H., "How to Break in the College Graduate," *Harvard Business Review* 42 (1964): 68–76.

_____, *Organizational Psychology,* Englewood Cliffs, N.J.: Prentice Hall, 1965, 1970.

_____, "The Problem of Moral Education for the Business Manager," *Industrial Management Review* 8 (1966): 3–14.

_____, "Attitude Change During Management Education," *Administrative Science Quarterly* 11 (1967): 601–628.

_____, "Organizational Socialization and the Profession of Management," *Industrial Management Review* (M.I.T.) 9 (1968): 1–15.

_____, *Process Consultation: Its Role in Organization Development,* Reading, Mass.: Addison-Wesley, 1969.

_____, "The Individual, the Organization, and the Career: A Conceptual Scheme," *Journal of Applied Behavioral Science* 7 (1971): 401–426.

_____, *Professional Education: Some New Directions,* New York: McGraw-Hill, 1972.

_____, "Personal Change through Interpersonal Relationships," in W. G. Bennis, D. E. Berlew, E. H. Schein, and F. L. Steele, eds., *Interpersonal Dynamics,* 3rd ed., Homewood, Ill.: Dorsey, 1973.

_____, "How 'Career Anchors' Hold Executives to Their Career Paths," *Personnel* 52, 3 (1975): 11–24.

Schein, E. H., and W. G. Bennis, *Personal and Organizational Change Through Group Methods,* New York: Wiley, 1965.

Schein, E. H., and G. L. Lippitt, "Supervisory Attitudes Toward the Legitimacy of Influencing Subordinates," *Journal of Applied Behavioral Science* 2 (1966): 199–209.

Schein, E. H., and J. S. Ott, "The Legitimacy of Organizational Influence," *American Journal of Sociology* 67 (1962): 682–689.

Schneider, B., *Staffing Organizations,* Pacific Palisades, Calif.: Goodyear, 1976.

Seidenberg, R., *Corporate Wives—Corporate Casualties,* New York: Anchor, 1975.

Sheehy, G., "Catch 30 and Other Predictable Crises of Growing Up Adult," *New York Magazine* (February 1974): 30–44.

_____, *Passages: Predictable Crises of Adult Life,* New York: Dutton, 1976.

*Shepard, H. A., and J. A. Hawley, *Life Planning: Personal and Organizational,* Washington, D.C.: National Training and Development Service, 1974.

Sofer, C., *Men in Mid-Career,* Cambridge, England: Cambridge University Press, 1970.

Steele, F. I., *Physical Settings and Organization Development,* Reading, Mass.: Addison-Wesley, 1973.

*Storey, W. D., *Career Dimensions,* Crotonville-on-Hudson, New York: General Electric Co., 1976.

Super, D. E., *The Psychology of Careers,* New York: Harper & Row, 1957.

Super, D. E., and M. J. Bohn, *Occupational Psychology,* Belmont, Calif.: Wadsworth, 1970.

Sze, W. C., *Human Life Cycle,* New York: Aronson, 1975.

Tarnowieski, D., *The Changing Success Ethic,* New York: AMACOM, 1973.

Thompson, P. H., and G. W. Dalton, "Are R & D Organizations Obsolete?" *Harvard Business Review* **54** (November–December 1976): 105–116.

Troll, L. E., *Early and Middle Adulthood,* Monterey, Calif.: Brooks-Cole, 1975.

Vaillant, G. E., *Adaptation to Life,* Boston: Little, Brown, 1977.

Vaillant, G. E., and C. C. McArthur, "Natural History of Male Psychological Health," *Seminars in Psychiatry* **4** (1972):417–429.

Van Maanen, J., "Observations on the Making of Policemen," *Human Organization* **4** (1973): 407–418.

_____, "Working the Streets: A Developmental View of Police Behavior," in H. Jacob, ed., *The Potential for Reform of Criminal Justice,* Beverly Hills, Calif.: Sage, 1974.

_____, "Breaking In: A Consideration of Organizational Socialization," in R. Dubin, ed., *Handbook of Work, Organization, and Society,"* Chicago: Rand-McNally, 1975.

Van Maanen, J. and E. H. Schein, "Improving the Quality of Work Life: Career Development," in J. R. Hackman, and J. L. Suttle, eds., *Improving Life at Work,"* Los Angeles: Goodyear, 1977.

Van Maanen, J., E. H. Schein, and L. Bailyn, "The Shape of Things to Come: A New Look At Organizational Careers," in J. R. Hackman, E. E. Lawler, and L. W. Porter, eds., *Perspectives on Behavior in Organizations,* New York: McGraw-Hill, 1977.

Wanous, J. P., "Effects of Realistic Job Preview on Job Acceptance, Job Attitudes and Job Survival," *Journal of Applied Psychology* **58** (1973): 327–332.

Whyte, W. H., *The Organization Man,* New York: Simon & Schuster, 1956.

Winterbotham, F. W., *The Ultra Secret,* New York: Dell, 1974.

Zytowski, D. G., *Vocational Behavior,* New York: Holt, Rinehart and Winston, 1968.